Designing and Building
Children's Furniture
with 61 Projects
2nd Edition

TAB FURNITURE WOODSHOP SERIES

Other Books in The TAB Furniture Woodshop Series

Designing and Building Colonial and Early American Furniture, with 47 Projects—2nd Edition

Capture the spirit and challenge of authentic Early American and Colonial craftsmanship.

A recognized expert provides first-rate illustrations and simple instructions on the art of reproducing fine furniture. Each piece is accompanied by exploded drawings, detailed materials lists, and plenty of suggestions for project variations. There are complete directions on how to recognize good furniture design, find solutions to specific design problems, use power tools, and more. Every project is an exquisite reproduction of centuries-old originals: a drop-leaf table . . . firehouse armchair . . . peasant chair . . . ladderback chair . . . gateleg table . . . dry sink . . . love seat . . . and other authentic, ''new'' antiques.

Designing and Building Outdoor Furniture, with 57 Projects—2nd Edition

Build beautiful, sturdy outdoor furniture and patio accessories.

This book is filled with practical, easy-to-understand instructions and detailed two-color illustrations. Even the novice woodworker will be able to make outdoor tables, chairs, benches, planters, and more. Advice is offered on tools, materials, and techniques. Fifty-seven projects are described in detail, from simple benches to a more complicated picnic table.

Designing and Building Space-Saving Furniture, with 28 Projects—2nd Edition

Unique ideas for saving money and space with built-in furniture you create!

Step-by-step directions, exploded drawings, detailed materials lists, and plenty of suggestions for project variations explain every aspect of making space-saving furniture. An excellent guide to designing and constructing built-in furniture, this book provides the novice craftsman with a complete course in measuring, marking, designing, and building furniture to meet specific space restrictions. Projects include complete instructions for building corner and hanging cabinets, room dividers, and units for kitchens, bedrooms, and other household areas.

No. 3064
$21.95

Designing and Building
Children's Furniture
with 61 Projects
2nd Edition

Percy W. Blandford

TAB BOOKS Inc.
Blue Ridge Summit, PA

SECOND EDITION
FIRST PRINTING

Copyright © 1989 by TAB BOOKS Inc.
First edition copyright © 1979 by TAB BOOKS Inc.
Printed in the United States of America

Library of Congress Cataloging in Publication Data

Blandford, Percy W.
   Designing and building children's furniture, with 61 projects / by
Percy W. Blandford. — 2nd ed.
    p. cm.
   Updated ed. of: 66 children's furniture projects.
   Includes index.
   ISBN 0-8306-9264-9   ISBN 0-8306-9364-5 (pbk.)
   1. Children's furniture.   I. Blandford, Percy W. 66 children's
furniture projects. II. Title.
   TT197.5.C5B55 1988
   684.1—dc19   88-24968
                                                         CIP

TAB BOOKS Inc. offers software for sale. For information and a catalog,
contact TAB Software Department, Blue Ridge Summit, PA 17294-0850.

Questions regarding the content of this book should be addressed to:
Reader Inquiry Branch
TAB BOOKS Inc.
Blue Ridge Summit, PA 17294-0214

Edited by Joanne M. Slike
Designed by Jaclyn B. Saunders

Contents

Introduction

One of the enjoyable parts of bringing up children is catering to their needs. With their smaller stature they cannot cope with many things of adult size. Yet they are growing and their needs change, so what may suit a baby will be far too small for him after a year or so. It is obvious with clothing, which is often outgrown before it has worn out, and it also applies to furniture, although much can be done to make it useful, over a longer growing span.

Parents enjoy being able to provide furniture and other equipment suitable for their children's size, but if it has to be replaced at intervals as the child grows, the cost might be more than the parents can afford. Making the furniture would be justified on the score of cost alone, but there are many other factors to consider. For instance, you can bring the cost of many items down to almost nothing by using salvaged wood. Even if you buy new wood, the cost might be no more than one-quarter than that of buying the furniture complete.

There is also the attraction of being able to make things to suit available space. Several items in a room can be made to fit in such a way as to make the most of the particular room size. If certain toys or books have to be stored, shelves and recesses can be made to suit, where a bought item might be just too small or far too big. Then there are some instances when there is no factory-made piece of furniture that will serve exactly the needs you have in mind. What you make can be perfect for its purpose.

In addition, you can take pride in having made something that is unique. It is for your child alone and nobody else has anything like it, so it furnishes a bond between you and the child that would not be quite the same with something bought in a store.

Also, you gain a satisfaction—a pride in achievement— that only comes with the practice of skill in a craft. Working with your hands is probably not the way you earn your living, yet there is a sense of accomplishment when you look at something and say, ''I made that,'' meaning that you saw the construction through from a few boards to a complete, functional, and attractive piece of furniture.

There is a particular attraction about making children's furniture for anyone who does not have sufficient skill to make many of the general pieces of furniture required in the home. Although much furniture intended for children can be made in the same way as that for adults and have a high-quality finish, in general, children's furniture can be made with simple joints, because it is not intended to have an indefinite life, and can be finished by painting. No craftsman would want to say that paint covers poor workmanship, but it can cover simpler construction that is quite satisfactory and acceptable. A painted finish also allows you to use woods that don't match each other and are of cheaper grades.

This means anyone who is uncertain of his or her woodworking skill can make simple furniture for children. With practice in handling tools, you will gain confidence and possibly progress to making more ambitious adult furniture. Of course, many items intended for a child's use can be made in larger sizes for adult use. In fact, many things in this book can be regarded as transitional furniture that will suit a child when small and also as he or she is growing up.

In preparing this book I have tried to cover a large range of furniture, often with several items intended for similar purposes, so each can be adopted to suit particular children or circumstances. The methods of construction vary from the very simplest to those that require traditional craftsman's skills, with alternatives suggested for many items. I hope there is something in the book for every lever of woodworking ability.

Most things can be made from solid wood, thick plywood, blockboard, particleboard, or framed thinner plywood. Each project is described as made in only one way, with the material list to suit. This should help avoid confusion due to multiple descriptions of the same thing. If you use a different form of wood, by referring to other projects you will be able to adapt your technique.

Material lists are provided for most pieces of furniture that include all the main wooden parts. Small parts are not listed as they can often be made from offcuts and scrap material, and would not have to be specially ordered. In any case, it is always a good idea to build up a stock of wood that can be drawn on. All sizes on drawings are in inches.

I hope you will get a great deal of pleasure and satisfaction out of making some of the things I have described for your son or daughter.

Planning Children's Furniture

THE OBVIOUS REASON for making furniture in children's sizes is that a child views a world that is out of proportion. If the child wants to sit on an adult chair, the adult has to lift the child on to it, and then the child's legs dangle. If the child wants to do things on a normal table from that chair, he or she has to kneel on the chair, and this is not what the chair was designed for. The child must constantly meet these frustrating experiences until growing up. A door handle placed at a convenient height for an adult might be out of reach. A coat hook might be too high. The child might need the help of a stool to get to toys put on a shelf.

Of course, a child has to adapt to an adult world as many things in it cannot be scaled down to suit the child. He or she has to accept that some things are intended for adult use and therefore, will not find them so convenient. The child is conditioned in earlier years to depend on the help of parents to do many things. This need for adult help might not frustrate the child in many tasks and simple situations like getting on a chair. However, when children get the opportunity to use things built to suit their size, enjoyment and comfort will increase. And that is what this book is all about.

Not everything is satisfactorily adaptable to smaller sizes. A child still has to get used to some things being too large. Children accept that their first view of a visitor might be at or below waist level. If they want to look into some shop windows, they might have to be lifted or stand on tiptoe. But a considerable range of furniture can be made to suit children's sizes that will add to their comfort and contribute to their education as they use these smaller things for everyday chores, work, and play.

It is much more satisfactory for a child to sit on a chair with feet on the ground, than to sit with legs hanging or kneel to get arms and head to a height comparable with an adult on an adjoining seat. They will find it more enjoyable to gather with friends on small chairs around a table of matching size, than to have to be lifted to a high chair to do things on a normal table. The child will appreciate having shelves and storage space at heights that can be reached without having to call for adult help.

This idea can be adapted to many things until a whole room is scaled to suit the child. If a room is set aside for a child's use only and equipped to suit the child he or she will be happier and so will the parents. He or she will also be more likely to learn care about tidiness. The room will serve as an educational background as the child develops into a young adult, knowing how to behave and exercise responsible independence.

Of course, children's furniture is not looked at by children as something formative and educational. They see it as something personal. It is so obviously theirs, as it is unsuitable for adults. They can take pride in their possessions. The things are managable in a way that comparable adult pieces of furniture are not.

A CHILD'S WORLD OF LEARNING

A child is always learning. Many things are new experiences and anything new has to be investigated. So many things that an adult regards as simple, a child might have to discover by trial and error. Every day brings new experiences, which the child's brain records. Giving a child an environment that suits his or her size should contribute to an accumulation of knowledge in a way that always being surrounded by oversize things will not.

Children have a great deal of physical energy. They need space to move about and anything they handle needs to be sufficiently robust to stand up to vigorous usage that an adult might not give it. This means that a child's room should have plenty of open space, have plenty of storage space for toys, and the furniture should be strong. Because it can't be moved built-in furniture has the advantage of being less likely to be damaged or cause accidents.

Toys are very important to children. They need not be elaborate. Adults might not always appreciate the imagination of a child. The value of a toy to a child may be nothing like the value an adult puts on a present. Something simple and cheap, like a set of building blocks, may be of much greater value in the eyes of a child than a very expensive mechanical toy.

This is not a book about making toys, but toys are related to furniture, and such things as tables and storage items will be used for toys. Also, some furniture may have play uses, although that was not the intention. Chairs might form a make-believe car or a fort. A table with a cloth draped over it becomes a den, or, turned upside-down, it becomes a ship or raft.

Some furniture might be specifically designed with a play purpose in mind. A box in which toys are put away might become a doll house, a garage, or anything else the child's imagination conjures up.

Young children find bright colors and pictures more appealing than the sober furniture of the adult world. They might be glad to have something that is made in the same design as a large piece familiar to them. A chair with turned legs like the one dad sits on might be appreciated by association, but in general, it is better to use plain strong construction and finish the furniture in bright colors, possibly with pictorial decorations.

This appeals to young children, but as they get older they might prefer something more like adult furniture. The child might not be big enough to use adult furniture conveniently, but if he or she has started moving about the adult world and has several years of school experience, brightly colored plain furniture might seem childish. He or she will then prefer more functional things, like working surfaces for hobbies and adult-looking desks for studies. The child might want a bunk with a cowboy or seagoing motif, instead of a straightforward bed. Most children want to put pictures on the walls, ceilings, and everywhere else. Furniture can be provided with plenty of space especially for this purpose, so pictures and posters can be put up and torn down without damaging the walls. Such pieces can serve as bulletin boards as a child's ideas and interests change with the process of growing up.

Because children spend much of their time outdoors running and playing games, there is a need for outdoor furniture or play equipment that helps the child get exercise as he plays. Such things as playhouses need not be elaborate. A basic structure can become a sedate home for parties or suddenly change to a fort or bandits' lair.

Children grow, sometimes too rapidly. Besides growing physically, they grow mentally. With increases in size their attitudes and desires also change. Furniture should be made to suit the child at the size he is. A chair that is made too high, with the intention that it will still be of use when his legs have grown longer, can be just as frustrating to the child as a full-size adult chair, and he might reject it. It is sometimes possible to design a chair so the legs can be lengthened, but too much alteration might cause other parts to no longer be in proportion.

Some things, like shelves, boxes, and beds, can be a compromised size to suit a growing child. However, chairs, tables, desks, and other articles will have to be designed for a period of no more than 2 years of a child's life and often much less. If there are other children to whom the item can be passed, it may have a longer, more useful life.

In addition, the materials used and the quality of workmanship will be affected by the expected life of the furniture. You can design something so all parts are screwed or otherwise temporarily fastened, so it can be dismantled without too much damage. Then you can salvage the wood to make something else. Design and construction have to be a compromise between making something that is attractive, strong enough for its purpose, and not more complicated than is justified by an expected short life.

Providing a child with furniture of the right size might also contribute to his safety. An adult trying to carry out daily tasks amidst furniture twice as big as needed, would soon find himself in trouble, having to climb on chairs, reach for tables, get at door handles, climb steps too high or use oversize tools. A child faces that sort of world everyday. But if the child has some things scaled down to suit, the child is less likely to have an accident with them. He or she can use and play with his own furniture with no more risk than an adult has with his. Of course, furniture for children should be made so that there are no weak joints or rough edges.

If all of the forementioned does not provide enough reasons for making children's furniture, there is another one concerning the parent-child relationship. Parents get considerable satisfaction out of making things for their children. They may talk about educational advantages and other reasons, but part of their motive is to do something for their family. This is a very good reason. At the other end of a child should appreciate what is being done for him, particularly when meeting other children. "My pop made this," is a real exclamation of pride. If what mom or dad made is something the other child does not have, the sense of pride is tremendous.

Another good reason for making furniture for children, even if they are not your own, is the opportunity of using your hands and brain to produce something complete from the raw materials to the finished object. Most of us never get that opportunity in our daily work. Not many people see a product right through. Most of us earn our living as part of a complex organization makes something, but what we do is only a small part of the process, often remotely connected with it. Many would-be amateur craftsmen hesitate at trying to make adult furniture, but in children's furniture construction is usually simpler and satisfactory results are easier to achieve. In any case, the final recipient will be much less critical than the user of an adult piece of furniture. If a joint does not fit perfectly or a leg is not absolutely upright, a child is unlikely to comment or regard it as of any importance, although an adult friend might remark on the error. But it is not really his concern.

SUGGESTED SIZES

Because children vary in their height and size, it is impossible to list certain sizes as being applicable to specific ages. Individual children have to be considered when furniture is made for them, but as a general guide to average sizes the measurements in TABLE 1-1 (in inches) are offered as suggestions for anyone producing their own designs.

Table 1-1. Suggested Sizes for Children's Furniture.

Furniture	Sizes for Various Ages in Inches			
	Adult	11 to 14	7 to 11	3 to 7
Chair height	18	16	13	10
Table height	30	27	22	18
Drawing table height	36	33	29	22
Drawing stool height	26	23	20	13
Table for standing	36	32	28	24
Door knob height	36	32	28	24
Tack or chalk board (bottom edge)	36	31	26	21
Book shelves (highest)	70	60	50	40
Coat hook (highest)	66	56	46	36
Bed length	78	72	66	60

2

Materials

ALTHOUGH THERE ARE NOW a great many natural and synthetic materials available that are used in making special furniture, the most commonly used material is wood. Wood has been the most commonly used material throughout history. It has so many properties that make it attractive, both in a finished piece of furniture and in the ease with which it can be worked with fairly simple tools. Most of the items described in this book are completely or mainly of wood. Wooden furniture is better able to stand up to rough usage and is generally less hazardous than some other possible materials.

There are actually thousands of species of wood, but those available at most lumber dealers are relatively few. Wood of value to furniture makers is broadly divided into softwoods and hardwoods. In general these names are a guide to relative hardness, although there are some borderline species where a hardwood is softer than some softwoods. The names are actually associated with the type of tree. Broad-leaf trees produce hardwoods, such as oak, mahogany, ash, chestnut, maple, walnut, and teak. The needle-leaf trees produce softwoods, some of which are cedar, fir larch, pine, redwood, and spruce.

Softwoods are suitable for most furniture that is to be painted. The appearance may be acceptable either untreated, or stained and varnished for a utility item, but by adult standards, softwoods are not the woods for better-quality furniture. Even when a piece of furniture is made of softwood, any bearing parts such as drawer runners, should be made out of a close-grained hardwood that will resist wear. Softwoods are mostly light in weight, so if a child is to move furniture around, they are the best choice.

Hardwoods are stronger than softwoods, as well as heavier. Some are more difficult to work. A leg for a table may be more slender in hardwood than in softwood if it is not to break in use. Most hardwoods have attractive grain. If you make something that will have other uses after the child has finished with it, you should use a hardwood with a clear varnish or polish.

On the other hand, softwoods are usually cheaper and more readily available than hardwoods. Within a species it is possible to get more than one grade. The quality of a lower grade, with its knots, flaws, and rough grain, might make it only suitable for unimportant outdoor carpentry. For children's furniture I advise you pay a little more for a higher grade. However, wood is a natural product that varies tremendously. There may be pieces amongst one grade that have qualities, at least in part, that should be in other grade. If it is possible to pick over lumber at the yard or dealers, you might find something suitable at a lower price than if you allow the supplier to select it in bulk.

When a tree grows, its increase in girth comes about by the addition of annual rings outside those already formed. It is these lines that make the grain. Sap goes up and down the tree. When the tree is felled there will be more moisture in the wood from the sap than would be acceptable for furniture making. This has to be dried out to an acceptable level by seasoning. Natural seasoning involves stacking the cut wood for years, but there are modern methods of hastening the drying. Even seasoned wood is never completely dry, and it is better for use with a very small amount of moisture in it. As wood is a porous material, it will take up more moisture from the atmosphere in damp and humid conditions or give it out in a very dry atmosphere, such as often occurs in a centrally heated room. This is inevitable and has to be accepted, but the changes in moisture content cause warping and shrinking.

Boards are cut from logs in many ways, but if the round log is cut across, the annual rings will have different relations to the board section according to where they were cut (FIG. 2-1A). Shrinkage is greatest along the lines of the annual rings. A board cut radially may shrink slightly in thickness if it dries out, but it will not usually become distorted (FIG. 2-1B). A board cut further from the center of the tree has curved lines and is more likely to warp if shrinkage occurs (FIG. 2-1C). If you look at the end of the board you want to use and want to know what would happen if it shrank, imagine the annual rings trying to straighten and that will give you a picture of the possible direction of warp.

Wood is normally supplied already seasoned, and the risk of shrinking or warping may be slight. However, if wood is cut to thinner sections, or sometimes when sawn wood is planed to expose a new surface, some distortion might occur. If possible, buy wood a few weeks before starting a project and keep it in a similar atmosphere to where the finished furniture will be. If any warping occurs, you can correct it when you prepare the wood for making it into furniture.

Fortunately, most wooden assemblies are made by fitting parts together so one piece holds another and any later tendency to warp is resisted. The whole carcass provides a sort of mutual support system. Exceptions are parts that extend without attachment to other parts, such as long legs without rails or a long handle. If possible, select wood with the grain across two faces. That piece is unlikely to go out of shape in use.

Softwoods are more susceptible to variations in moisture content than hardwoods. A piece of wood that has been prepared to 2-inch width might actually

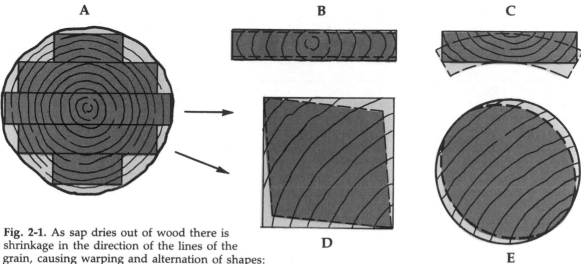

Fig. 2-1. As sap dries out of wood there is shrinkage in the direction of the lines of the grain, causing warping and alternation of shapes: (A) annual rings; (B) radial cut; (C) curved lines cut; (D) diagonal grain lines; (E) elliptical.

shrink to $1^{15}\!/_{16}$ inches by the time you get it. This will not generally matter, but it means that when you construct anything, the actual pieces of wood measure particularly if cutting joints, and don't assume the measurement is correct. What might be more of a nuisance would be a piece of wood that started square and changed to a diamond section due to shrinkage in the direction of diagonal grain lines (FIG. 2-1D), or a round that became elliptical for the same reason (FIG. 2-1E). Most wood that has been properly seasoned should not warp or shrink to any appreciable extent.

The designs described later are accompanied by material lists. It is usually best to take a copy of the list to the lumber dealer and let him select sizes to suit, or go over his stock and select them yourself. It is unwise to merely total the lengths of a particular section and ask for that. For instance, you might need six pieces of a 2-×-1-inch section of wood, each 2 feet long. If you ask for one piece 12 feet long, it will probably cost you more than if you tell the dealer what you need to cut and let him select random lengths that will give you the same results.

Available wood can only be as big as the tree it comes from. You should be able to get any length you need, but in some woods the widths are very limited because of the tree thickness. Wide boards in a particular species might be impossible. Even when wide boards are available, you might pay proportionately more for them than if you scheme your work to narrower boards. Fortunately, plywood and other manufactured boards have removed much of the need for very wide natural boards.

Wood is converted into a large number of stock sizes that have been found to suit the majority of uses. I advise that you check what is available locally and arrange your work accordingly for economy. If you want stock sizes altered to other sizes, you have to pay extra. Sizes quoted are usually as sawn. Also, if the wood ordered is machine-planed, it is likely to be about ⅛ inch under size. This means that what is bought as a 1-inch board will actually be ⅞ inch as planed. For most purposes this is acceptable, providing the work is laid out to allow for the actual dimensions of the wood. If you insist that the planed wood should finish at 1 inch you will pay much more because it will have to be specially prepared from thicker wood.

Most of the things described later in this book can be made from stock sections of wood, but if the locally available sections are different, it will not matter in most cases if the actual wood used is slightly thicker or thinner. For instance, if a piece of plywood is to be framed around with solid wood that is specified as ¾ × 1½ inches (⅝ × 1⅜ inches when planed), it would be just as satisfactory as much as ½ inch wider or ¼ inch thicker, providing the difference is allowed for when cutting joints or fitting adjoining parts.

If you plan to do alot of woodwork, you should build up a stock of the common sections of wood. When buying wood for a particular project, get more than you need and put it into stock. Besides giving you a variety of woods to draw on when you get an idea for an alteration or a new small project, the wood stored will complete its seasoning in your shop. When you come to use it, you can be certain that it has settled to a stable condition.

Also consider other sources of supply. You can find a large amount of useful lumber in discarded crates, pallets, and various sorts of packing material and containers. Some of this might be inferior grade wood and of little value to you except for rough outdoor uses, but sometimes excellent lumber can be found. Do not be put off by the roughly sawn surface, even if it is dirty or covered with painted details of the one-time contents. You might need to plane the wood extensively, but test an edge to see if it is worth salvaging.

Old furniture might also yield useful wood. Someone's discarded table or bookcase, damaged and bought cheaply at a yard sale, may be taken apart to provide plywood panels and framing that can be used again.

PLYWOOD

Plywood is one of the most useful materials for making children's furniture. Its most attractive features are its availability in large flawless sheets without visible joints and its resistance to expansion and contraction. Plywood is all wood, bonded with glue. It is made by joining veneers, which are thin pieces of wood, so alternate layers are perpendicular to each other. There are always an odd number of layers of veneer so the grains of the outside pieces are the same way.

The simplest form of plywood has three layers and is often referred to as three-ply (FIG. 2-2A). Veneers can be as thick as ⅛ inch, so three-ply can be up to ⅜ inch thick, but over ¼ inch thick it is also possible to get plywood with five or more veneers (FIG. 2-2B). The greater the number of veneers in a given thickness, the stiffer the panel will be. This could be important if the plywood is to form a flap or door without framing, but if it is to be framed with solid wood, the number of veneers does not matter.

Some plywood is bonded with a nonwaterproof glue, but most modern plywood is made with synthetic resin glue that has a good resistance to moisture. The type and quality of the veneers affect the plywood and many grades are available. You need not buy the best quality if a lesser grade will do. Many woods are used for plywood. Douglas fir is common. It has a rather prominent coarse grain that makes finishing to a smooth finish difficult, but this might not be important in most children's furniture. Other plywood is made from more close-grained wood, many of them reddish in color.

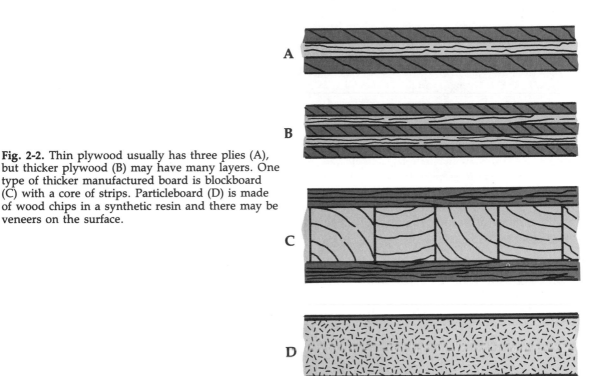

Fig. 2-2. Thin plywood usually has three plies (A), but thicker plywood (B) may have many layers. One type of thicker manufactured board is blockboard (C) with a core of strips. Particleboard (D) is made of wood chips in a synthetic resin and there may be veneers on the surface.

Some plywood has one or both outer veneers of good quality wood and inner layers of a poorer quality wood. If only one side will show, that need be the only good one. Most plywood has both sides sanded, in any case. Veneers are quite wide, but there are joints between their edges. In lower grade plywood these joints might be poor and obvious. In some plywood inside veneers have gaps between their edges. Better plywood has the same wood used throughout and all edge joints are close.

If plywood is described as exterior grade, the glue used has a very high resistance to moisture. If it is called marine grade, besides the glue being waterproof, the quality of veneer is uniformly high. Exterior grade may have poorer veneers inside.

Plywood made from any wood may have a further thin veneer applied to one or both surfaces. This can be wood that is similar to the solid wood that surrounds it, to make panelled furniture with all exposed surfaces matching.

Plywood is made in thickness from about ⅛ to 1 inch and in several stock size panels. The largest panels commonly available are 4 × 8 feet, although larger sizes are made. There are several smaller standard-size panels. A supplier will cut what you need, but there will be a charge for this. Therefore, it is always more economical to scheme your requirements so you can buy a standard panel and cut it to suit yourself. Often if you are making several items of children's furniture, offcuts from one job will be used on another, so spare pieces of plywood are always worth having.

Although plywood is made up to about 1 inch thick, there are some alternatives in the thicker grades, although these are not as common. One type of blockboard or stripboard has a core made up of solid strips of wood sandwiched between veneers, which may be single or double thickness on each side (FIG. 2-2C).

MANUFACTURED BOARDS

Another thick manufactured board is made of small shreds of wood embedded in resin and called particleboard, chipboard, or flakeboard. This is made in thicknesses from ½ inch upwards. It is made in similar panel sizes to plywood and most of it has a drab gray/brown appearance. Surfaces are smooth and it is possible to work the material with ordinary woodworking tools. In its normal form it is a constructional material, suitable for parts that are not normally visible, so its appearance is unimportant.

However, particleboard can be obtained with its surfaces covered with wood veneers, laminated plastic, and other materials (FIG. 2-2D). It is also possible to get these materials in strips to cover cut edges, so surfaced particleboard can be used instead of wood for many things. A laminated plastic surface makes a working top to a table or bench that resists moisture and heat and can be wiped clean. A real wood or plastic imitation wood surface covering allows the flat, rigid qualities of particleboard to be used in making modern-style furniture, suitable for children.

Hardboard (not to be confused with hardwood) is a compressed material made from wood or vegetable fibers. It is normally available ⅛ inch thick and in similar-size panels to plywood. Hardboard is compressed and normally has one smooth glossy hard surface, while the other side is patterned. The smooth side takes paint well and hardboard can be substituted for plywood in some paneled work. The quality of the reverse side is unimportant.

There are several grades of hardboard, mainly dependent on relative hardness and stiffness. The lowest grade, with characteristics little better than cardboard, is not much use for furniture, but the harder grades are worth considering. You might not need hardboards with fluted or decorated surfaces, but there is a type with a regular pattern of holes that can take special hooks and allow the young user to arrange different methods of hanging toys and clothing.

Most makers of hardboard offer a grade described as oil-tempered, or something similar. Ordinary hardboard does not have much resistance to dampness, but the oil-tempered grade is one of the hardest with a good water resistance, although not as good as exterior or marine grades of plywood.

A large range of prepared moldings are also available. Some types have rabbets for framing pictures or mirrors. Others may be shaped for particular purposes, but the majority are purely decorative. It is unlikely that a child will take much notice of these finer points of decoration—an adult viewer will be more likely to notice them. The use of prepared moldings on children's furniture should be limited, but one use for them is to break up the plainness of a large panel. Mitered molding shapes on the plywood can give the effect of a solid framed door or other structure, with enclosed panels. Alternatively, colored or cut-out pictures can be framed where they are mounted on a panel of a piece of furniture.

OTHER MATERIALS

Glass should be avoided in children's furniture, because of its danger if broken. Plexiglass or other transparent plastic is better. This also has the advantage of being more easily worked. It can be bent, cut to shaped outlines, and is easily drilled. A disadvantage is its comparative softness. It can be scratched and its original gloss and clarity may become impaired with anything abrasive. This means that it should not be used where it gets frequent rubbing; but for windows, inspection panels, and framed pictures, it is better than glass in a child's room.

Other plastics are best used for knobs and handles. Fittings made of nylon and other plastics work well too. There is not much use for sheet plastic used alone, but it is best employed as an easy-clean facing for particleboard or hardboard, when it can be bought already attached.

The majority of people who turn to making children's furniture will be content to restrict most of their activity to wood, but anyone with a little skill at metalwork can introduce metal parts, although entire construction in metal is unlikely. Metal tubes can make rails in hanging closets or be used as struts in some types of furniture. For most metal parts associated with wood, aluminum is usually the best choice, as it does not corrode and will keep its appearance for a long time. Also, it is easy to saw, file and drill.

Steel is less suitable because of the risk of rust, but if it is well painted, there should be no trouble. Steel is much stronger than aluminum and for this reason it may have to be used for substantial outdoor furniture, then thoroughly painted to protect it from dampness. For some indoor furniture, chromium or other plating on steel will produce an attractive effect when used with painted or polished wood.

Brass and copper can also be used instead of aluminum. If metal parts are to be soldered, these are the metals to use, as it is difficult to solder steel and almost impossible to solder aluminum. Lead has some use where weight is needed. It can be used in the base of anything tall, like a lamp standard or a clothing rack, to increase stability. Its density allows maximum weight to be put into a small space. It has the advantage of a low melting point, so it can be made liquid with commonly available heat sources and poured into a mold of the shape required

If furniture is to be upholstered I suggest you use synthetic materials, mainly because it is easy to clean and is comparatively moisture resistant. Fillings may be plastic or rubber foam of the closed-cell type, which will not absorb water. Polyester and other synthetic fabrics are available in many attractive colors and patterns. For the easiest cleaning, choose fabric-backed plastic, or imitation leather-type for covering.

3

Hardware
and Adhesives

MANY GREAT METAL FITTINGS, fasteners for special purposes, and hinges are available that can be used in making furniture. Knobs, handles, and catches can be decorative as well as functional. If furniture is to be built-in, there are special attachments to help you. If doors are to slide instead of swing, or the furniture is to be movable, there are devices to facilitate this. Many of these things will be described in connection with particular pieces of furniture, but this chapter can serve as an overview to the bewildering array of hardware, accessories, and adhesives.

NAILS

A cabinetmaker or other expert maker of adult furniture has little use for nails and tends to associate them with poor-quality furniture. However, because children's furniture does not usually have to last indefinitely, you need not spend a lot of time cutting special joints. For many places on children's furniture, nails will work fine. Of course, there are places where traditional joints are preferred and other places where screws would be a better choice than nails. Nails can be difficult to withdraw without damaging the wood, so if parts have to be separated later, possibly to allow the wood to be used for something else after the child has grown too big for the item, it may be wiser to use screws.

All general-purpose nails are made of mild steel, often loosely described as iron. Zinc plating may be used as a protection against corrosion for exterior use. Nails are also made of other metals with better resistance to corrosion, but most are not as strong and stiff as mild steel. Tempered tool steel nails are made for driving directly into masonry.

Common nails may be collectively called *wire* nails. They are round, parallel, and have flat heads. Points may be tapered squares (FIG. 3-1A), as with *common* or *box* nails. Thicknesses increase with length and common nails are slightly thicker than box nails of the same length.

Nails are available in a great many lengths up to about 6 inches. It is probably best to order nails by their lengths, but you can also order them by penny sizes. For instance, a two-penny nail is 1 inch long and there are about 840 to one pound. This system continues through other sizes, such as 10 penny, which is 3 inches long and 65 per pound to six penny, which is 6 inches long and 11 to one pound. Quoting the length needed may be less confusing to the occasional user.

For use on roofing there are shingle and roofing nails with larger heads (FIG. 3-1B). Some nails might have barbed shanks (FIG. 3-1C), while others have twisted square shanks to produce *screw nails*. Both of these have increased grip.

Ordinary nail heads appear prominently on the surface of the wood. Other types have finer heads that do not show as much if left on the surface, but they are particularly intended for punching below the surface and covering with stopping. Of course, a reduced head does not have quite the holding power, but it is adequate for most purposes and is useful in making children's furniture. Small nails with reduced heads are called *panel* or *veneer* pins (FIG. 3-1D). Bigger nails of this type are *casing* nails. A variation on the head is the *brad* head of *finishing* nails.

A staple is a double-ended nail (FIG. 3-1E). A *tack* is a small tapered nail (FIG. 3-1F), used mostly in upholstery. Its taper means it does not have much strength in a direct pull, but where the strain is across it, as in fixing cloth to wood, it is strong enough.

In many circumstances nails can be driven directly without drilling first. However, if there seems a risk of splitting, it is better to drill the top piece of wood with a hole the same size as the nail or very slightly smaller. In most cases there is no need to drill the lower piece of wood, but if there is, the hole should be undersize. When a withdrawing type of load comes on a nail, this is taken between the head pressing down on the top piece of wood and the friction holding the nail in the bottom piece, so too much should not be removed there by drilling. Even when there is not much risk of splitting anticipated, it might still be wiser to drill for nails that come near an edge. For extra strength at a part liable to greatest strain, there should be closer nail spacing (FIG. 3-2A). Driving vertically to a surface is common, but greater strength can be obtained by angling the nails a little in alternate directions to produce dovetail nailing (FIG. 3-2B).

The choice of nail length is a matter of experience. Nails hold tighter in hardwoods than in softwoods, and are stronger in cross grain than in end grain, so adjust the lengths and spacing accordingly. If the lower part is stout enough, a penetration of 1 inch into it for light construction is probably right, with increasing depths for heavier work.

For nails that are to be sunk below the surface, use a nail punch or sett (FIG. 3-3A). The flat end of the punch should be about the same diameter as the nail head. Some punches have hollow ends, but there seems little advantage in this.

Punches are cheap and it is worthwhile to have a few of different sizes. Normally a head is punched about ⅛ inch below the surface and the hole filled

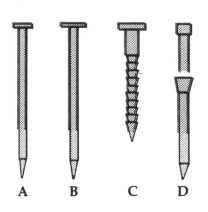

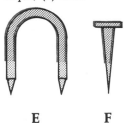

Fig. 3-1. Nails may have different sized heads, there may be rings to provide grip and they can be intended to drive below the surface. A double-ended nail is a staple and a tapered one is a tack: (A) common nails; (B) roofing nails; (C) screw nail; (D) panel pins; (E) staple; (F) tack.

A B C D E F

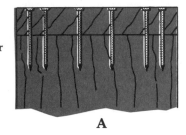

Fig. 3-2. Nails should be driven closer near edges (A). Driving at alternate angles is stronger than straight nailing (B).

A B

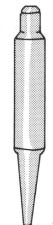

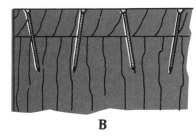

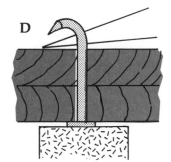

Fig. 3-3. A nail can be punched below the surface (A), then the hole filled with stopping (B). A projecting point may be clenched (C), but it is stronger and safer to end the point first (D).

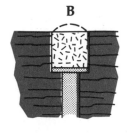

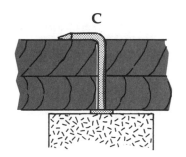

A B C D

with a stopping, which sets hard and can be sanded level with the surface (FIG. 3-3B). If the work is to be painted, it does not matter what color the stopping is, but there are some stoppings that will take stain like wood, and others that are already colored to match different kinds of wood. Both are for use on furniture with a clear finish.

In some constructions, particularly in garden furniture, a nail can be taken right through, so the projecting point can be turned back into the wood and *clenched*. This increases strength to the point where the wood would have to be broken before the nail gave way. Although the simplest way to do this is to flatten the nail end (FIG. 3-3C), it is better to bury the point by clenching in two stages. First, hold an iron block, or another hammer, against the nail head. Then put a spike close to the nail end, which is curved over it by hammering (FIG. 3-3D). Withdraw the spike so that the nail end is buried in the wood. Although neatest along the grain, hammer the end across or diagonal to the grain for added strength.

When nailing light parts that cannot be supported on a bench or something else solid, hold an iron block or second hammer against the far side to reduce rebound. Without this there is a risk that the act of driving one nail will loosen another further along the row.

SCREWS

Wood screws make better joints than nails as they will pull parts tighter together by the action of driving. They have a more positive grip and can be withdrawn without damaging the wood. Some special wood screws are produced, but in general the screws commonly available have parallel plain shanks for a short distance under the head, then threads with sharp edges, finishing in a sharp point (FIG. 3-4A). The word *screw* is also applied to what most people call a *bolt*, which is really a screwed fastener used with a nut. Therefore, it is safer to speak of *wood screws*, if that is what you mean.

Some screws that look very similar, but usually have threads right to the head, are hardened-steel, self-taping screws, intended to cut their way into sheet metal as they are driven. Although they can be driven into wood, that is not what they are intended for.

Common screws have flat heads (FIG. 3-4B). These should be countersunk so they finish flush with the surface of the wood. Another type has a round head, which is almost semicircular and stands above the surface (FIG. 3-4C). Between

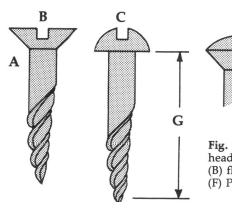
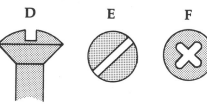

Fig. 3-4. Screw length is from the wood surface. There are several heads and two types of sockets for screwdrivers: (A) plain shanks; (B) flat heads; (C) round head; (D) oval head; (E) slotted heads; (F) Phillips head; (G) length of screw.

the two is an oval head (FIG. 3-4D). This looks better than a flat head when attaching metal fittings with countersunk holes.

Slotted screw heads (FIG. 3-4E) have been the only type in use for a long time and are still satisfactory for hand driving. The star-shaped socket of the Phillips head (FIG. 3-4F) was developed for power screwdrivers in mass production, but screws with heads of this type are available for ordinary use and require screwdrivers with special points. Three different sizes should cover the range of screws normally used in furniture.

The quoted length of a screw is from the surface of the wood to the point (FIG. 3-4G), so the overall length of a screw that stands above the wood is greater than a flat head one. Lengths range from ¼ inch to sizes bigger than needed in furniture. The shorter screws come in ⅛-inch steps, then ¼-inch steps up to 3 inch, and ½ inch steps above that. Thicknesses are by a gauge size—the lower the number, the thinner the screw.

No hardware store stocks the whole range of screws made, but there is a guide to the sizes available and useful in furniture making. Larger screws are only commonly available in even-number sizes, but for screws under ½ inch, you can find gauges of 2 or 3, for screws from ⅜ to ¾ inch, gauges of 4 or 5, for screws from ½ to 2 inches, gauges of 6 or 8 (and sometimes 7), and for screws from 8 to 12 inches, gauges over 2 inches. However, there are other combinations of length and gauges available.

Steel is the usual metal for screws, but there are brass screws that resist corrosion and look better for places in furniture where the heads show. Both metals may be plated in several ways in order to protect them or to improve appearance. Other screws available are made of bronze, aluminum, stainless steel and even plastics.

Although you can often drive a nail without first drilling a hole, you should always make a hole for a screw in the top piece, to allow it to slide through. A screw holds by compressing the top piece of wood against the other between its head and the pull of the screw threads. The hole in the top piece should not grip the screw neck. If the screw is forced into the top piece, this will interfere with its tightening of the joint, so always choose a drill for the top piece to match the diameter of the screw (FIG. 3-5A). The size and depth of the hole in the lower piece depends on the wood as well as the diameter and length of the screw. For the smallest screws in soft wood it might be sufficient to give the screw a light tap with a hammer and then let it cut its own way in. Other screws need a small hole with only part of the depth of the screw penetrating the soft wood (FIG. 3-5B). A slightly bigger hole is needed for the full depth in harder wood (FIG. 3-5C).

In some softer woods a flathead screw will pull in level with the surface as it is driven, but in harder woods use a countersink bit to prepare the hole (FIG. 3-5D). It is wisest to try one screw first. If it does not pull in enough, it might be sufficient to countersink only slightly as full countersinking might result in the screw head actually going too far.

Holes for screws can be made with the small twist drills primarily intended for metal. For the lower hole for small screws, a convenient simple tool is a *bradawl* (FIG. 3-5E). Its cutting end is thrust in and turned backwards and forwards, to make a hole by severing fibers, then the screw threads get a better grip than in a cleaned-out hole made by a drill.

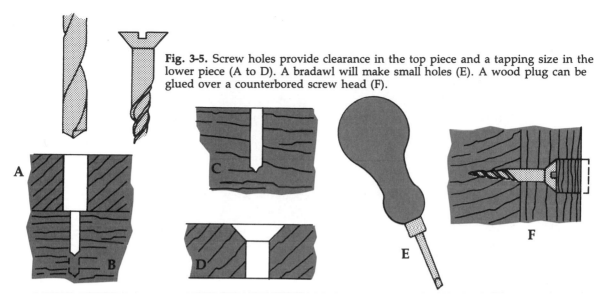

Fig. 3-5. Screw holes provide clearance in the top piece and a tapping size in the lower piece (A to D). A bradawl will make small holes (E). A wood plug can be glued over a counterbored screw head (F).

When screws are driven through a surface that will be exposed in the completed furniture, they can be sunk and the holes plugged so the screw heads do not show. Plugs can be made with a plug cutter from similar wood to that in the furniture, with its grain across to match the surrounding wood. A plug cutter is like a hollow drill and is used in a drill press or a hand electric drill mounted in a stand. For a hole to suit the plug, drill about ¼ inch deep, then drill for and drive the screw (FIG. 3-5F). Glue the plug over the screw head so it stands above the surface and can be trimmed level after the glue has set.

Besides plain screwdrivers there are ratchet and pump-action types. Both of these are convenient, but it is better to spend a limited amount of money on an assortment of sizes and lengths of plain screwdrivers than to spend it all on one of these special types. The end of a screwdriver should be a fairly close fit in the screw head or it might jump out and damage the surrounding wood. If the end is much narrower than the slot, leverage is reduced and the screw head may be damaged. A long screwdriver is less likely to be misdirected, but some short ones are needed to get into confined spaces.

As with nails, the choice of screws and their spacing is largely a matter of experience, but a penetration of 1 inch into the lower part and a spacing of 2 inches can be regarded as a guide to increase or decrease according to particular needs. Thicker screws have a stronger grip than thinner screws of the same length.

For built-in furniture you can screw directly into wooden walls. Screws are best located where they can enter studding. For cavity walls there are several fasteners that go through and expand on the far side of a panel (FIG. 3-6A). Solid walls have to be plugged.

There are special drills for use on stone and brick and other tools to use with a hammer. It is possible to plug with wood, but fiber or plastic plugs are preferred. The action of driving a screw expands the plug to grip the hole, but it might also cause its end to rise. Because of this I advise that you position the plug end slightly below the surface. This is particularly important if attaching

Fig. 3-6. Attachment to a hollow wall can be made with a device that expands when tightened (A). A solid wall has to be drilled and plugged to take a screw (B).

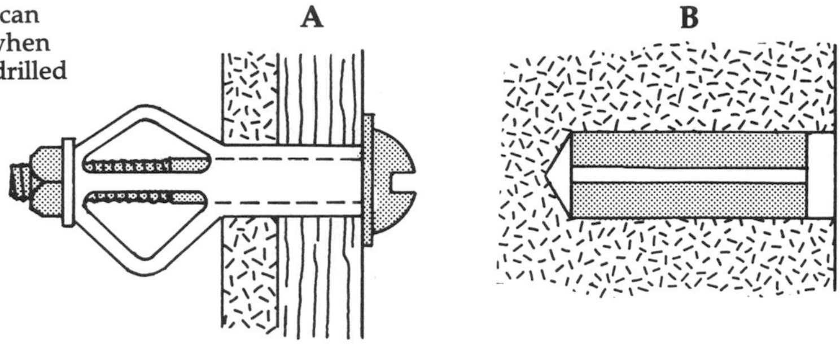

A

B

with a metal plate, where part of the unthreaded neck of the screw will enter the hole, making the last few turns difficult and causing a flush plug to lift the plate above the wall level (FIG. 3-6B).

BOLTS

For some parts of furniture the most convenient fastening is by nut and bolt. This is particularly so when there is a folding framework and the parts can pivot on a bolt.

Technically, a *bolt* is a fastener with threads only partly along its length (FIG. 3-7A). If the threads go to the head, it is a *machine screw* (FIG. 3-7B). This applies whatever the head, which can be of any of the forms used on wood screws, although a bolt is more likely to have a head to take a wrench. This, and the nut, can be square or hexagonal. A *carriage bolt* is a useful type for folding furniture, as it has a square neck under a shallow head, to pull into and grip the wood to prevent the bolt from turning (FIG. 3-7C).

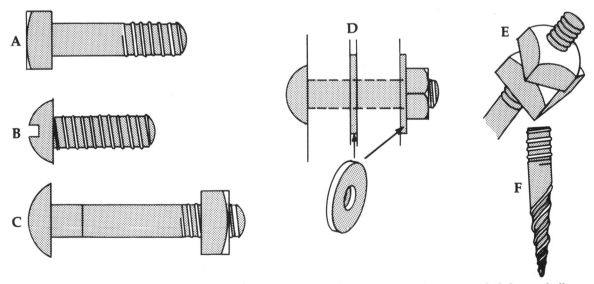

Fig. 3-7. A bolt has a short thread (A), a screw has a full-length thread (B) and a carriage bolt has a shallow head and square neck (C). Washers should be put between wood and a nut (D). Two nuts tightened together provide locking (E). A wood screw with a threaded neck (F) allows bolting directly to wood.

Washers are used under nuts to prevent them from pulling into the wood, as well as between moving parts (FIG. 3-7D). If parts move on a bolt, it will be necessary to do something to prevent the nut from coming loose. There are adhesives in tubes that can be squeezed on the bolt to prevent the nut from loosening accidentally, yet a wrench will still turn the nut off. You can spread the bolt end by hammering, but that makes dismantling difficult or impossible. There are nuts that incorporate fiber or other friction material to resist loosening.

Another way is to use two nuts (FIG. 3-7E). Do not merely tighten the second nut on the first. To achieve a good lock, use two wrenches and tighten the under nut back against the top one.

A *stud* is a piece of screwed rod without a bolt head. Although studs are intended for use in machinery, they can also be used to assemble furniture with folding frames. A stud can be put through several pieces of wood and nuts used on the ends, so a stud is then like a double-ended bolt.

Another method sometimes useful for attaching a metal part to wood involves a combination of machine and wood screw (FIG. 3-7F). With the wood screw part driven into wood, the extending part can be used with a nut to hold down another part, which can be removed and replaced as often as you wish. To drive the screw, lock two nuts against each other on the machine screw part and drill a suitable hole in the wood. Use a wrench on the top nut to drive the screw, then remove the nuts.

HINGES

The basic type of hinge is often called a *butt hinge* and consists of two flaps joined by a pin through a knuckle. It is already drilled for flathead screws (FIG. 3-8A). Steel and brass are the common metals used. Hinge sizes range from quite tiny to ones larger than are needed for furniture construction.

Butt hinges are particularly useful for doors and lids, when the hinge is let into one or both parts so the gap between the two parts is narrow when closed. The knuckle must be clear of the edges so the door swings clear of the frame (FIG. 3-8B). Be sure to line the knuckles of the hinges when you use two or more on an edge.

A *flush hinge* works in a similar way, but it is made of thin metal and one part fits inside the other (FIG. 3-8C). The total thickness is no more than the gap left between a door, lid or flap and its frame, so these hinges do not have to be let in. This is an advantage when using particleboard, as it is not very easy to cut a neat recess in that material.

Ordinary hinges do not swing open much more than 180°. This is sufficient for the usual door or lid, but for circumstances where the flap has to go further, there are *backflap hinges* (FIG. 3-8D). The hinge can also be used with its knuckle let into the wood for a flap that swings back (FIG. 3-8E). This is necessary in some types of tables where the top turns and has hanging flaps or leaves.

A different type of hinge fits on the top and bottom edges of a door. This *angle pivot hinge* turns on a pivot point that is offset (FIG. 3-8F). The door swings clear, possibly to miss a surrounding molding or other projection.

Other hinges are intended to be screwed on a surface. These *cabinet hinges* usually have decorative outlines (FIG. 3-8G). Some are cranked (FIG. 3-8H), with one leg on a surface level with the inside of the door.

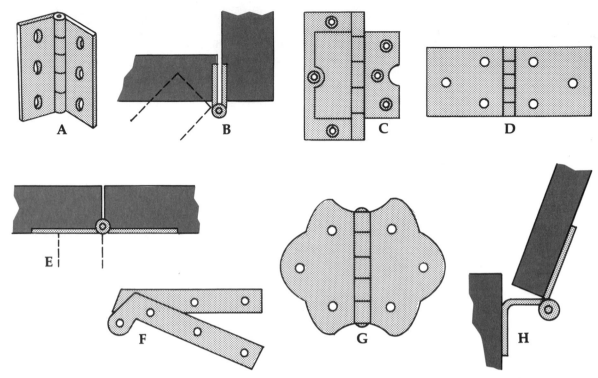

Fig. 3-8. Hinges take many forms and most depend on a pivot pin through a knuckle; (A) butt hinge; (B) cleared knuckle; (C) flush hinge; (D) backflap hinge; (E) swinging flap; (F) angle pivot hinge; (G) cabinet hinge; (H) cranked hinge.

Several ingenious hinges, used on adult furniture, are mostly concealed when the door is shut. The large hinges are for heavy construction and outdoor use. Some hinges have combined actions that lock things like table legs. All of these should be used for adult furniture. For most children's furniture use a butt hinge to suit the strong construction necessary.

BRACKETS

For added strength in furniture that a child might treat roughly during play, reinforce the wood with metal, particularly at joints that could be strained or broken.

There are shelf brackets in many forms and sizes, some with angle pieces projecting, but the type made from pressed sheet metal (FIG. 3-9A) does not project much from the wood. Brackets can be used to strengthen right-angled corners, as well as for their intended use of supporting shelves.

Repair plates are made like brackets but are flat or T shaped (FIG. 3-9B). They can be used across wood-to–wood joints where extra strength is required. Use these plates at joints where a risk of strain is anticipated, rather than wait until weakening occurs before screwing them on.

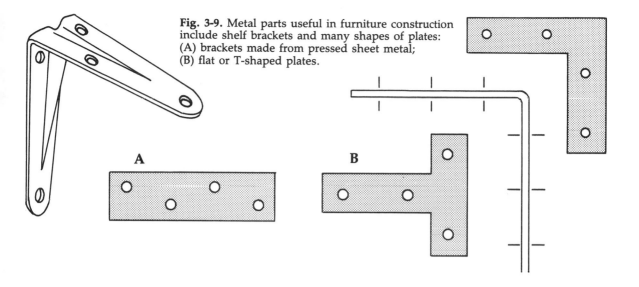

Fig. 3-9. Metal parts useful in furniture construction include shelf brackets and many shapes of plates: (A) brackets made from pressed sheet metal; (B) flat or T-shaped plates.

A

B

CASTERS

If furniture will be moved, it might be sufficient to merely take off the sharp corners of the feet or other bottom edges, so it can be pushed without catching. This will work on a plain wooden floor, but if there is any covering, particularly carpets, something else is needed to avoid damage to the surface.

Casters are wheels, offset on arms, that allow furniture to roll. A simple and satisfactory version has a round projection to fit into a hole in the wood (FIG. 3-10A). Other types work the same way, and with a more attractive appearance, but the basic caster will do for most children's furniture. For anything heavy, or where the bottom of the furniture is unsuitable for drilling, it is better to have the type mounted on a plate to screw in place (FIG. 3-10B). A caster raises the furniture about 2 inches and this should be allowed for in the original design. Otherwise, the legs will have to be shortened.

A metal glide is a simpler way of reducing damage when furniture is moved over a carpet. It is a polished metal dome with projecting teeth to drive into the wood (FIG. 3-10C). Clicks do not raise the furniture any appreciable amount. One

Fig. 3-10. Casters (A and B) allow furniture to be moved about. Glides (C) are simpler and are suitable for light furniture.

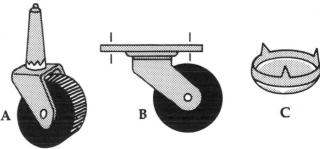

A

B

C

possible advantage with some furniture for children is that these are less likely than casters to allow unintentional sliding if the child leans against or knocks the table or cabinet.

KNOBS, CATCHES AND LOCKS

A very young child may not have the ability or patience to operate any sort of device that requires thought and possibly more than one action. For instance, if a pair of doors has to be fastened by first using a bolt on one, then turning a catch against it on the other, the child is likely to leave the doors undone. This might be out of frustration at not knowing how to operate the assembly or because the child is in a hurry to get to some other activity. Consequently, you should make the handling of such things as doors and drawers as simple as possible.

You do not always need to add anything. A cutaway to admit a small hand will allow a door or drawer to be pulled (FIG. 3-11A). You could also provide two well-rounded holes to put fingers through (FIG. 3-11B). If you want to use handles or knobs, they should be simple and without projections. Avoid handles, appropriate for adult furniture, that have raised and intricate decorations. Turned wooden or plastic knobs offer a good grip without roughness (FIG. 3-11C). They should be fitted with machine or wood screws from the back, although one simple type glues into a hole (FIG. 3-11D).

Long handles have advantages. If a child needs to use both hands to pull a drawer, they allow him a broad grip. If there is a door to be opened, a long handle gives a grip at a child's height and an adult can use a higher portion without bending too much. A drawer handle in wood or plastic can have a hooked section (FIG. 3-11E), while a door handle might have a symmetrical section (FIG. 3-11F). Both are attached with screws from the back. Thoroughly round the ends of these handles, which can be bought in long pieces for cutting to suit the job.

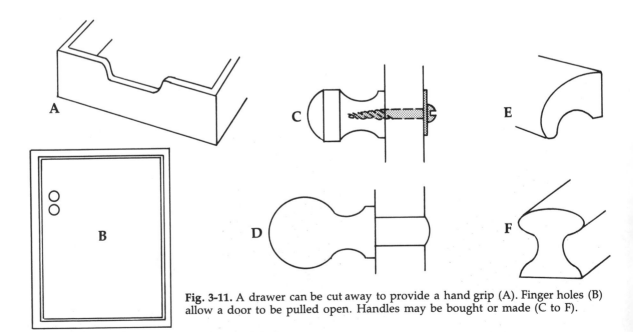

Fig. 3-11. A drawer can be cut away to provide a hand grip (A). Finger holes (B) allow a door to be pulled open. Handles may be bought or made (C to F).

With several types of door catches you must lift or turn them to operate. You might want to use more complicated door catches in a child's room for storage places he is not supposed to reach or open. However for doors he will open and close, it is better to have something that only requires a push or pull on the door handle. Magnetic catches are useful. A magnet on one part engages with a steel plate on the other part. There are several types to suit particular situations, but a magnet mounted on the frame and a plate on the door will suit most furniture (FIG. 3-12A).

One or two rollers may spring over a hump on the other part to grip it. They can be plastic or metal and can fit on a drawer or the frame behind a door (FIG. 3-12B). The many types of sprung ball catches also operate with a pull. Some types engage with a hole in a metal plate. Another type has two facing sprung balls and a thickened piece for them to engage and grip (FIG. 3-12C). Avoid catches with sharp edges or projections. Plastics are usually smoother than metals.

Sliding bolts that are satisfactory inside adult furniture doors might be too complicated for a child. Therefore, he either wrenches the door back and breaks or bends the bolt, or he leaves the door swinging open. Handles that turn catches inside are also unsuitable. A child needs to see what is happening, so a catch with its movements visible on the front should be used.

It is a good idea to provide a door or flap with some sort of support to prevent it from closing unintentionally and possibly hurting the child. There are lid supports that fold and have to be operated in some way to secure them; some by a cam action, others by locating a slot on a peg, and some with the aid of a screw or nut. Use a simple folding stay that pivots in the middle (FIG. 3-12D). The pivot should be a friction joint that can be adjusted to prevent accidental closing. It can be used to hold a lid open, a door at any position, or for a swing-down flap for a writing surface.

Locks, with their loose keys, have no place on furniture to be used by a child. Nothing should be capable of being fastened so it cannot be opened from either side. If something is big enough for a child to get inside, he should be able to push his way out. Any catch that requires a positive action on the outside could be dangerous if the child was inside. I wouldn't advise you to lock anything intended for adult use in a child's room. It would be better to store it elsewhere.

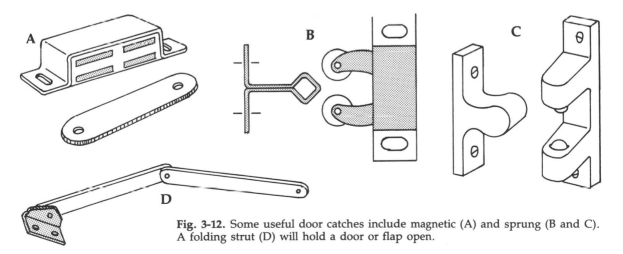

Fig. 3-12. Some useful door catches include magnetic (A) and sprung (B and C). A folding strut (D) will hold a door or flap open.

GLUES

Because of the changes in glues in recent years, I suggest you carefully read the description and instructions that accompany a supply of glue, as such information might be very different from those applicable to earlier glues. The following notes give a clue to the main types of wood glues available, but when buying, make sure that the glue is for wood and nothing else. If a glue is described as suitable for paper, cardboard, cloth, and other things besides wood, it is probably a general-purpose adhesive that is strong enough for toys and the like, but is not really suitable for furniture and the stress put on their joints.

Most glues supplied premixed depend on the evaporation of a solvent, which may be water, to make them set. They have to be held in contact until the glue has set, usually by light clamping. Warming the joint might speed setting, but do not heat excessively, as this will damage some glues. Some older glues required very tight clamping, but most modern glues need only just enough pressure to keep the surfaces in close contact. Excessive tightening causes *glue starvation*, which occurs when much of the glue is pressed out of the joint.

For general furniture work there are several makes of white glue, which is plastic-based and usually supplied in a semi-flexible applicator bottle. These glues have good moisture resistance, but would not stand up to really wet conditions. The strength, however, is adequate for most children's furniture.

The strongest and most waterproof glues are in two parts, with the glue itself accompanied by a hardener that causes it to set. There are several trade names, but anything packed in two parts can be assumed to be in this group.

One two-part, waterproof synthetic glue is *ureaformaldehyde* or resin glue. You mix either a resin, already a thick creamy consistency, or a powder with water. With it is a hardener, which is a mild acid. In some glues the hardener is added to the resin just before use. In another type the hardener is put on one surface and the resin on the other then setting starts when they meet. Another type has a dry powder hardener mixed with the dry powder resin. Setting commences after water is added and there is a limited time for use. Any excess mixture will harden in the pot.

Another two-part glue is *resorcinol*. It has a reddish color and is often used in plywood, but it does not have much use in furniture construction. The strongest and most waterproof glue is epoxy. It is more expensive than the other glues and unnecessary for children's furniture, except it is the only wood glue that will also join most other materials, including metals, to themselves or to wood.

The strength of most wood glues builds up progressively. Instructions usually give clamping times. Clamps can then be removed and further work done on the wood, but the glue might not gain its full strength for several days.

Some glues cause discoloring of the wood if in contact with metals. They should not be mixed in metal containers and any brushes used should not have metal bindings around the bristles. Screws or nails in contact with the glue may cause staining. Check the instructions provided with the glue.

Another type of adhesive used with wood is generally known as *contact adhesive*, because it sticks as soon as the surfaces are brought together. It is not used for wood-to-wood, but it is the adhesive for attaching melamime and other hard plastic sheets to woodtops and panels. Usually, both surfaces are coated and left until almost dry. As incorrect positioning cannot be corrected, the plastic sheet has to be sprung to a curve, located at one edge and then lowered progressively on to the wood.

STOPPINGS

Materials used to fill holes and cracks are collectively called *stoppings*. They are mostly putty-like pastes that may be squeezed from a tube or used with a knife from a can. They do not provide strength like glue, but merely fill spaces. They set without expanding or contracting, usually in a few minutes. It is normal to let them stand slightly above the surface and sand them level afterwards.

Stoppings colored to match many woods are available. Some are waterproof, but that is not important for furniture. If the wood is to be stained, the chosen stopping should be one that will take stain like the surrounding wood or be of the final color.

There are flexible stoppings intended for wood in boats and other situations where the wood may be expected to expand and contract. These stoppings never completely harden and will always be sufficiently flexible to allow for slight wood movements. They may have uses in outdoor children's furniture.

Nearly all glues are not gap-filling. This means that for a successful joint the wood parts should meet closely. If parts do not meet as they should or there are holes or cracks to fill where some strength would be welcomed, and this would not be provided by a stopping, it is possible to mix sawdust with glue and use this to fill the space. Sawdust from similar wood to that being stopped should be mixed with glue to a thick paste and pressed into the space, so a little is left standing above the surface. Leave this to harden completely, then sand level. Most untreated glues if put into an open space will craze—they set with minute cracks that weaken the glue. By mixing in sawdust, the glue is given more small particles of wood to adhere to and crazing is avoided.

Stoppings should not be confused with fillers. Some woods have very open grain. Spaces in the grain pattern on a surface can be clearly seen. Fillers are used all over such a surface to close these small spaces and present a level surface for polishing or another finish. A filler may be like a more liquid stopping, but the two names are not interchangable. More information on fillers is given in the instructions on finishing.

4

Joints

FURNITURE OF ANY KIND is made from pieces of wood joined together. Even the simplest things have to be made with joints of some sort. Some traditional furniture was put together with quite complicated joints. We have to admire the craftsmen who did that work mainly with hand tools. Fortunately we have the benefit of better nails and screws, as well as more powerful glues, so it is now possible to get satisfactory results and ample strength by simpler methods.

Many of us have the advantage of power tools, which help in achieving a precision difficult to obtain with some of the older hand tools, and the modern hand tools we have are much more exact and easier to use. Coupled with this there are plywoods and other manufactured boards that allow constructions that were impossible in earlier days when furniture makers were constantly having to contend with the limited widths of wood available and the tendency of wide boards to shrink and warp.

It is still, of course, possible for anyone interested in traditional craftsmanship to produce children's furniture with similar joints to those used a century ago. But those who prefer to make furniture using the advantages of modern materials and methods get results quicker and just as satisfactorily. For children's furniture that is only expected to have a limited life, simple and strong construction may be all that is needed, while something expected to be of use through several generations would justify a higher quality construction based on traditional methods, if the maker desires.

TOOLS

This is not a book on basic woodworking. I have assumed that the reader possesses some of the tools common to any sort of woodworking and has enough skill in their use to obtain satisfactory results. Anyone unaccustomed to woodworking and who is starting without a stock of tools, will find guidance and instructions in *The Woodworker's Bible* (TAB Book No. 860).

Children's furniture can be made with a few hand tools, an elaborately-equipped powered woodworking shop, or anything in between.

Power tools might seem attractive, and they are, but they are not as essential as many aspiring woodworkers imagine. Much of this feeling is due to the power of advertising. Even when an assortment of power tools are at your disposal, there will still be some work that has to be done by hand. It may be impossible to use a power tool for a particular function and setting it up for a simple operation might not be justified. This means that whatever power tools you acquire, you will still need hand tools. More importantly you need enough skill to use them. Because of this, I suggest you approach any project as if it was to be made by hand and regard power tools that can help as an added bonus. The better cabinetmakers and furniture makers are able to do all their work by hand, although they make use of any power tools available for certain tasks.

Any tool should be regarded as an extension of your hand. It gives you scope to do things that you could not do with your fingers. It is your skill in using the tool that gets results. This applies to power tools as well as hand tools. A power tool is not a machine that does things for you. You have to control it. Sometimes more skill is needed to make a power tool do exactly what you want than there is in controlling a hand tool. Drilling too deeply, rabbeting too far, or planing off too much are all more likely when you substitute electric power for human power.

The basic hand tools should include saws, planes, chisels, hammers, screwdrivers, and drills. A hand bit brace is better than the usual small electric drill for larger holes, but the first power tool acquired is probably an electric drill, preferably with a chuck capacity up to ⅜ inch. Anything bigger is heavy to handle and clumsy when making small holes.

There are attachments available for many drills that allow it to be converted to such things as saw and sander, but some time is taken in changing over and tools with their own motor built in are preferred. Larger power tools, such as a table saw and planer, are only justified if a woodworking shop is being set up for a lot of work besides making children's furniture. However, money spent on quality tools can be regarded as a good investment of considerable long term value.

NAILED AND SCREWED JOINTS

In the simplest box or carcass construction, one piece of wood overlaps another and is nailed or screwed, usually at right angles. It is best to let the piece that overhangs the other project slightly, to be leveled later. This is much less trouble than cutting it exactly to length and finding after joining that the large surface has to be planed because the end is slightly below it. When marking out and cutting, use inside and outside guidelines. Nails driven a short distance at intervals can temporarily join two pieces together (FIG. 4-1A), then be withdrawn after fitting. Use a sharp, finely-set plane diagonally on the end grain and towards

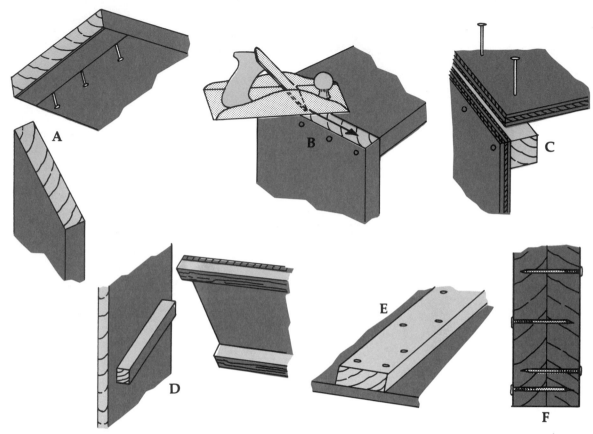

Fig. 4-1. Nails on a line provide a guide for joining (A). Plane a corner inwards (B). Edges can be thickened for nailing (C and D). Stagger nails in a stiffening batten (E). Thin pieces can be nailed from both sides (F).

the other part to avoid grain breaking out (FIG. 4-1B). Sanding can come later, but it is wise to avoid the use of a sander until all tool work has been done, otherwise particles of sanding grit will blunt tools.

If plywood or other thin panels are to be joined, the corner can be thickened with a strip of wood inside (FIG. 4-1C). Attach the strip to one piece with a slight projection to plane off before adding the other panel. Strips can be put under shelves and similar places. If a shelf is thin plywood, one or both edges can be stiffened and the support cut back (FIG. 4-1D). Always nail or screw through a thin piece into a thick piece. If a broad strip is put across another, arrange the fastenings diagonally (FIG. 4-1E). If pieces are the same thickness, nails or screws can be driven from opposite sides (FIG. 4-1F).

It is often possible to arrange an assembly so nail and screw heads are hidden because they are driven from inside or are covered by other parts. If not, they can be sunk and covered with stopping. One way of hiding screws is by pocket screwing. The appearance of a top of a table or cabinet might be spoiled, even with counterbored and plugged screws, so it is better to fasten from below. Drill

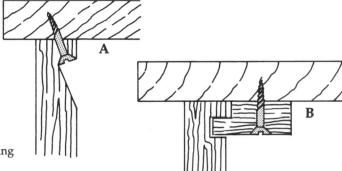

Fig. 4-2. A tabletop can be attached with pocket screwing or screwed buttons engaging with grooves:(A) diagonal cut; (B) space permits movement.

a hole diagonally through a rail, then cut away with a chisel to admit the screw head (FIG. 4-2A). A series of these screws around the rails under a top will secure it inconspicuously.

A wide top made from solid wood will expand and contract a little If it is fixed down rigidly, something might break or crack. A better method of fixing is to use buttons underneath. The rails have grooves plowed around them before assembly. Small buttons are made with a hole in each for a screw. Cut each button to fit the groove, then glue and screw to the top so it does not touch the bottom of the groove and there is space to permit movement (FIG. 4-2B).

EDGE JOINTS

Plywood and manufactured boards have provided modern alternatives to the broad panels that had to be made up by gluing boards edge to edge. However, in certain places, pieces have to be joined along their edges and the joint should be as strong as possible. With modern glues there should be no need for dowels or other reinforcement in the joint.

Edges should be planed and one piece propped on the other to check with a straightedge (FIG. 4-3A). Look through the joint to see that there are no gaps. Even if the edges are machine-planed, you should take off a shaving from each edge with a hand plane. If the cutters of a power planer are not absolutely sharp, they pound the wood as well as cut it so the surface becomes case-hardened and resists the penetration of glue. Hand planing opens the surface again.

If the edges are planed very slightly hollow, a single central clamp will pull the joint close and the ends will remain tight (FIG. 4-3B). *Pinch dogs* or *joiner's dogs* are simple clamps. Their outsides are parallel and the insides tapered, so when they are driven into the ends of boards, they force them together (FIG. 4-3C). If there is any doubt about which way boards should go together, pencil across the joints before applying glue (FIG. 4-3D).

If boards joined to make up a width are not very thick, I suggest that you put battens across (FIG. 4-3E) to keep them flat. However, because of the possibility of expansion and contraction, it is better to fasten without glue and give the outer screws slots in where slight movement can be taken care of (FIG. 4-3F). Holes near the center can be round.

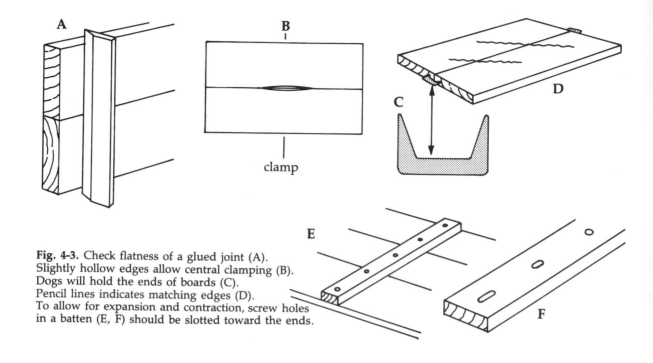

Fig. 4-3. Check flatness of a glued joint (A).
Slightly hollow edges allow central clamping (B).
Dogs will hold the ends of boards (C).
Pencil lines indicates matching edges (D).
To allow for expansion and contraction, screw holes
in a batten (E, F) should be slotted toward the ends.

NOTCHED JOINTS

There are several places where one piece of wood has to be cut away to fit against
another. The obvious example is where two pieces cross at the same level and
each is cut away in a halving or half lap joint (FIG. 4-4A). Besides a crossing in
the length of each piece, they map lap at a corner (FIG. 4-4B) or where the end
of one meets the other (FIG. 4-4C). These are the joints to use in strips stiffening
plywood.

When preparing these joints, mark the face side of each piece to come together the same way and do any measuring or gauging from those sides. Use
the actual pieces of wood to mark the widths to cut away and mark where saw
cuts comes across the grain with a knife. After the fibers are severed, use the
saw on the waste side of the line to make a clean cut. Waste can be removed
with a power router, but if you use a chisel, cut at a slope from each side (FIG.
4-4D) before trimming across level.

A similar sequence of cuts can be used if the joint comes together at an end,
but use a saw throughout. Saw across the grain, then make diagonal cuts on the
waste side of the line (FIG. 4-4E), before cutting straight through (FIG. 4-4F). If a table
saw is available, a clean cut can be made by setting the fence at the thickness
needed (FIG. 4-4G).

If the crossing pieces are different thicknesses, do not cut halfway through
the thinner piece. By only cutting a small amount from that and more from the
thicker piece, you will make a stronger joint.

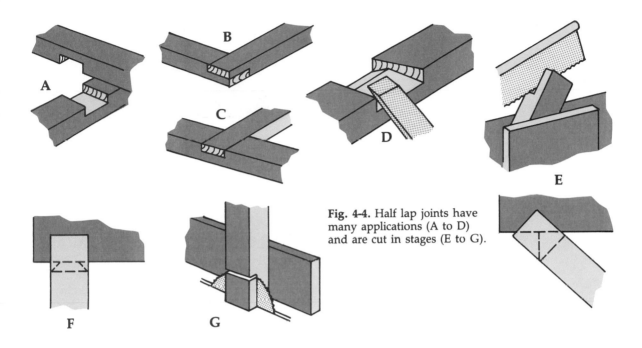

Fig. 4-4. Half lap joints have many applications (A to D) and are cut in stages (E to G).

DADO JOINTS

In a dado or housing joint, the end of one piece goes into a slot in the other piece. The most common example is the end of a shelf (FIG. 4-5A). The shelf end is cut true, but not shaped in any way. The groove in the other part is made in the same way as a part of a half lap joint, by sawing the sides and removing the waste with a chisel or router.

In this type of joint the end grain of one part is against the side grain of the other part. Glue does not bond very well in these circumstances. If the complete assembly will ensure the joint being supported, it will be strong enough, but if it is something like a block of open shelves, some strengthening might be necessary. Driving screws from the outside will help, but if it would be better for the outer surface to remain plain, drive the screw upwards, something like pocket screwing (FIG. 4-5B). The joint can also be stiffened with a strip of wood glued underneath (FIG. 4-5C).

If a dado joint is cut the full width of the upright, the exposed end might not be attractive. It would look better if the notch could not be seen. The joint to use then is a stopped dado (FIG. 4-5D). It is still open at the back, but the front edge of the shelf is notched around an uncut part. Use knife lines to mark the notch to be cut on the shelf, for a clean finish.

To cut the dado by hand, the closed end has to be chopped out with a chisel, but do not go right to the line at the end (FIG. 4-5E) until after sawing. If this cutout is about 1 inch long it is sufficient to use a backsaw with short strokes to cut down the sides of the notch ready for chiseling out the waste. If you use a power router, there is no need for the first cutout, but you still need to square the closed end of the notch with a chisel.

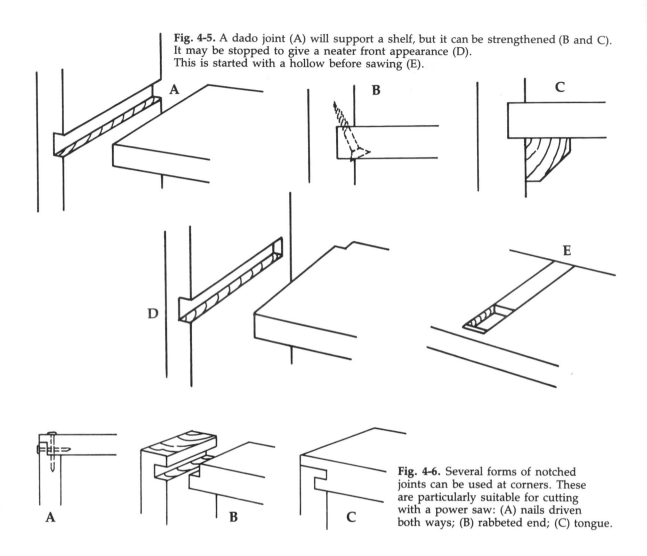

Fig. 4-5. A dado joint (A) will support a shelf, but it can be strengthened (B and C). It may be stopped to give a neater front appearance (D). This is started with a hollow before sawing (E).

Fig. 4-6. Several forms of notched joints can be used at corners. These are particularly suitable for cutting with a power saw: (A) nails driven both ways; (B) rabbeted end; (C) tongue.

If power tools are available for cutting dados and rabbets, other corner joints can be used. If both parts are rabbeted, nails can be driven both ways (FIG. 4-6A) to make a securely locked corner. Another possibility is to let the rabbeted end of one piece into a dado (FIG. 4-6B). A further development gives the first piece a tongue to go over the other part for a neater finish (FIG. 4-6C). Because these last two joints include some short grain, do not cut with hand tools. But with the control and precision of power tools, they can be cut cleanly with little risk of short grain breaking out.

MORTISE AND TENON JOINTS

At one time mortise and tenon joints were used extensively in all parts of a piece of furniture, but with the change in materials, stronger glues, and the availability of power tools, they are not as essential. Today, dowels are used in many places

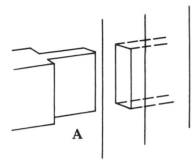

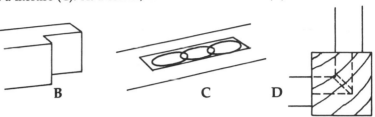

Fig. 4-7. Mortise and tenon joints are the traditional construction joint (A). If the tenon is one-sided it is called bare-faced (B). Waste can be drilled from a mortise (C). At a corner, tenons can be mitered (D).

A B C D

where a traditional craftsman would have used mortise and tenon joints. However, in some places mortise and tenon joints are still the best joints to use, although there is rarely any need to master some of the more complicated variations.

For things like the end of a rail into a table leg, a mortise and tenon joint makes the strongest connection. The mortise is a slot, into which the tenon fits. The mortise may go right through, but it can also be *blind* or *stub*, when the tenon only goes partly into the other part, as it would when joining a rail to a table leg.

It is common for the tenon to be one-third the thickness of the wood (FIG. 4-7A). If the other part is thicker, the joint is stronger when the tenon is thicker, even to the extent of making it "bare-faced" (FIG. 4-7B). This is a convenient form for a beginner to use, as it is easier to get a neat finish.

The traditional way to remove the waste wood from the mortise was by chopping with a chisel, but with modern tools it is better to drill away most of it (FIG. 4-7C), then trim to shape with a chisel. With a *through mortise*, work from both sides with the drill and chisel to keep grain from breaking out. In a *blind mortise*, make the mortise slightly deeper, otherwise the shoulders of the tenon will not close properly. If rails into a leg meet at the same level, miter their ends, but leave a gap there (FIG. 4-7D).

DOWEL JOINTS

Dowels are round wood rods that fit into holes. Lengths of prepared dowel rod can be bought and cut to length or precut. Any doweled joint should have at least two dowels (FIG. 4-8A). Make holes slightly deeper than the dowel's length, bevel the ends of the dowels, and saw a groove along each dowel so air and surplus glue can escape, otherwise there is a risk of bursting as the joint is forced together (FIG. 4-8B). As a rough guide, the dowel diameter should be about half the thickness of the thinner of the pieces of wood being joined.

Although the principle of doweling is simple, the main problem is ensuring accuracy. Mating holes must come exactly opposite and must be drilled perpendicularly to the meeting surfaces. Discrepancies in a row of dowels will prevent the joint from going together properly. Making holes with a drill press or an electric drill mounted in a stand will help to ensure that the holes are vertical. There are doweling jigs in which the drill is guided by bushings to ensure accurate location and direction.

Whenever possible, mark parts together (FIG. 4-8C). There are special pegs to fit into the holes in one part, so they can be pressed against the other part to mark hole centers. Make a template or jig to mark hole centers in such constructions as table rails into a leg (FIG. 4-8D).

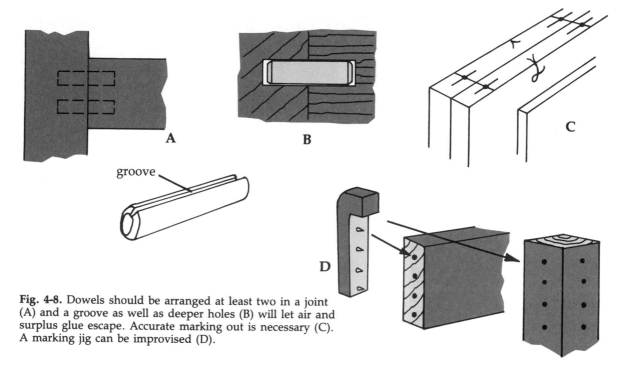

Fig. 4-8. Dowels should be arranged at least two in a joint (A) and a groove as well as deeper holes (B) will let air and surplus glue escape. Accurate marking out is necessary (C). A marking jig can be improvised (D).

OTHER JOINTS

A joint frequently used and regarded as evidence of a cabinetmaker's skill was the dovetail in its many variations. It is possible to get tools to make machined dovetails and anyone interested in traditional methods can find plenty of use for handcut ones, but in the making of most children's furniture they are not necessary.

The place where a dovetail is superior to other joints is where any expected load will try to pull the joint apart. With modern glues most other joints would take the strain, but the dovetail provides interlocking that holds, even with the uncertain strength of older glues.

In a basic single dovetail, the dovetail is cut in one part (FIG. 4-9A). The angle of the sides should be between 1 in 6 and 1 in 8. A socket is cut to match the other piece (FIG. 4-9B). A multiple dovetail is found in a box corner, such as is found in drawers (FIG. 4-9C). In a machine-made dovetail joint the dovetails and the pins between them are the same width. In a handcut dovetail joint it is common to make the pins narrower. A variation that can be used in some children's furniture combines the dovetail with a half lap (FIG. 4-9D), in a place where there might be a pull on the extending part.

Plywood panels can be let into plowed grooves (FIG. 4-10A). If they are to be flush with a side, they can rest on or be let into rabbets (FIG. 4-10B). Backing a piece of thin plywood with framing is satisfactory if it is part of an assembly that will hold it in shape, but if it is otherwise unsupported as it would be for a door, the uneven strain in the section might cause it to warp or twist. It is better then to have plywood on both sides, possibly with a narrow strip of wood as a lip at the edges (FIG. 4-10C).

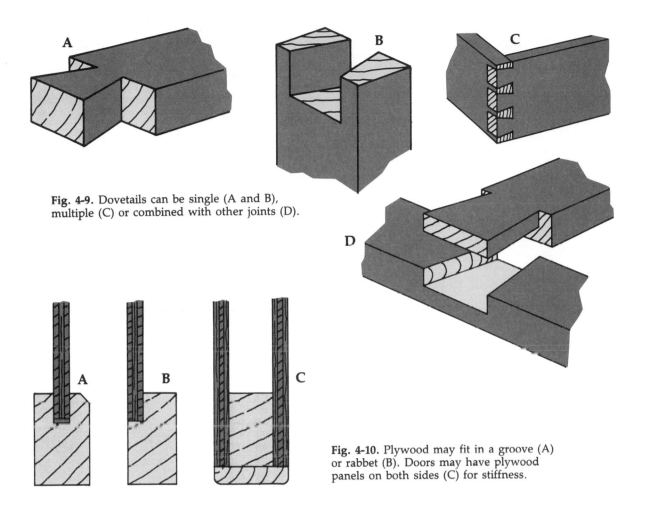

Fig. 4-9. Dovetails can be single (A and B), multiple (C) or combined with other joints (D).

Fig. 4-10. Plywood may fit in a groove (A) or rabbet (B). Doors may have plywood panels on both sides (C) for stiffness.

Miter joints are used at the corners of picture frames. There can be nails both ways to provide some strength (FIG. 4-11A), but this is a rather weak joint to use elsewhere. A stronger joint is created when pieces of veneer are glued into saw cuts (FIG. 4-11B). A picture or mirror can be held into a frame with a backing of hardboard or cardboard and then nailed at intervals (FIG. 4-11C). A glass or transparent plastic panel can be held with a strip of wood and fine nails (FIG. 4-11D).

If pieces of wood have to be joined to make up a length, there is no need to use any of the complicated joints used with weaker glues in the past. Instead, plane both parts to an acute angle and glue this scarf joint (FIG. 4-12A). Although no glue holds well on end grain, a taper across the grain of 1 in 7 or flatter (FIG. 4-12B) allows a modern two-part glue to bond very strongly.

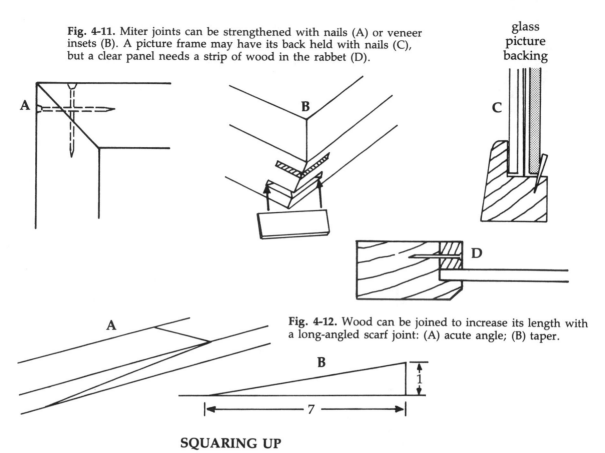

Fig. 4-11. Miter joints can be strengthened with nails (A) or veneer insets (B). A picture frame may have its back held with nails (C), but a clear panel needs a strip of wood in the rabbet (D).

glass
picture
backing

Fig. 4-12. Wood can be joined to increase its length with a long-angled scarf joint: (A) acute angle; (B) taper.

SQUARING UP

It is important to assemble an item of furniture squarely, otherwise any error in shape will be obvious, even to casual observers. Be sure to keep this in mind right from the start. If parts which should be the same size vary slightly, it might be impossible to finish squarely. If there are four identical legs, they should be marked together and all the positions of rails and other parts should be located at the same time (FIG. 4-13A). A similar scheme should be used with other parts that have to match. Particularly note the distances between shoulders of tenons, which are more important than the overall lengths of those parts.

Use a try square to mark and check anything that has to be square to an edge. This takes care of wood that comes within the length of the blade of the try square, but for larger panels or assemblies, there is a risk of error if you merely extend the try square blade line. If you want to mark a right angle on a large panel of plywood, it is safer to do it geometrically. There are several geometric constructions that will give you a right angle, but a useful one is the *3:4:5 method*. If a triangle has sides in that proportion, the angle between the "3" and "4" sides will be 90 degrees.

From the point where the right-angled line is to come, measure four units along the edge to another mark (FIG. 4-13B) Away from the edge in a direction that will clearly be about a right angle, make a mark at a 3-unit distance (FIG. 4-13C). Now measure from the other edge mark 5 units and mark where this point comes

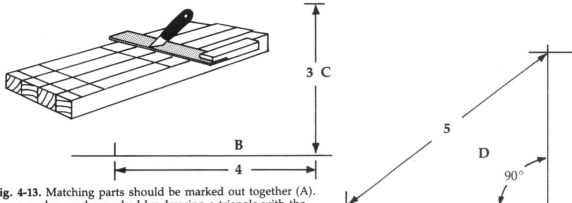

Fig. 4-13. Matching parts should be marked out together (A). Large angles can be marked by drawing a triangle with the sides in the proportion 3:4:5.

on the 3-unit line (FIG. 4-13D). A line through this crossing and the base mark will be square with the edge.

Choose units of a size that will take the crossing further from the edge than the final line is intended to be, to ensure maximum accuracy. For instance, if the line needed is 30 inches long from the edge and you make the unit 12 inches, the crossing will be 36 inches to ensure accuracy at 30 inches. If several long lines are needed at right angles to the edge, the others can be marked by measuring parallel with the first line.

Coupled with this is the method of ensuring accuracy of frames. If four pieces of wood are joined and they are properly squared up, their diagonals should measure the same (FIG. 4-14A). Measuring can be with a tape rule, but a straight scrap piece of wood can also be used and the distances pencilled for comparison (FIG. 4-14B.) This will alleviate the risk of misreading measurements along a rule. If there is a matching frame to go at the other side of the final assembly, try this on the first in the correct relative position, with what will be inner or outer surfaces together, not one of each.

Besides measuring cornerwise, the frames must be checked flat. Sight across one rail to the one at the other side. This will show any twist. Press the assembly flat. Leave it under weights, if necessary until the glue has set. Although it might be necessary to go on to further assembly right away, accurate shaping of the whole assembly is easier to obtain if the glue in the opposite pair of sides is allowed to lock them securely before going on.

When assembling parts that make up the other direction, stand the carcass on a flat surface and make similar diagonal checks on the two new sides. (FIG. 4-14C). These are only part of the checks needed. You must also check the squareness when viewed from above by measuring diagonals on top (FIG. 4-14D). It would help if they can also be checked at the bottom, but this is not always possible. If you can sight over rails from about it is possible to see if there is any twist in the assembly that way.

The final check is to stand back as far as possible and look at the assembly from several directions. Legs should appear upright in relation to each other. Move around and look to see if the sight lines of any of them appear to cross at a slight angle, which can be corrected. Although the example is an open frame, similar checks should be made with enclosed cabinets, although the panels will ensure

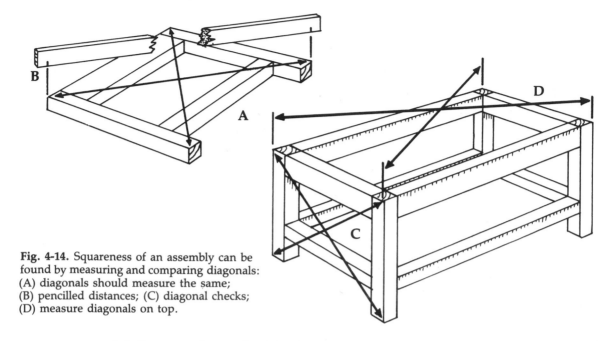

Fig. 4-14. Squareness of an assembly can be found by measuring and comparing diagonals: (A) diagonals should measure the same; (B) pencilled distances; (C) diagonal checks; (D) measure diagonals on top.

squareness over their flat areas. There will still be the problem of correct angles between joining parts.

PARTICLEBOARD JOINTS

Surfaced particleboard is being used more and more in the making of furniture, sometimes with special designs intended for it, or as an alternative in a design intended for wood. It has the advantages of being available in large flat pieces that are more stable than solid wood or even plywood, and it can be used in rectangular panels, but is not so satisfactory if you want to use solid wood or plywood to be cut to a shaped profile. Consequently, particleboard construction mostly involves joints with straight edges meeting at right angles.

Particleboard without any surface covering can be used for internal parts or for items where the surface appearance is unimportant. For most purposes the particleboard is bought with its surfaces and long edges covered with plain or grained plastic or wood veneer. In either case be careful not to damage the surfaces. Pad vise jaws with newspaper and have newspaper on the bench top when working on a surface.

Saw with any fine woodworking saw, power or hand. For a more accurate edge, use a finely-set close-mouthed plane. A power sander might cause a slight rounding. Plane towards the center from the edges to avoid breaking out.

Accurate edges are needed to make close joints. If an edge will be exposed, iron on a strip of self-adhesive plastic or wood to match the surface with a domestic iron at a hot setting over a piece of paper (FIG. 4-15A). Follow by rubbing with a piece of cloth. Allow sufficient time for the glue to set. Then plane the edges of the strip level. A small block plane in one hand is convenient for this. Turn it towards the board so the cut is a slice inward (FIG. 4-15B). Finish to size with fine abrasive paper wrapped around a piece of wood and used at a slight angle, but

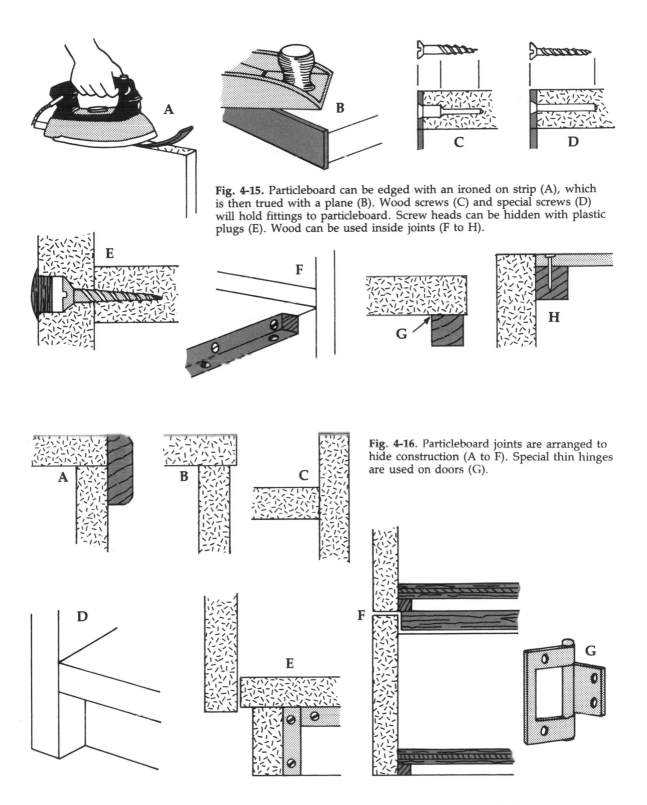

Fig. 4-15. Particleboard can be edged with an ironed on strip (A), which is then trued with a plane (B). Wood screws (C) and special screws (D) will hold fittings to particleboard. Screw heads can be hidden with plastic plugs (E). Wood can be used inside joints (F to H).

Fig. 4-16. Particleboard joints are arranged to hide construction (A to F). Special thin hinges are used on doors (G).

be careful not to take off so much that the particleboard shows through the edges.

Joints appropriate to solid wood are mostly unsuitable for particleboard. Instead, dowels should be used. Keep them no more than one-third the thickness of the board, to reduce the risk of breaking out. It is also important to have grooves for air and surplus glue to escape.

Many metal and plastic devices are available for joining particleboard sheets at right angles, but most of these are intended to allow the furniture to be supplied in a ready-to assemble form. They are more appropriate to quantity production. Unless you are making a single piece of furniture to be taken apart later, there is no need to use this equipment. If you do not use dowels, screw the joint together.

Ordinary wood screws can be used for particleboard, but there are several special screws made for the material. Most have sharper thread forms and many have double threads, carried almost to the thread. The solid neck of a wood screw might have too much of a bursting action if it is forced into an undersized hole, as particleboard does not have the elasticity of the fibers in wood. This means that there should be a clearance hole as deep as the screw neck goes and a tapping size hole slightly deeper than the threaded part will go (FIG. 4-15C). A screw cannot be expected to penetrate without a full-depth hole. With the special screws there is no neck to need a clearance hole (FIG. 4-15D).

If the screw heads will not show, there can be a row of screws through one board into the edge of another. If the surface is visible, it is possible to counterbore the screw heads and cover them with shallow plastic plugs that match the surface material (FIG. 4-15E). They can then be held in with a spot of glue.

If it would be better to have nothing showing outside, the joints can be screwed from inside. There are ready-drilled plastic blocks available to go in the angles, but strips of wood are just as satisfactory (FIG. 4-15F). If the wood is first screwed to the end, but set back very slightly (FIG. 4-15G), the joint will be pulled close.

This is also the way to fit a plywood or hardboard back to a cabinet (FIG. 4-15H), as cutting a clean rabbet in the edge of particleboard is difficult.

Even with a perfectly planed edge, a simple butt joint at a corner might show some roughness along the joint line. To disguise it, use wood molding or a plain strip may come over the joint (FIG. 4-16A). Another possibility is to allow the top to overlap the upright a bit (FIG. 4-16B). In some furniture the upright could stand above the top (FIG. 4-16C), so the meeting line is not obvious. At the bottom, the sides could reach the floor and a plinth at the front be set back a little (FIG. 4-16D) so the shelf meeting with the uprights is hidden. Drawers may overhang runners so a rail between is avoided (FIG. 4-16F).

Example furniture in shops to observe the way designs have been arranged so meeting surfaces in particleboard are disguised.

Several hinges, knobs, and fasteners are available especially for use with particleboard. It is possible to drill the material, even with fairly large-diameter holes, and there are several hinges made to fit into holes. Some are quite ingenious with throw clear actions. However, these are more appropriate for kitchen equipment than children's furniture. Particleboard is unsuitable for the usual hinges, as there is too much risk of it crumbling to cause ragged edges. Instead there are hinges with a total thickness of no more than the clearance that would be allowed at the edge of a door, with one side fitting into the other to keep the space needed minimal (FIG. 4-16G). These are the most suitable type for doors and flaps on particleboard children's furniture.

5

Simple Furniture

EVEN IF A CHILD does not have a room of his or her own, there are several things that can be made for the child's use, either amongst or on other furniture or to put in a corner. Some of these things can be quite simple to make and they provide an opportunity for anyone doubtful about their skill to try furniture making with a good prospect of success. There are also some things that are not strictly furniture for the child's use, but they are needed for his safety or to keep him within bounds.

It is important to make things with the child's safety in mind. All parents know that a child is liable to do the most unexpected things and handle or use furniture or toys in a way that would seem illogical to an adult. Even where there is a simple assembly for temporary use, it must be treated as potentially hazardous to the young user. It should be impossible for anything to be pulled apart. If a child finds that a joint will move, he will try to make it move more.

In particular, nailed joints should be firm. It is better to use nails too large than to depend on short, thin ones that might allow a joint to open. Dovetail nailing and clenching at least some of the nails so their points are buried are security and safety precautions.

Corners and edges should be rounded or beveled. This applies to some of the less obvious places. A child might turn a table over, so the bottoms of legs should have their sharpness removed (FIG. 5-1A). Sharpness should be taken off the edges of legs, as well. The outer corner should be well rounded, but less curve would be enough on the other three corners (FIG. 5-1B).

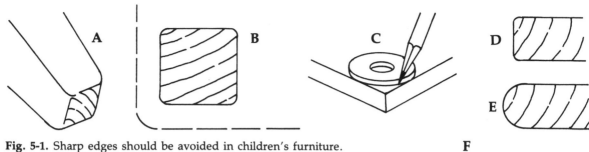

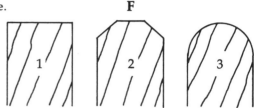

Fig. 5-1. Sharp edges should be avoided in children's furniture. Corners as well as edges are better if rounded: (A) sharpness removed from bottom of legs; (B) sharpness removed from edge of legs; (C) large washer; (D) removing sharpness; (E) full rounding; (F) removing angles.

Overhanging tops could be most hazardous. This also applies to adult furniture, where a tabletop might be at a child's head level. Even the child's table, built purposefully lower, could be dangerous to a stooping or running child. There should be no angular corners left exposed anywhere. The corner of a top should be given a small radius curve.

To make a curve, it is simpler to mark around a guide like a small can or washer, than to use compasses. (FIG. 5-1C). Keep a stock of suitable round things as corner templates.

Edges of tops should also be rounded in section. Merely taking off the sharpness might be sufficient, particularly if the furniture is for older children (FIG. 5-1D), but a full rounding is better for younger ones (FIG. 5-1E). Rounding can be done in steps without marking out. Use a plane at about 45° and take the angles off until what is left between them is the same width as the bevels (FIG. 5-1F). Take off those corners with the plane, remove any high spots left, then thoroughly hand sand with abrasive paper. Take the rounded section around curves. This can be done by careful work with a chisel or Surform tool.

Check the condition of any fittings, such as catches and hinges. Mass-produced metal parts might have rough edges or sharp corners. If you use a hinge on an edge, any sharpness can be covered, but if the hinge is on a surface, deal with sharp edges with a file and abrasive paper. Plastic parts should not be found as sharp, but there still might be roughness left from molding that should be removed.

WORKING BOARD

A board can be used for painting, drawing, clay modeling or any activity that might harm an ordinary table. It can be put on a table or a shelf not particularly intended for children. Sizes can suit circumstances, but those given will suit a young child's play needs and still be of use to him when he moves on to more ambitious drawing or painting.

The material needed for this project are listed in TABLE 5-1. The top is plywood. Trim its corners squarely, then plane and round the edges (FIG. 5-2A). If the board might later be used as a straight edge, do no more than take off their sharpness.

Table 5-1. Materials List for a Working Board.

1 board	12	×	18	× ⅜ plywood
2 supports	3	×	12	× ¾
1 rail	¾	×	15	× ½
1 socket				
rail	2	×	15	× 1
or	1	×	15	× 1
and	1	×	15	× ⅜

The supports can be parallel, particularly for a modeling board, so things cannot roll off, but for drawing purposes a slight slope is preferred. First plane both pieces together (FIG. 5-2B). Then fit them fairly close to the ends of the board, so pressure on one end of the surface is unlikely to tilt it (FIG. 5-2C). Use glue and nails, which are set below the surface and covered with stopping, but as the plywood top may be thin, do not punch so far that there is little wood left for the nail head to grip.

Such a board might be sufficient for the child's needs, but there are some possible additions. A rounded rail along the lower edge will prevent things from

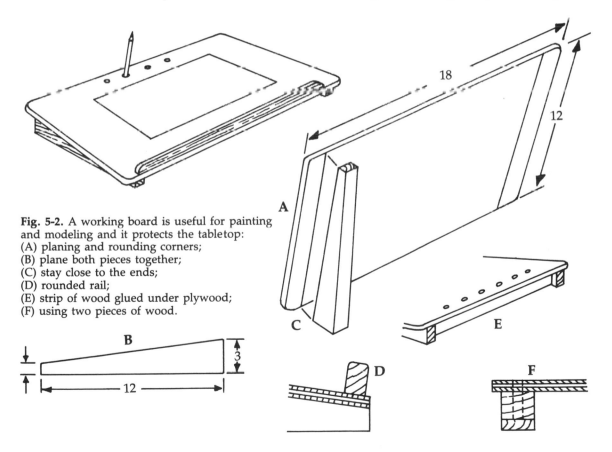

Fig. 5-2. A working board is useful for painting and modeling and it protects the tabletop:
(A) planing and rounding corners;
(B) plane both pieces together;
(C) stay close to the ends;
(D) rounded rail;
(E) strip of wood glued under plywood;
(F) using two pieces of wood.

rolling off (FIG. 5-2D). Sockets for pencils, pens, and brushes can be drilled near the top edge. This could encourage tidiness at an early age. To give sufficient depth for the holes, glue a strip of wood under the plywood, either a short piece for a few holes, or taken from one support to the other (FIG. 5-2E).

Check the sizes of things to be accommodated, but ⅜ inch holes will hold most pens and pencils. Use a depth stop on the drill to keep all holes the same depth. An alternative is to use two pieces of wood. Drill through the thick one and glue and nail a strip below it (FIG. 5-2F).

GATE

A child can be stopped from falling downstairs or going out of his room by a gate that he cannot move. The arrangement has to be temporary as it will not be required for very long. The gate described here is intended to be lifted out and be fitted between battens at each side of the opening. TABLE 5-2 lists the necessary materials. The battens can be held in place with thin nails (FIG. 5-3A), then when the gate is no longer required, they can be pulled away and the nail holes filled with stopping.

Table 5-2. Materials List for a Gate.

Uprights as required	5 × 25 × ⅝
2 rails	3 × ⅝ × length to suit
4 battens	1½ × 23 × ⅝

The number and widths of the upright parts will depend on the space to be filled. They should be wider than the space between them and the spaces kept too narrow for a child to get a foot through and use a crossbar as a step.

Cut and plane the upright material, then mark all parts together for length and the positions of the crossbars. Round the tops to discourage climbing over (FIG. 5-3B) and take off sharp edges all around. The crossbars should be long enough to almost reach the supporting battens. Round or bevel their ends and assemble the gate so there is enough clearance at the sides for easy fitting (FIG. 5-3C). The gate goes into its slots with the crossbars on the side away from the child. Use glue as well as nails or screws in each joint to prevent the whole thing from loosening and becoming slack.

There should be some sort of fastener, arranged low on the side away from the child, to prevent the gate from being lifted. Bolts can be arranged on the lower crossbar (FIG. 5-3D) to enter holes in the battens. Paint the battens before finally fitting them, to avoid the risk of marking the surfaces they are fixed to.

STOOL

Quite early in life a child will welcome something that is at a suitable height to sit on. Chairs are described later, but a stool will suit his early needs, then can become a step for reaching things or helping a parent at a normal table. Eventually it can even be used as an adult footstool.

For the materials listed for this project, see TABLE 5-3. The stool is designed to be cut from one piece of wood (FIG. 5-4A). Sizes can be altered to suit an available piece.

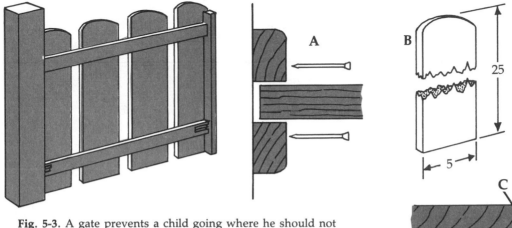

Fig. 5-3. A gate prevents a child going where he should not and is particularly useful at the top of stairs: (A) use thin nails; (B) round the tops; (C) bevel the ends; (D) bolt the lower crossbars.

Table 5-3. Materials List for a Stool.

7 × 15 × ⅝	1 top
3 × 15 × ⅝	2 sides
7 × 8 × ⅝	2 legs
7 × 48 × ⅝	or all from 1 piece

Be sure the stool is stable. It should not be possible to stand near one edge of the top and tilt it. The floor area outlined by the feet must be at least as large as the top to prevent this.

The legs should slope at the ends (FIG. 5-4B) and should be drawn full size to obtain sizes and angles. The top is a plain rectangle (FIG. 5-4C). The two sides fit under it and are made by cutting a board of similar length along its middle (FIG. 5-4D). Mark where the legs will come on the sides.

Mark out the legs together (FIG. 5-4E). Bevel their ends, using the full-size drawing as a guide to the angles and lengths. To make the cutouts, locate and drill the holes, then saw into them. Clean these edges by paring with a chisel. Take off sharpness, particularly where the cuts join the holes.

Use the actual sides, rather than measurements, to mark the depths to be cut at the tops of the legs (FIG. 5-4F). Assemble with nails or screws to one side, then add the other side and check for squareness by measuring diagonals. If necessary, plane the tops of the legs level with the sides. It should be sufficient to fasten the top to the sides and legs, but if you want extra stiffness, put blocks inside the legs (FIG. 5-4G).

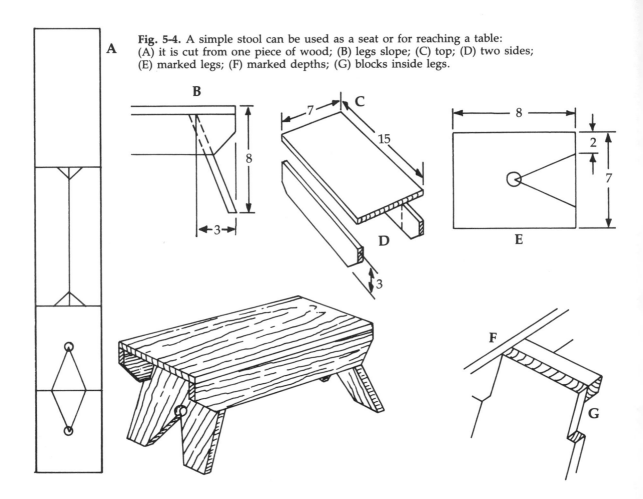

Fig. 5-4. A simple stool can be used as a seat or for reaching a table: (A) it is cut from one piece of wood; (B) legs slope; (C) top; (D) two sides; (E) marked legs; (F) marked depths; (G) blocks inside legs.

TABLE

A table or desk can be made in a similar way to the stool as a companion to it. Its height should be related to the stool and have a top 9 inches above the stool top.

The materials list for this table is found in TABLE 5-4. The top overhangs and has rounded corners. The ends are made in a similar way to those of the stool, but they are upright. Because the legs have to be marked with most of the

Table 5-4. Materials List for a Table.

1 top	20 × 22 × ⅝
2 legs	18 × 18 × ⅝
1 front	3 × 20 × ⅝
1 back	8 × 20 × ⅝
1 shelf	8 × 19 × ⅝
1 ledge	⅝ × 19 × ½

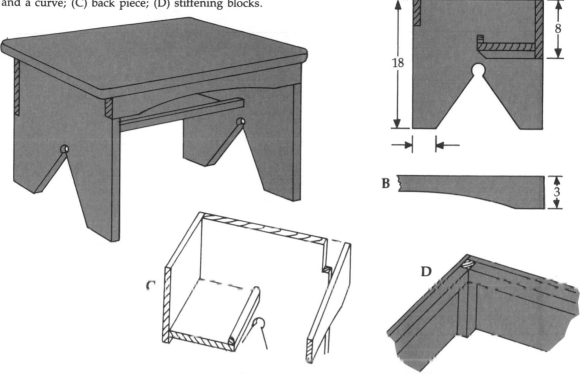

Fig. 5-5. A stool built at a height to serve as a table for a young child can have a storage shelf underneath: (A) marked legs; (B) deep ends and a curve; (C) back piece; (D) stiffening blocks.

measurements of the assembly, they should be made first (FIG. 5-5A). The front piece could be made narrow enough to clear the sitting child's legs, but the assembly will be stronger if the ends of the piece are deeper and there is a curve for clearance in the lower edge (FIG. 5-5B).

The back piece is deeper and provides support for a shelf, which rests on strips on the legs and, preferably, is given a ledge across the front (FIG. 5-5C). Do not make the shelf too wide or it will touch the sitter's knees, but it will be appreciated as somewhere to put or hide things. It also reinforces the table. If you use plywood, you can place stiffening blocks under the top (FIG. 5-5D); but if you use solid wood, glue and screws should be enough.

BULLETIN OR CHALKBOARD

A child's natural inclination is to mark everything within reach. If the child gets a picture or is able to cut shapes from paper, he or she wants to display them. If he is given something on which he knows he can do whatever he likes in the way of decoration without incurring the wrath of an adult, he may keep his activities within bounds and be more content.

Suitable boards need not be elaborate, but they should be framed for appearance and to show limits. For a bulletin board to which things are to be pinned, the main area should be one of the softer types of wallboard or building board. If things are to be fixed with adhesive, self-adhesive tape, or one of the pressure clay-like substances, use a piece of plywood or particleboard. For a chalkboard, plywood is the usual choice.

An unframed board might be used, but there is a risk that things put on it might overflow on to the surrounding wall, with subsequent trouble. TABLE 5-5 lists the materials needed for this project. The simplest frame is added to the surface and need only be strips of wood with their edges rounded (FIG. 5-6A). They should be thick enough to allow screws to be driven from the back.

The corners of the frame can be mitered (FIG. 5-6B). Plywood or particleboard would support these joints, but it might be better to use a strong joint if a soft

Table 5-5. Materials List for a Bulletin or Chalkboard.

Sizes to suit space
Back: building board about ½ or plywood about ¼
Frame: ⅝ × 1⅜

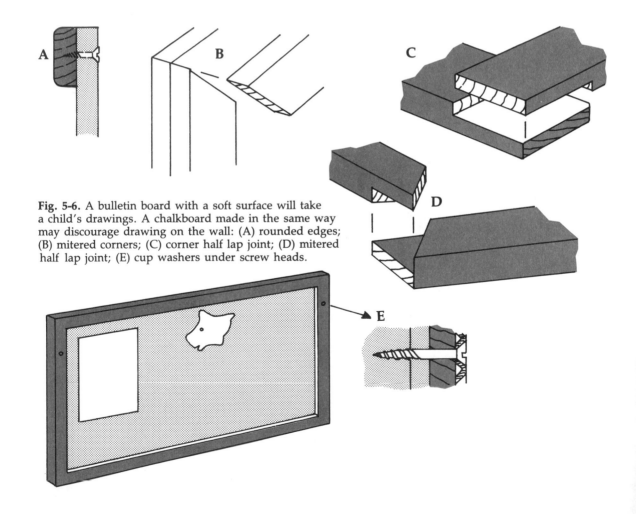

Fig. 5-6. A bulletin board with a soft surface will take a child's drawings. A chalkboard made in the same way may discourage drawing on the wall: (A) rounded edges; (B) mitered corners; (C) corner half lap joint; (D) mitered half lap joint; (E) cup washers under screw heads.

building board comes behind it. This might be a corner half lap joint (FIG. 5-6C). Fastening through the back of the joint could be driven before the frame is put on the backboard. A mitered half lap joint is particularly appropriate for this sort of frame (FIG. 5-6D).

For the neatest finish leave final trimming of the backboard until after the frame is fitted, then plane the outside level. Green seems to be the commonly acceptable color for a bulletin board, if it is not to be left in its natural color. A chalkboard should be black or dark gray without any gloss. As several coats of paint might be needed, it is best to paint the front of the board and separately paint or varnish the frame, before putting them together.

Affix to the wall with screws through the frame. For the best appearance use cup washers under the screw heads (FIG. 5-6E).

BOOKRACK

A young child should not be expected to deal with loose bookends and he or she might not have enough books to justify a proper bookcase, but a definite place for books is helpful, both for the sake of tidiness and training in putting things away.

The materials list for a bookrack is found in TABLE 5-6. This rack is (FIG. 5-7) intended for a rather small number of books of the larger page size, common for children. Proportions can be altered to suit the thicker and smaller books that come later.

Table 5-6. Materials List for a Bookrack.

Suggested sizes:

1 bottom	$8 \times 20 \times 5/8$
2 supports	$8 \times 8 \times 5/8$
1 back	$2 \times 10 \times 5/8$
2 feet	$2 \times 8 \times 5/8$
2 figures, as required	

The bottom is a board about 12 inches longer than the thickness of the books to be accommodated. It could be raised on thin strips (FIG. 5-7A), which will give a steadier base on an uneven surface than if the whole bottom was bearing on the table. The book supports are shown rectangular with rounded corners, but they can be cut to animal designs or other outlines, providing there was enough area left to bear against the books. Notch the back into the supports (FIG. 5-8B). Then check its length against the marked positions on the base and nail or screw the parts together.

The rack would be functional as it is, but the attraction to a child would be enhanced by some decorative figures at the ends. The choice of these is almost limitless. One way to personalize the rack is to use the child's own initials, but some letters are better than others for this. Cut the letters from thick wood and attach them with screws through flattened parts (FIG. 5-7C). Other possibilities are cutouts of the child's favorite characters or something from a picture in a book (FIG. 5-7D). Whatever you choose must be made so that the flattened parts are at right angles to each other, so as to bear against the two surfaces.

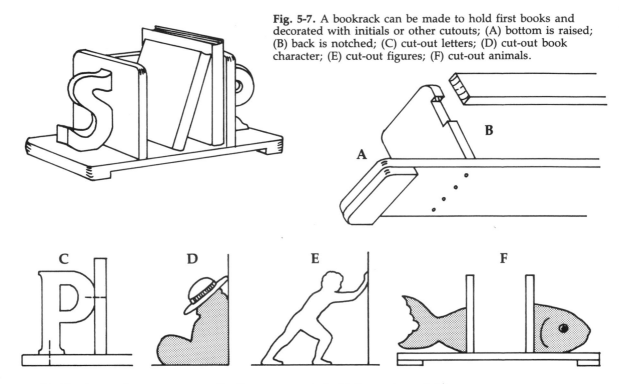

Fig. 5-7. A bookrack can be made to hold first books and decorated with initials or other cutouts; (A) bottom is raised; (B) back is notched; (C) cut-out letters; (D) cut-out book character; (E) cut-out figures; (F) cut-out animals.

Besides improving appearance, the figures serve to hold the ends upright. If figures can be made to show they are doing this (FIG. 5-7E), that will appeal to the child also. Another treatment that might amuse the child would be an arrangement where the animal or other figure appears to go through the books (FIG. 5-7F).

For a young child the rack could be finished in bright colors. As the figures will usually be in a contrasting color to the rest of the wood, first make a trial assembly, then remove the figures for painting and not replace them until all paint is dry.

TRAYS

Shallow boxes or trays are useful at many stages in a child's development. They will keep the youngest child's experiments with paint and clay within bounds, preventing or reducing spillage onto more important surfaces. A small tray that a child can carry, allows him to take his toys around. A tray will also allow a parent to put an actual meal in front of the child with the minimum risk of accidents.

The basic tray is a simple nailed box (FIG. 5-8A). The materials list for this project is found in TABLE 5-7. For general use the top edges are well rounded and the sharpness taken off all other angles. A deeper box can be used by an older child to contain sand for making a model garden. An even older child might use the box to contain equipment for electrical or chemical experiments. Any strain the tray is likely to suffer will come at the top corners, so nail closely there. The parts could be joined with rabbets that allow nailing both ways, or the more advanced woodworker could use dovetails.

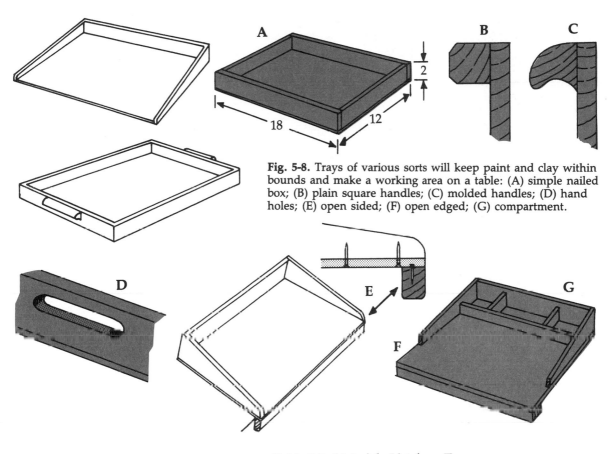

Fig. 5-8. Trays of various sorts will keep paint and clay within bounds and make a working area on a table: (A) simple nailed box; (B) plain square handles; (C) molded handles; (D) hand holes; (E) open sided; (F) open edged; (G) compartment.

Table 5-7. Materials List for a Tray.

1 bottom	12 × 18 × ⅛–¼ plywood or hardboard
2 sides	2 × 18 × ⅜
2 ends	2 × 11 × ⅜
1 ledge (optional)	1 × 18 × ⅝
2 handles (optional)	1 × 6 × 1

If the box is to be carried, attach metal or plastic tray handles at each end. Simpler handles can be blocks of wood, either plain square sections (FIG. 5-8B) or molded (FIG. 5-8C). If the box is deep enough, hand holes can be cut through instead (FIG. 5-8D).

A tray with an open side (FIG. 5-8E) can be used in front of a young child sitting at a table to keep play materials together, while not obstructing the child's reach with a bordering piece. The bottom can be plywood, up to ¼ inch thick, or it could be hardboard. The side pieces can taper and their ends toward the child should be well rounded.

Although painted or varnished wood is satisfactory, a tray or box can be made more attractive to a child if the bottom is covered with a plastic place mat of the type with a nursery rhyme scene or an alphabet with animals. For a child who has grown beyond that stage, the bottom could be covered with plastic, either the self-adhesive flexible type or a hard laminated plastic for easy cleaning.

On an open-edged tray, you might want to attach a piece of wood projecting downward to hold the tray against the table edge (see FIG. 5-8F). This tray could be developed into a tabletop work bench for an older child interested in making models or some similar activity. The tray bottom could then be made of thicker plywood and the ledge downward be made deep and strong enough to permit a small vise or clamps to be attached. This could develop into a complete work area, with compartments at the back for small items (FIG. 5-8G).

CLOTHES RACK

A young child cannot be expected to hang up his or her coat if the only hooks are out of reach. The child is also liable to rip or damage a coat by pulling it off from a high peg.

One possibility is to attach a temporary low row of pegs for his use. Wooden pegs with rounded ends are safer than the majority of metal hooks. (The materials list for such a project is found in TABLE 5-8.) You can buy turned wooden pegs with enlarged ends that merely require drilling a hole for each. Shaker pegs are one type (FIG. 5-9A). If a lathe is available, you can make suitable pegs yourself. For a child's use, it is better if the pegs do not project quite as much as the standard adult types (FIG. 5-9B).

Table 5-8. Materials List for a Clothes Rack.

Sizes to suit space

1 backboard	4 × 20 × ¾
4 pegs	3 × ¾ dowel rod
2 hangers (optional)	3 × 20 × ½

An alternative to pegs is to use pieces of dowel rod. As there is no knob to prevent things from falling off, be sure to enter them at a slight angle (FIG. 5-9C) and round the ends well. For the sake of appearance it is important that all holes along a row are drilled at the same angle. If you drill them by hand, place a piece of scrap wood cut to the intended angle alongside the drill (FIG. 5-9D). If you use a drill press, tilt the wood with a packing (FIG. 5-9E). An angle of about 15° to horizontal should be satisfactory.

If you use prepared pegs with the ends shouldered to fit holes, make sure the joints are strong enough if using glue alone. If you use pieces of dowel rod, you might only have to glue in place; however, for added strength, use wedges as well. Make a saw cut across the end of the dowel before gluing it in the hole. Put glue on a wedge and drive this into the saw cut (FIG. 5-9F). When the glue has set, cut off any projecting wood and plane the end level.

A strip of wood with several pegs can be screwed to the wall in a child's room or fixed below adult pegs or hooks. Such a rack will be of use for several years and afterwards it might have other adult uses. In that case it can be attached permanently. Another idea is to adapt a Shaker practice and give the child's rack

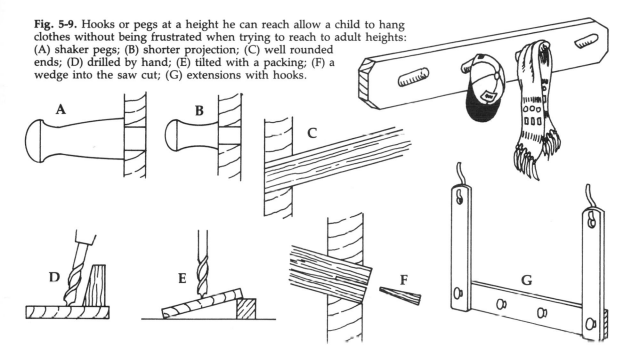

Fig. 5-9. Hooks or pegs at a height he can reach allow a child to hang clothes without being frustrated when trying to reach to adult heights: (A) shaker pegs; (B) shorter projection; (C) well rounded ends; (D) drilled by hand; (E) tilted with a packing; (F) a wedge into the saw cut; (G) extensions with hooks.

extensions that hang from adult clothes hooks (FIG. 5-9G). Spacing will have to suit the existing hooks. To keep the child's rack as close as possible to the wall, the hangers should be fixed to its front.

SHOE RACK

Shoes, slippers, and sandals might be tossed anywhere if there is no definite place to put them. This rack is intended to be attached to a wall or inside a closet door and should accommodate most of the child's footwear. Sizes are obtained by measuring the present shoes and allowing some extra space for larger sizes. One compartment might be made to accommodate two soft shoes, but boots and heavier shoes might need a space each. In any case, you will have to arrange the overall size to suit the available space. One long rack might be best (FIG. 5-10), but there could also be two shorter rows on one backboard if necessary. TABLE 5-9 lists the necessary materials.

The back is a piece of plywood. It need not project much above the compartments if the wall or door behind has a surface that will not be damaged by putting shoes in, but usually it is better to let it come as high as the shoes will project (FIG. 5-10A). The front is a narrower piece of plywood and it should not reach the bottom, so there is a space left for dirt to be removed (FIG. 5-10B).

The important parts are the dividers, which are better if made of solid wood. They must all be the same (FIG. 5-10C). They could be cut from a strip, but the tapered widths should be planed together (FIG. 5-10D). Be sure to round their top edges.

Assembly is better with screws than with nails since the young user pulling shoes out might put considerable leverage on the front and that could loosen nails.

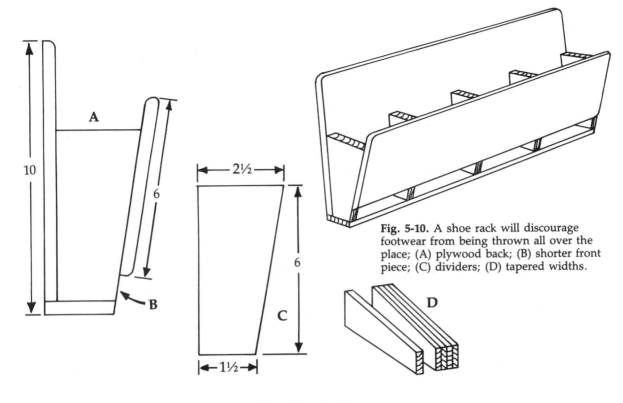

Fig. 5-10. A shoe rack will discourage footwear from being thrown all over the place; (A) plywood back; (B) shorter front piece; (C) dividers; (D) tapered widths.

Table 5-9. Materials List for a Shoe Rack.

Sizes to suit space

1 back	10 × 20 × ⅜ plywood
1 front	6 × 20 × ⅜ plywood
1 bottom	2 × 20 × ⅜
5 dividers	2½ × 6 × ½

FOLDING BOOKLET RACK

A young child collects a great many comics, and magazine-size books, which are usually quite thin. None of these are really suitable for storage in a bookcase, yet the child might want to keep them and will appreciate having them displayed where they can be seen. This folding screen is intended to hold a large number of these paper booklets and anything else to similar proportions. (The materials list is found in TABLE 5-10.) It will stand to show its contents or it can be folded flat for storage. With a cloth draped over it, the young user can imagine it as a home or a tent.

Construction of each part is similar to the bulletin board (FIG. 5-11) with similar joints in the framing attached to plywood. If the rack is to stand on the floor, extend the frame to form feet (FIG. 5-11A) or attach separate feet (FIG. 5-11B).

Put dividers across at suitable distances to allow for the books and other things to be accommodated. Deep things can be kept low, but the child will have little

Table 5-10. Materials List for a Folding Booklet Rack.

2 panels	36 × 36 × ⅛—¼ plywood or hardboard
4 legs	1¼ × 40 × 1¼
8 rails	1¼ × 36 × 1¼
1 strut	1¼ × 18 × ¼

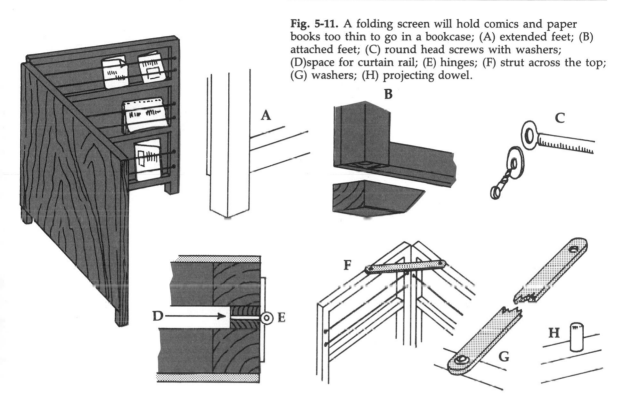

Fig. 5-11. A folding screen will hold comics and paper books too thin to go in a bookcase; (A) extended feet; (B) attached feet; (C) round head screws with washers; (D)space for curtain rail; (E) hinges; (F) strut across the top; (G) washers; (H) projecting dowel.

regard for this and will put things where he wishes, so it might be better to keep all spaces the same. The dividers can be cut close to the uprights and fixed to the plywood, although a T half lap could be used, or even a mortise and tenon joint, if you wish to show your skill.

If there is some flexibility in the way of storing the books and comics, varying thicknesses can be held and it will be easier to put things in or take them out. This is arranged by using an expanding spring-type curtain rail covered with plastic, into which screw eyes can be driven after cutting to length. For hanging curtains or drapes the eyes usually engage with hooks, but in this case there are round head screws through washers (FIG. 5-11C). Use two strands in front of each book space, with one at about half height and the other below it.

The sides that meet for hinging have to be thickened so the frames will close against each other and allow space for the screwed curtain rails (FIG. 5-13D). Hinges can be let into these thickening pieces or screwed on the surface (FIG. 5-13E).

It might be satisfactory to allow the rack to open and close to any position without any retaining strut. Fully open, it could rest against a wall. If it is to stand free, place a strut across the top for stability. This can be a folding metal type, such as is used for closet doors.

A simple type that can be made is shown in FIG. 5-11F. Hardwood is preferable to softwood. One end pivots on a screw, with washers above and below (FIG. 5-11G). At the other end there is a projecting dowel in the frame and a hole in the wooden strut can be put over it (FIG. 5-11H). You will have to do some experimenting to get a position where the strut can fold along the top of one side of the rack, then will lock the assembly at a suitable open position, which is usually a little more than a right angle. Drill several holes in the strut to allow different open positions.

6

Tables
and Chairs

ONE OF THE FIRST NEEDS of a child after the stage of lying or crawling is a place to sit with something in front of him on which he can do things with his hands. It might be a chair with a tray attached and this could be at a high position where he is at the same level as adults sitting at a table, or it could be nearer floor level.

From this the child will want to progress to an independent seat and work or play surface. The seat might be anything from a stool or form to a well-upholstered small version of an adult chair. The play surface might be a simple bench that is intended for rough treatment, or a table of better construction and appearance, more like a small version of an adult table.

Other variations might combine the table and chair but not as closely as the first chair with a tray. An arrangement where the child is free to get in and out of the chair is popular. The chair is kept at the right distance from the table by a permanent or temporary attachment.

When the child starts school he or she will ask for something like a school desk for use at home. Obviously these interests should be encouraged, and a desk with a sloping top and storage underneath can be provided. This might have a built-in seat or a matching chair. An older child might be better served with a flat-top table and a stack of drawers or shelves, more like a scaled-down version of an office desk or table.

In some rooms a tabletop can be built into an alcove or attached to a wall. As the child grows, it may be moved up. Later needs will always be higher, so the early table may become a shelf under a new top, or its attachments hidden if it is repositioned.

The variety is endless and this chapter includes examples of many types. Most of these can be adapted to other sizes and situations. It is also possible to incorporate features of one design in another. The chairs are mostly related to particular designs for tables or desks, but they could be used independently. With several children in a family, it would be interesting to make a set of matching chairs in different sizes.

Chairmaking in the traditional adult sizes is a skill that is more advanced than a beginner craftsman might realize. A chair can get quite rough usage, particularly if it is rocked on two legs, yet the parts are mostly of quite light sections and there is dependence on the security of properly fitting joints.

If the same type of chair is scaled down without any modifications, sections of wood and glue areas in joints become so small that the assembly will not stand up to the rough treatment given it by the small user. Consequently junior chairs have to be given a relatively stouter construction if they are to be strong enough. This means that a certain clumsiness might be evident to an adult, but this must be accepted. However, making a chair for a child will give an enthusiastic woodworker an opportunity to see the problems involved if he later wants to make an adult chair of a more conventional design.

TODDLER'S TABLE

This is a table for the smallest child, who wants to sit on the floor or a very low stool and play with coloring books and similar things at a convenient height. TABLE 6-1 lists the necessary materials. The whole construction is of ½-inch plywood, which can be painted all over, or the top covered with laminated plastic and framed all around to prevent things from falling. The size allows for a possible future use when the child no longer wants a table on the floor. It could then be used as a bed table, resting on the bed over the legs of the user.

Table 6-1. Materials List for a Toddler's Table.

1 top	18 × 30 × ½ plywood
2 sides	14 × 30 × ½ plywood
2 ends	14 × 18 × ½ plywood
2 stiffeners	¾ × 30 × ¾
2 stiffeners	¾ × 18 × ¾

The leg assemblies are all the same shape. To achieve uniformity, make a template for marking them (FIG. 6-1A). Using this on a sheet of plywood will also allow for scheming cuts economically. In any case, waste from between the legs can make the top in two parts.

A good idea is to overlap corners and glue and nail them, with reinforcing strips inside (FIG. 6-1B). If the suitable tools are available, even neater corners can be made by rabbeting one part (FIG. 6-1C). The top can fit inside the leg frame and rest on strips of wood (FIG. 6-1D). This would be satisfactory if the top is made in two parts and will be covered with laminated plastic, but otherwise it will be easier to achieve a neat finish if the top goes over the leg frame and the edges are planed close afterwards (FIG. 6-1E).

To complete the basic table, all edges should be very thoroughly rounded and sanded smooth before painting.

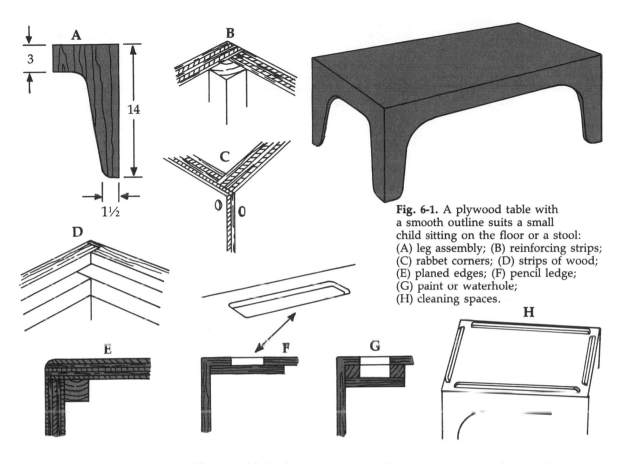

Fig. 6-1. A plywood table with a smooth outline suits a small child sitting on the floor or a stool: (A) leg assembly; (B) reinforcing strips; (C) rabbet corners; (D) strips of wood; (E) planed edges; (F) pencil ledge; (G) paint or waterhole; (H) cleaning spaces.

There could also be one or more wells or recesses cut in the top. For pencils there could be a piece cut out and another piece of plywood put below (FIG. 6-1F). If a deeper recess is needed, possibly to hold a pot of paint or water, the hole could be framed around and the plywood put below that (FIG. 6-1G). Plugs can be made to fill the wells when a level top is needed.

Although you could frame around the outside of the table to prevent things from rolling off, it might be neater and easier to put strips on the top a short distance in from the edges and leave spaces at the corners for cleaning (FIG. 6-1H). Nails can then be set below the surface and covered with stopping.

BUILT-IN TABLE

If you have a suitable alcove in a room, make the simplest table like a shelf. It can be a single board resting on strips screwed to the walls. Instead of a piece of solid wood, it might be a piece of surfaced particleboard or a piece of plywood. Although something strong enough in itself can be used, it would be more economical and lighter to use thinner plywood or hardboard and stiffen it below with framing. A further development would be the addition of one or more drawers.

An unstiffened board might seem strong enough at first, but it might develop a sag in time. Even if the rear edge is left unsupported, it is stronger and looks

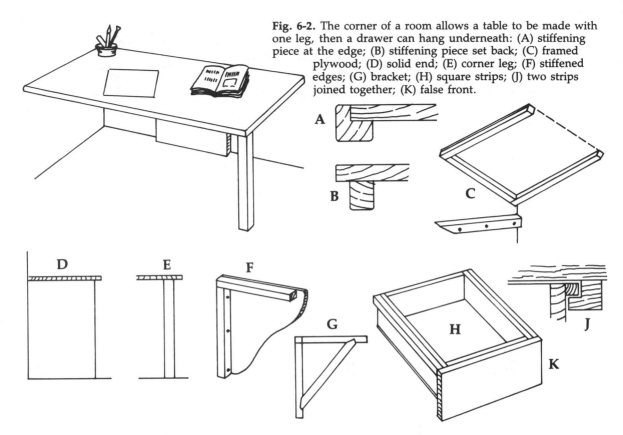

Fig. 6-2. The corner of a room allows a table to be made with one leg, then a drawer can hang underneath: (A) stiffening piece at the edge; (B) stiffening piece set back; (C) framed plywood; (D) solid end; (E) corner leg; (F) stiffened edges; (G) bracket; (H) square strips; (J) two strips joined together; (K) false front.

better if you include a stiffening piece under the front, either at the edge and rabbeted (FIG. 6-2A), or set back a short distance (FIG. 6-2B).

If you use thinner plywood, frame all around (FIG. 6-2C), and rabbet the front edge for the neatest finish. If both ends can be supported by walls, screw strips of wood in place, but be careful that the result will be level. Don't always assume that a floor is level and merely make the tabletop parallel with it. Instead put a level across a length of scrap straight wood to check that the supporting pieces really are level.

If only one end can be supported in a corner, the other end can have a solid end (FIG. 6-2D) or a corner leg (FIG. 6-2E). In both cases, attach the bottom to the floor, either with blocks screwed on or with small metal brackets. They have to resist occasional lifting loads as well as the normal downward thrusts.

In some places it is better not to obstruct the floor at an open end. Support then can be achieved by a bracket off the wall. For maximum strength it should extend most of the width of the table and the vertical part should be longer than the horizontal part. It could be shaped from plywood with stiffened edges (FIG. 6-2F).

Another bracket can be built up from strips (FIG. 6-2G). The top corner would be strongest if made with a dovetail and the diagonal strut should be notched into the other parts.

In both brackets the actual angle should be a degree or so above a right angle. If you make a bracket exactly a right angle the tabletop will almost certainly slope very slightly at the front. Walls are not always as accurate as they should be, so first put the bracket in place and check the top with a level, then adjust the surface if necessary.

A fairly simple task is to sling a simple drawer below this type of table. This would be useful, particularly for an older child to keep small items and paper together. Although drawers can be made with special joints, the one shown here has a simple nailed construction. The drawer itself is a plain box with the corners nailed and a plywood bottom nailed on. The runners are small square strips screwed to the sides (FIG. 6-2H). They hang from strips screwed below the table top, either solid with rabbets or made from two strips joined together (FIG. 6-2J). A false front to the drawer serves as a handle by projecting below and hides the ends of the runners (FIG. 6-2K).

If the tabletop is a flat board, the guides fit directly to it. However, if the top is framed plywood, you will need thickening pieces to make the runners the same level as the front. Arrange the length of the drawer so when it stops against the wall, its front is a short distance back from the table edge.

DESK

A desk with a sloping top that lifts to expose storage space below can keep things tidy and be made as a freestanding unit, as a top to rest on a table or shelf, or be built into a combined unit with a seat. The desk described here is a basic unit that can be adapted to other designs. The necessary materials are listed in TABLE 6-2.

Table 6-2. Materials List for a Desk.

2 ends	7 × 20 × ⅝
1 back	7 × 22 × ⅝
1 front	3 × 22 × ⅝
1 flap	18 × 24 × ¾ plywood
1 top	3 × 24 × ¾ plywood
1 bottom	20 × 22 × ¼ plywood
2 legs	6 × 22 × ⅝
2 feet	1¼ × 20 × 1¼
4 feet	1¼ × 2 × ⅝
1 rail (optional)	3 × 24 × ⅝
1 rail (optional)	1¼ × 24 × 1¼

Construction can be entirely of plywood, but it might be simpler and cheaper to use softwood for the box frame and the legs, with plywood for the top flap and bottom. The sloping top flap might warp if made of unstiffened solid wood. If you alter the sizes, do not make the desk front too deep. Try sitting the child and check that the bottom of the box will clear his knees easily, while the top is at a convenient height for him to use his hands on it.

Next, make the box ends (FIG. 6-3A). The back is a plain rectangular piece. Plane the top of the front to the same angle as the slope of the ends. Corners may be overlapped and nailed. They can be rabbeted or the ends can fit into dados (FIG. 6-3B).

Check squareness as you glue and nail on the bottom. If the desk is to be supported on legs, make the top and flap long enough to cover their tops. There

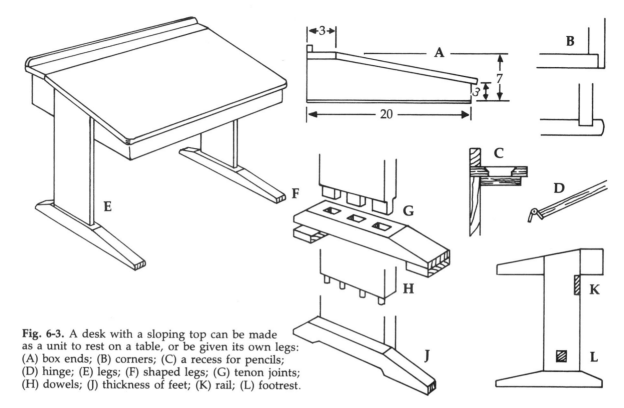

Fig. 6-3. A desk with a sloping top can be made as a unit to rest on a table, or be given its own legs: (A) box ends; (B) corners; (C) a recess for pencils; (D) hinge; (E) legs; (F) shaped legs; (G) tenon joints; (H) dowels; (J) thickness of feet; (K) rail; (L) footrest.

should be a strip at the back to prevent things from falling off. This can be screwed from below before the top is attached to the box. There could also be a recess in the top to take pencils. The simplest way to make this is to cut through the top and fix a piece of plywood below (FIG. 6-3C). Round the exposed edges.

The flap is made of plywood the same thickness as the top. Cut meeting edges to match and round the other edges and corners. The best hinge for the top is a full-length piano hinge, but two or three small butt hinges will also work (FIG. 6-3D).

This completes the construction of a desk to stand on a table. To prevent it from sliding on a smooth surface, glue pieces of rubber or cloth under the corners.

Legs can be made from pieces screwed to the box ends. They can be central or set back to allow easier access when the child gets into a chair near the desk (FIG. 6-3E). The feet have to extend far enough to prevent the desk from tipping. This means that at the back and front they should extend as far as the corners of the desktop.

The best feet are slightly thicker than the legs and cut so only their ends rest on the floor. They could be built up (FIG. 6-3F) or bandsawn to shape. The tops of the extremities of the feet should be rounded. The traditional method of joining the legs to the feet would be with multiple mortise and tenon joints (FIG. 6-3G), however, dowels work almost as well (FIG. 6-3H). A simpler treatment is to make the feet about the same thickness as the legs and screw them outside (FIG. 6-3J).

There will almost certainly be enough rigidity in a small desk built this way without extra bracing. However, if some stiffening seems necessary, attach a rail across the backs of the legs close under the desk (FIG. 6-3K) or near the bottom of the desk legs to serve as a footrest (FIG. 6-3L).

DESK WITH SEAT

Although a separate stool or chair might be used with a desk, there is the problem of it not always being there. A child is more likely to be attracted to his desk if the seat is always in front of it. This design uses a central attachment between the desk and seat, so the child sits astride it. The example here has a plain seat, but some comfort could be provided with loose padding held in place with tapes, which would be more convenient for cleaning than fixed upholstery. (For the necessary materials, see TABLE 6-3.)

Table 6-3. Materials List for a Desk with Seat.

2 ends	$7 \times 20 \times \frac{5}{8}$
1 back	$7 \times 22 \times \frac{5}{8}$
1 front	$3 \times 22 \times \frac{5}{8}$
1 flap	$18 \times 24 \times \frac{3}{4}$ plywood
1 top	$3 \times 24 \times \frac{3}{4}$ plywood
1 bottom	$20 \times 22 \times \frac{3}{4}$ plywood
1 back leg	$15 \times 22 \times \frac{3}{4}$ plywood
1 beam	$15 \times 33 \times \frac{3}{4}$ plywood
1 seat	$8 \times 9 \times \frac{3}{4}$ plywood
1 seat back	$7 \times 25 \times \frac{3}{4}$ plywood
stiffeners from	$\frac{3}{4} \times 70 \times \frac{3}{4}$

The desktop is made the same as in the last example (FIG. 6-3), except the bottom of the box might be kept back so the sloping front gives more leg clearance (FIG. 6-4A).

Cut the back two legs as a unit from ¾-inch plywood, with its outer grain upright (FIG. 6-4B). The central beam should come against the bottom of the desk box, then cut down to give the sitter leg clearance and raised to seat level (FIG. 6-4C). It could butt against the back legs and be stiffened with blocks glued and screwed (FIG. 6-4D); but it would be stronger if tenons were taken through (FIG. 6-4E). Dowels would be unsatisfactory edgewise in plywood. Instead, screw through and use glued blocks under the box.

The seat needn't have a back, which might be a better design for a very active child, constantly wanting to get on and off; however, the seat would be more comfortable if a back was provided. If no back is to be included, the leg assembly could be upright under the seat top, but for a back it would be more comfortable if the plywood forming the leg and back piece is given a slight slope (FIG. 6-4F).

The beam is attached at the seat end in the same way as to the back leg unit. The bottom of the beam and chair leg could rest on the floor in their full widths, but there is less risk of rocking if they are cut away a little (FIG. 6-4G).

Shape the seat top to give some leg clearance, well rounding the edges, then screw in place (FIG. 6-4H). Holes through the beam and the seat back will allow tape to secure any seat padding.

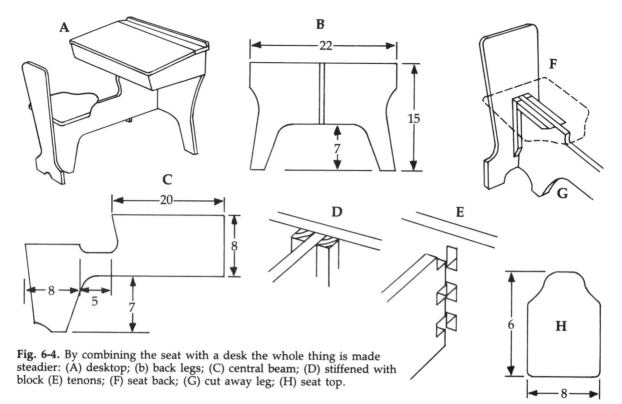

Fig. 6-4. By combining the seat with a desk the whole thing is made steadier: (A) desktop; (b) back legs; (C) central beam; (D) stiffened with block (E) tenons; (F) seat back; (G) cut away leg; (H) seat top.

STANDARD TABLE

This project is a flat-topped table that will serve as a play or work area, or a junior dining table for an older child. It is included here as an example of traditional methods of construction for the benefit of a woodworker interested in the older techniques of cabinetwork, with much of the detail cutting being done by hand. There are other ways of making tables of similar size, using simplified constructions and methods appropriate to power tools. For this table, a materials list is found in TABLE 6-4.

Table 6-4. Materials List for a Standard Table.

1 top	24	×	36	×	1 solid or framed plywood
1 rail	5	×	34	×	¾
2 rails	5	×	22	×	¾
2 front rails	3	×	34	×	¾
1 front rail and drawer	3½	×	34	×	¾
4 legs	2	×	24	×	2
4 drawer guides	1½	×	22	×	¾
4 drawer guides	¾	×	22	×	¾
2 drawer sides	3½	×	22	×	½
1 drawer back	3	×	12	×	½
1 drawer bottom	12	×	22	×	¼ plywood

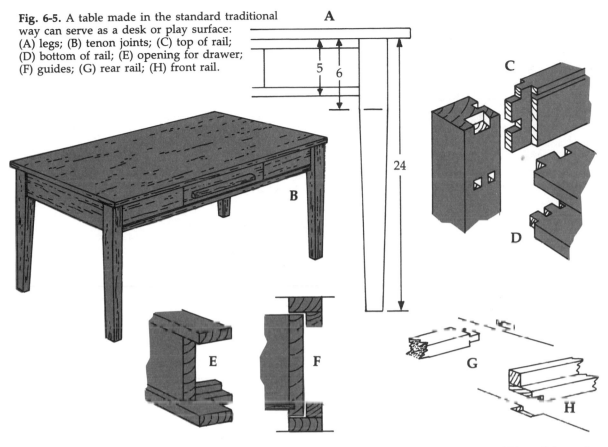

Fig. 6-5. A table made in the standard traditional way can serve as a desk or play surface: (A) legs; (B) tenon joints; (C) top of rail; (D) bottom of rail; (E) opening for drawer; (F) guides; (G) rear rail; (H) front rail.

All parts are best if made of attractive hardwood. The top could be solid wood, perhaps with a veneered plywood center section. The drawer shown in FIG. 6-5 is an example of traditional drawer construction. The legs are without lower rails and straight grained wood should be used so there is no risk of warping.

The legs are parallel to a short distance below where the rails join, then are tapered slightly (FIG. 6-5A). Leave some excess length at the tops until after the mortises have been cut.

The end and rear rails are solid wood. Their joints into the legs are haunched mortise and tenons (FIG. 6-5B). Plow grooves a short distance down from the top edges if the tabletop is to be affixed with buttons. A framed top might also be affixed with pocket screws. The front rail can be a single piece with an opening cut for the drawer, but a built-up rail is shown.

The top part is a broad piece dovetailed into the legs and taken around to butt against the end rails (FIG. 6-5C). The bottom part is similar, but a dovetail cannot be used and it is tenoned instead (FIG. 6-5D). Between these parts are pieces that can be affixed against the legs, be tenoned into them, or dowelled. They are screwed from above and below, leaving an opening to suit the drawer (FIG. 6-5E).

The drawer fits between guides, which are called *runners* at the bottom and *kickers* at the top, but they all have the same section (FIG. 6-5F). At the rear rail they are tenoned (FIG. 6-5G), but at the front lap joints can be used (FIG. 6-5H). It is important that the surfaces against which the drawer will slide follow smoothly back from the opening in the front rail. If the drawer is to fit properly, they must be at right angles to the front rail. They should be at right angles elsewhere, but if there are to be any slight errors in assembly, at least get the front angles correct.

It is also important that the guides are parallel. Obviously a drawer cannot be wider at the back than the front or it would not pull out. Sometimes a drawer is made very slightly narrower at the back than the front for ease of movement, but the runners and kickers should still be parallel.

Usually, the table is assembled at this stage. With the table standing on its legs and the top open, it is possible to fit the drawer more accurately as any irregularities can be seen and adjusted. The top can be made and the outline finished to give an even overhang, then the framework inverted and fitted to it.

If you use solid wood to make the top, you might have to glue boards to make up the width. If plywood is to be framed around, the simplest way is to use rabbets in the framing and let in the plywood with glue and punched pins (FIG. 6-6A).

If you use thicker plywood, rabbet the plywood first so it fits into grooves in the frame (FIG. 6-6B). The corners of the framing should be mitered in both cases. If you use buttons as the method of fastening, make the frame pieces wide enough to take buttons underneath. Otherwise, put packings under the plywood in each position (FIG. 6-6C).

At the front you could also put screws up through the wide rail, or use pocket screws upward on the insides of the other rails (FIG. 6-6D) instead of buttons.

The drawer front should match the front rail. If the three parts are cut from the same piece of wood, the grain pattern can follow through. Make the drawer front first, to be a fairly close fit in the opening. If necessary it can be eased a little after the drawer has been made up. Cut the wood for the drawer sides. Try the pieces in their guides. They should slide freely without much play. Leave them overlength at this stage.

The drawer bottom is a piece of plywood. Plow grooves to take it in the front and sides. It helps to keep the drawer in shape if the bottom fits tightly, so it is common to plow the grooves a little too narrow and bevel the underside of the plywood so that it is forced in (FIG. 6-7A).

The front corners are half blind dovetails. They can be machine-made with a suitable jig, but if cut by hand, make sure that the tails are wider than the pins

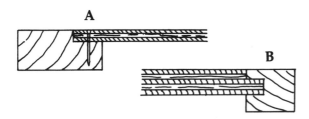
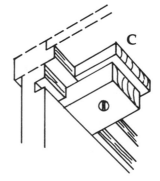
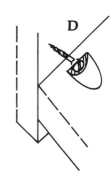

Fig. 6-6. The top of the standard table can be framed plywood held with buttons or pocket screws: (A) punched pin; (B) rabbet the plywood; (C) packings; (D) pocket screws.

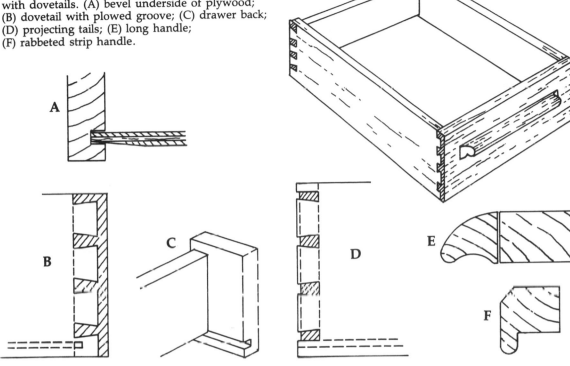

Fig. 6-7. To match the traditional construction of the standard table, its drawer can be made with dovetails. (A) bevel underside of plywood; (B) dovetail with plowed groove; (C) drawer back; (D) projecting tails; (E) long handle; (F) rabbeted strip handle.

between them. There is also a bottom part dovetail that contains the plowed groove and hides it (FIG. 6-7B). Cut the joints, but do not assemble them yet.

After cutting these joints, check the lengths of each side. It should stop against the back rail so the drawer front will be level, but leaving them a very small amount too long at this stage is better than finishing with them too short.

The drawer back goes above the plowed groove and need not be taken quite as high as the sides (FIG. 6-7C). It is joined with through dovetails, but set in a little so the tails project (FIG. 6-7D). After assembly they can be planed until the drawer closes properly with its front level with the front rail. If a drawer is made too short, glue veneer or paper inside the back rail to make a stop.

Next, assemble the four drawer parts. Check squareness and leave them for the glue to set. Remove surplus glue, particularly in the grooves for the bottom and level any side projection in the joints. Try the drawer in position and adjust the rear ends of the sides to make a good fit. It is best to not use glue when fitting the bottom. Bevel the edges of the plywood and tap it into the grooves from the back. Drive a few screws upwards into the drawer back.

A metal or plastic drawer pull can be fitted with one or a pair of knobs. For a wide drawer a child might find a long wooden handle better. It can be shaped on the edge of a wider board and cut off (FIG. 6-7E) or a simple rabbeted strip can be used (FIG. 6-7F). If the drawer sticks, do not put oil on it, but rub its edges with a piece of candle or hard wax.

BOOKCASE AND TABLE

An older child usually has a need for plenty of book storage. This desk or table is of a unit construction with two bookcases as supports that might have enough stiffness in themselves. A drawer unit fits centrally between the supports. If the units are screwed together from below, the whole thing will be a rigid piece of furniture. It will be possible to disassemble it, however, so that there are two bookcases that could be used alone, a top that might serve as a drawing board, and a drawer unit that could be put under another table. This materials list is found in TABLE 6-5.

Table 6-5. Materials List for a Bookcase and Table.

4 uprights	8 × 27 × ¾	
8 shelves	8 × 20 × ¾	
4 plinths	2¼ × 20 × ¾	
4 plinths	2¼ × 7½ × ¾	
2 backs	20 × 27 × ¼ plywood	
4 drawer rails	1½ × 18 × ¾	
4 drawer rails	¾ × 20 × ¾	
2 unit sides	5 × 20 × ¼ plywood	
1 unit back	5 × 18 × ¼ plywood	
1 drawer front	3½ × 18 × ⅝	
1 drawer front	5 × 18 × ⅝	
1 drawer back	3 × 18 × ⅝	
1 drawer bottom	18 × 20 × ¼ plywood	
1 top	20 × 36 × ¾ solid wood or framed plywood	

The height shown would suit a child of 12 years old and yet could still be useful for an adult. For a young child the whole thing could be made lower, although if the bookcases are first made to stand without plinths, these can be added later to give an extra 2 inches or more when needed. If this is anticipated, make the plinths at the same time as the other parts so they can be finished with paint, stain, or varnish to match the other parts. They can then be kept and screwed on when needed.

Several joints can be used in the bookcases, but those shown are rabbets at top and bottom (FIG. 6-8A) and stopped dado joints for the shelves (FIG. 6-8B). Mark out the four sides together (FIG. 6-8C). You might have to adjust the spacing of the shelves to the actual books. There is no need for the two bookcases to have the same spacings, although overall lengths should be marked across all four pieces together to get the heights uniform.

The plywood backs fit into rabbets in the sides and can overlap the top and bottom (FIG. 6-8D). These rabbets and those across the ends of the side pieces are deeper than the dados. Make the tops and bottoms and put them temporarily in position so the lengths of the shelves can be measured.

When the bookcases are assembled, pull the sides to the tops and bottoms with clamps, while gluing and screwing into the sides (FIG. 6-8E). The screw heads will be hidden so there is no need to sink and plug them. The shelves should be a good fit, but be careful of making them overlong, forcing the sides to become

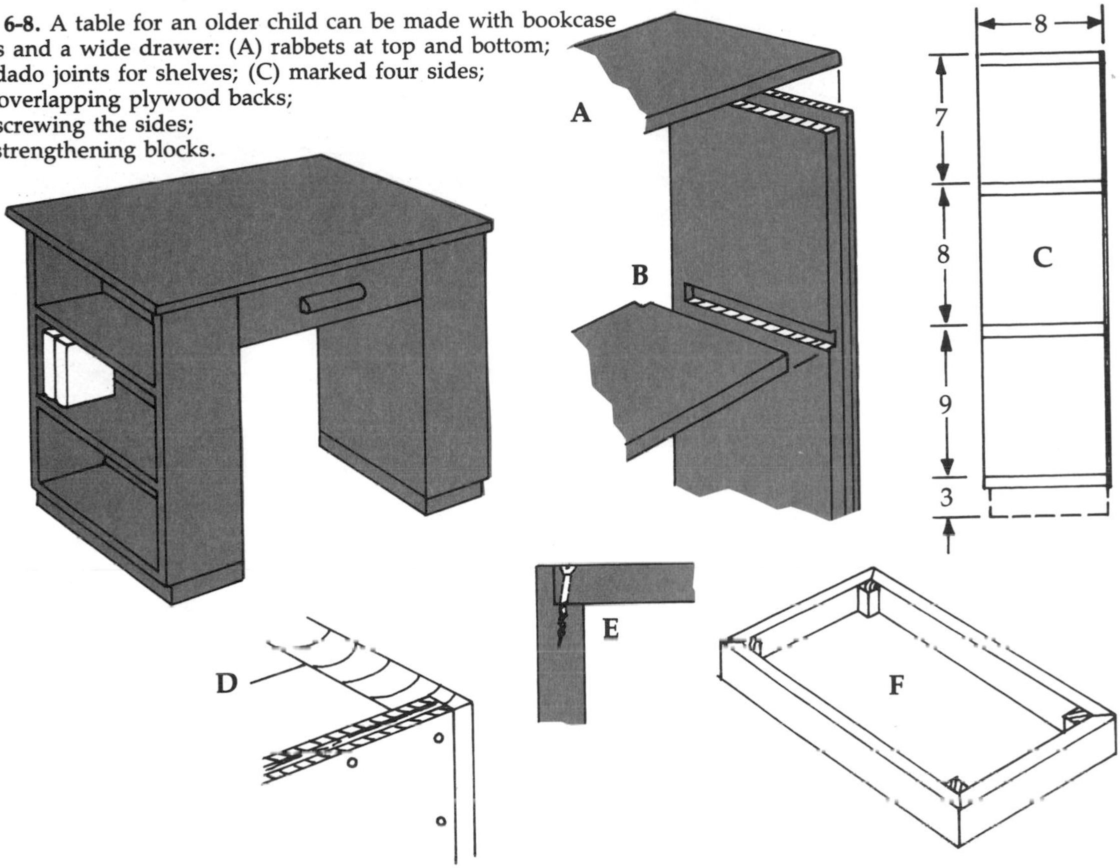

Fig. 6-8. A table for an older child can be made with bookcase ends and a wide drawer: (A) rabbets at top and bottom; (B) dado joints for shelves; (C) marked four sides; (D) overlapping plywood backs; (E) screwing the sides; (F) strengthening blocks.

bowed outwards when they are forced in. Glue alone should be sufficient in the dados, but if a shelf is loose, it can be screwed from below.

If the plywood backs of the bookcases are carefully squared, there should be no difficulty in getting the bookcases assembled true, but try one on the other to see that they match. Put the plywood in the rabbets with glue and drive light nails into the sides and the crosswise parts.

The plinths have mitered corners with strengthening blocks inside (FIG. 6-8F). They are set in from three edges of the bottoms of the bookcases, but are level with the plywood backs. Attach them with pocket screws inside.

The top can be made of solid wood, with several pieces glued to make up the width. Thinner plywood can be framed as described for the standard table (FIGS. 6-5 and 6-6). The top shown (FIG. 6-9A) is made of thick plywood with a frame of the same thickness. It could be faced particleboard treated in the same way.

Plow a groove all around the top and fit a solid wood edging into it with a tongue (FIG. 6-9B). Then miter the framing pieces at the corners. To allow for slight errors in cutting the matching parts, the edging pieces should be made a little too thick, so they can be planed and sanded level after gluing.

It is possible to assemble the top to the two bookcases and use the table, but there might be some lack of stiffness (that might not matter) and the appearance

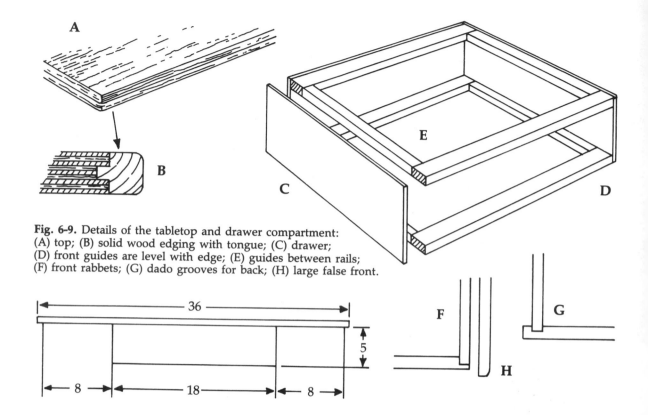

Fig. 6-9. Details of the tabletop and drawer compartment: (A) top; (B) solid wood edging with tongue; (C) drawer; (D) front guides are level with edge; (E) guides between rails; (F) front rabbets; (G) dado grooves for back; (H) large false front.

of the comparatively thin top without framing below would not be very attractive. Besides its usefulness, the drawer unit provides stability in the assembly and improves appearance.

The drawer unit is made like a box with an open top and bottom and plywood sides and back. The drawer has a false front that overlaps the plywood sides of the box and the top and bottom rails.

First, make the plywood sides. Their length should be the same as the width of the bookcases and deep enough to accommodate the drawer and its guides (FIG. 6-9C). Four rails fit between the pieces of plywood. At the rear they are set in enough to take the plywood back, but at the front they are level with the edge (FIG. 6-9D). Screw through the plywood into the ends of the rails and nail on the back. Put guides between the rails (FIG. 6-9E), making sure to get the surfaces that will come next to the drawer level. Check that the whole assembly is square.

The drawer is given a false front, but otherwise could be made with dovetails. A simplified method is described here. There are grooves for the plywood bottom in the sides and the front, and the sides are screwed into rabbets in the front (FIG. 6-9F). The back goes into dado grooves above the plywood grooves (FIG. 6-9G). The complete drawer at this stage should fit into the box with its front level.

The wood you use for the drawer parts need not be as good quality as for the other parts, but make the false front of wood to match the rest of the table. It should be large enough to overlap the plywood sides (FIG. 6-9H) and the top and bottom rails. Round the exposed edges. Attach it with glue and screws from inside the drawer. If the handle you choose has to be attached with screws through the wood, it might be better to fit the handle to the false front before fitting that to the drawer.

PEDESTAL TABLE

Bookcase supports might suit some children's needs, but others might want places to store more bulky and awkwardly shaped things as well as books. This table has a pedestal with one drawer and storage room below it to hold fairly large toys or models. The pedestal is matched for height by a pair of legs in the manner of some office desks.

It is possible to combine features of this and the previous table to suit particular situations. For instance, a table that is to fit into a corner could have a pedestal against the two walls and a bookcase support at the open end. If the table is to be more of a work bench for a hobby than a desk, the pedestal can be fitted as a tool cabinet and the bookcase part altered to make racks for other tools.

The pedestal can be treated as a unit, except that instead of a plinth around its base there is a single foot joined with a footrail to the other leg assembly. For a materials list, see TABLE 6-6.

Table 6-6. Materials List for a Pedestal Table.

4 pedestal frames	¾ × 26 × ¾	
5 pedestal frames	¾ × 12 × ¾	
1 pedestal frame	1 × 12 × 1	
4 pedestal frames	1½ × 15 × ¾	
2 pedestal frames	¾ × 15 × ¾	
2 pedestal sides	15 × 25 × ¼ plywood	
1 pedestal back	12 × 25 × ¼ plywood	
1 pedestal bottom	12 × 15 × ¼ plywood	
1 drawer front	6¼ × 11 × ¾	
2 drawer sides	6¼ × 15 × ⅝	
1 drawer back	6 × 11 × ⅝	
1 drawer bottom	11 × 15 × ¼ plywood	
1 door	11 × 18 × ¾ plywood	
2 legs	3 × 28 × 1	
2 leg rails	3 × 10 × 1	
2 leg rails	4 × 8 × 1	
1 pedestal foot	4 × 15 × 1½	
1 footrail	2¼ × 24 × 1	
2 rails	3 × 16 × 1	
1 rail	3 × 15 × 1	
1 top	17 × 30 × ¾ solid wood or framed plywood	

The sides of the pedestal are made of plywood on wood framing. There could be mortise and tenon joints between the parts of the framing, but it should be satisfactory to notch and lap the parts as glue and thin nails through the plywood will provide sufficient reinforcement. Back and front parts of the frames are the full height and the other parts fit to them (FIG. 6-10A).

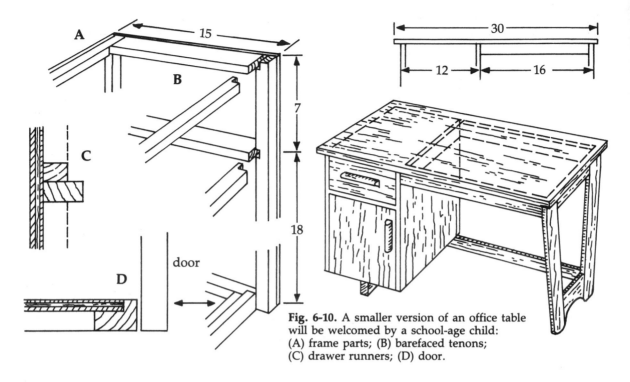

Fig. 6-10. A smaller version of an office table will be welcomed by a school-age child: (A) frame parts; (B) barefaced tenons; (C) drawer runners; (D) door.

The six rails that cross to unite the sides can be attached with barefaced tenons (FIG. 6-10B). The back plywood comes between the side pieces. Allow the plywood to extend over the framing enough for edges to be planed level after assembly.

The top and intermediate rails across the sides should be wider than the front and back parts of the framing so they will act as drawer runners and guides (FIG. 6-10C).

The bottom should be set back enough for the door to overlap it and fit between the sides. You can nail plywood to the front rail, but it will look better if the edge fits into a rabbet in the rail. To allow for this the edge must be fitted higher than the other rails (FIG. 6-10D).

Hinge the door between the sides so that it closes against the bottom rail, but you can also put a small block of wood on the drawer rail to act as a stop at the top. For the door you can use a piece of ¾-inch plywood. For a painted finish, the door can be left with nothing over the edges, but otherwise it would be better treated with a narrow strip tongued and grooved as described for the table top (FIG. 6-9B).

Attach a handle at a convenient height for reaching from a sitting position. Use a spring or magnetic catch. Make the drawer in one of the ways described earlier in this chapter and provide it with a handle to match the one on the door.

The leg assembly is made up with framing to go under the top and a footrail connecting with the piece under the pedestal (FIG. 6-11A). The legs are made with their tops upright for a depth that will include the top rails, then slope towards each other and are joined with a crossbar (FIG. 6-11B). Hollow the crossbar on the lower edge and shape the bottoms of the legs to match. Then join the crossbar and the top straight crossbar with the legs with dowels.

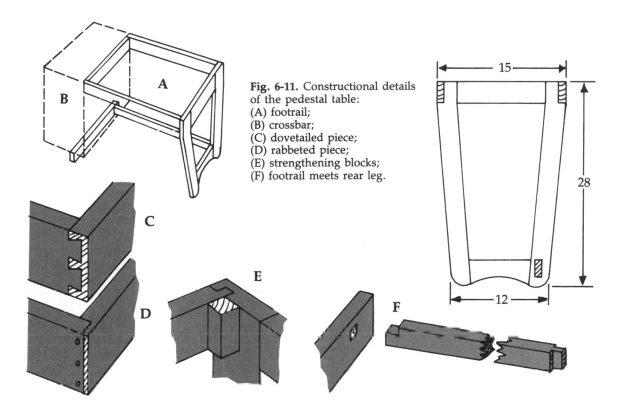

Fig. 6-11. Constructional details of the pedestal table: (A) footrail; (B) crossbar; (C) dovetailed piece; (D) rabbeted piece; (E) strengthening blocks; (F) footrail meets rear leg.

Link the two top rails that join the leg assembly with a piece across at the pedestal end, which can be dovetailed (FIG. 6-11C) or rabbeted (FIG. 6-11D). At the leg end, barefaced tenons are best with strengthening blocks glued inside (FIG. 6-11E). Round the lower edges of the rails. The front one can be hollowed to give more leg room if desired.

Below the pedestal, notch the block of wood forming the foot to fit against the plywood bottom and hollow its lower edge slightly in a way similar to the bottom of the leg assembly. Attach it by screwing from inside. The footrail should cross at a suitable position to come under the pedestal and meet the rear leg (FIG. 6-11F). Its end can be tenoned with a screw upward into the pedestal framing.

Points to watch include:

- squareness at all stages
- that the leg assembly finishes the same width as the pedestal and its height finishes the same as the pedestal plus its foot
- that when the leg and rail assembly are brought to the pedestal, the legs are upright when viewed from the front.

You can make the top in one of the ways described for the last two tables. Attach it by screwing upward through the top framing of the pedestal, along with pocket screws through the rails.

LOW CHAIR

This chair is intended to give a small child a safe seat in comfort with a tray big enough to provide a play area for toys. The size should suit a child from the time the child is first able to sit up. The footrest is located to suit the smallest child's legs, but when the child gets bigger, it can be removed so his feet will reach the ground. The chair outline is part of a square cone, so the spread of the feet on the floor is larger than the top and the whole thing should stand firm no matter how active the young user may be.

At a later stage, with tray and footrest removed, the chair can be used by a child alongside one of the tables already described. When no longer required as a seat, the back can be removed and a top added so the leg assembly then becomes part of a small table. TABLE 6-7 lists the necessary materials.

Table 6-7. Materials List for a Low Chair.

4 legs	3 × 22 × 1
2 top rails	2 × 12 × 1
6 rails	1½ × 20 × ¾
1 seat	20 × 20 × ½ plywood
1 back	15 × 10 × ½ plywood
1 tray	12 × 20 × ½ plywood
1 tray frame	1 × 20 × ½
2 tray frames	1 × 12 × ½
1 footrest	3 × 20 × ½ plywood
2 brackets	3 × 3 × ¾
1 tabletop (optional)	22 × 22 × ¾

The design shown in FIG. 6-12 includes some simple upholstery—foam padding and a plastic covering that can be wiped clean. You can also make cushions with tapes, so the padding can be removed for cleaning. So the cushions will not move, drill holes to take the tapes through the edges of the seat rails and back.

Although the chair framework slopes both ways, there are no complicated compound angles to cut. Make the two side assemblies first and join them with the crosswise parts. Although some of the wood has to be bevelled, those parts that are not square all have the same bevels. One setting of an adjustable bevel will mark and test these surfaces.

Start by drawing the side view full size (FIG. 6-12A). The edges should slope inward 2 inches in the height of 20 inches. This should be the same in the other direction also (FIG. 6-12B). This angle is the one to which the adjustable bevel is set.

The legs should taper from 3 inches to 1½ inches. Check that they match and mark them out together from your full-size drawing. Then join the top rails to them with dowels (FIG. 6-13A). Leave some excess length on the tops of the legs to trim level after assembly.

The seat rails are better joined with mortise and tenon joints (FIG. 6-13B), although they can also be dowelled. Assemble the two sides over your full-size drawing and check them against each other. See that they are kept flat while the glue is setting. The joints in the other directions can be prepared after the sides are completed.

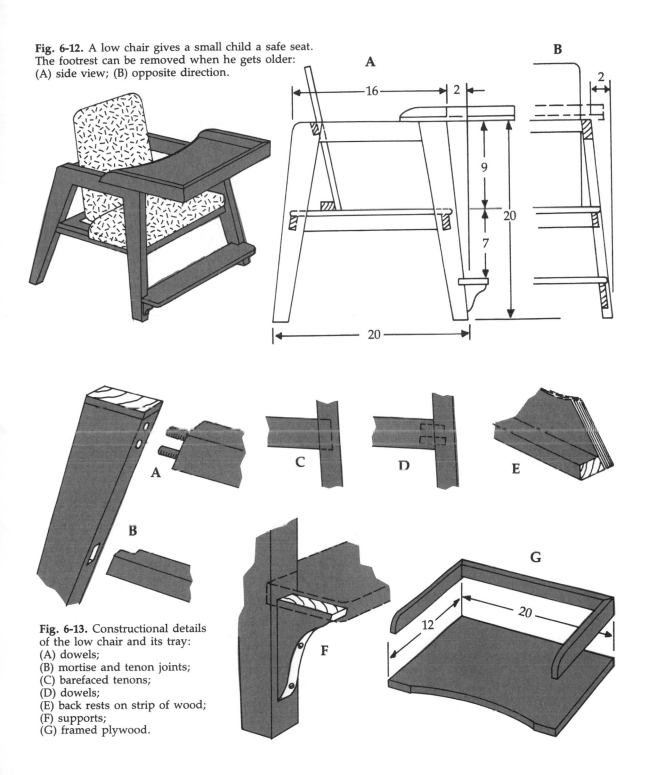

Fig. 6-12. A low chair gives a small child a safe seat. The footrest can be removed when he gets older: (A) side view; (B) opposite direction.

Fig. 6-13. Constructional details of the low chair and its tray:
(A) dowels;
(B) mortise and tenon joints;
(C) barefaced tenons;
(D) dowels;
(E) back rests on strip of wood;
(F) supports;
(G) framed plywood.

In the other direction, the assembly is set to shape by the two rails under the seat and the one behind the back. Cut their ends to the standard bevel. (The lengths are indicated in the full-size drawing.) The two seat rails can be kept level with the inner faces of the legs and joined with barefaced tenons (FIG. 6-13C) or dowels (FIG. 6-13D).

In this sort of joint, dowels are always fitted in line with the wood, although its end is cut at an angle. Never drill at right angles to the sloping face. The rail behind the back can be tenoned or dowelled. Plane the top edges of all these rails to the standard bevel before assembly.

Next, notch the piece of plywood that forms the seat around the legs. To ensure squareness of the chair, this should be prepared and fitted at the same time as the crosswise rails, to which it is attached with glue and nails. The plywood edges overlap the rails and should be rounded. If the chair will eventually be converted into a table, the seat can remain as a shelf, so it can be fastened down permanently.

The back is a piece of plywood with its top corners and edges rounded, cut to fit between the sides. At the bottom it rests against a strip of wood on the seat (FIG. 6-13E). You can put screws into the rail and the attachment to the seat, so the back can be removed later for a table conversion.

The footrest is a piece of plywood notched around the legs. It does not have to bear much load, so there is no need to stiffen it. The supports underneath could be small metal shelf brackets, but wood supports are shown in FIG. 6-13F. Shape the outline so two screws can be driven into each leg, so that it is possible to remove the footrest. Leave only small holes to fill with stopping and sand level after the parts are no longer needed.

The tray is based on a piece of plywood, framed around (FIG. 6-13G). At the side toward the child, hollow the edge slightly and thoroughly around it. The sides of the framing should taper down to the plywood and be rounded. Then join the tray to the sides with two screws into their tops. If you wish to be able to remove the tray occasionally for cleaning the chair, place a bolt at each side through the top rails, with a nut underneath. In any case, do not use glue, as the tray as well as the footrest will be removed when the child gets bigger and wants to sit at a table.

A painted finish might be best for a young child, but if the chair will be converted to a table later, it would look better if you give the leg assemblies and seat a finish to match the furniture that will be around the table. This will probably be stained, varnished, or lacquered. The footrest, tray and back can still be brightly painted to attract the child. The tray surface can be decorated with a decal or painted design. Apply the chosen finish at this stage, even if the chair is to be upholstered.

The back is easier to upholster before it is fitted into the chair, although it can be done in position. It is best to make a trial assembly, then withdraw the screws and do the upholstering on the loose piece of wood. The bottom screws can be driven from the plywood into the supporting strip of wood, as they will not be covered by upholstery, but at the rail the screws should be from the solid wood into the plywood, otherwise their heads will be covered. The seat has to be upholstered in position.

Padding can be plastic or rubber foam, not more than 1½ inches thick. Fit a piece of vinyl or other plastic coated fabric over the padding. Do not use a woven porous fabric covering, as this will collect dirt and be difficult to dry if it gets wet.

Most foams are soft enough to pull down at the edges, but if a piece is not, do not cut its top surface. Bevel its lower surface by cutting with a sharp thin-bladed knife. This will allow the padding to pull to a curve with a smooth surface towards the covering (FIG. 6-14A). Trim the foam so it is slightly bigger than the area to be covered, so that the covering will pull it into a neat fit.

Attach the covering with tacks. On the back, the pull should be just enough to hold the padding. Drive the tacks a short distance in from the edge (FIG. 6-14B). At the bottom, turn under the covering and fit with a few tacks on the front surface of the plywood (FIG. 6-14C). At the top curved corners there will have to be some folding. Two folds at each corner will probably be enough (FIG. 6-14D).

Keep the tacks at an even distance from the edge, then trim the fabric inside them (FIG. 6-14E). For the neatest finish, use another piece of the same fabric, cut to go over the tacks and turn under, with more tacks holding it in place (FIG. 6-14F).

Notch the padding for the seat at the front corners to fit around the legs, but do not cut away very much since the covering will compress the foam. At the back it can be taken close to the plywood below the rear upholstery.

As there is no space for tacking under the seat, unless the covering also goes below the rails, drive tacks into the sides of the rails (FIG. 6-14G). At the rear edge there should be sufficient tension on the turned-in edge to compress the padding, without putting any tacks across the width of the seat. At the front corners, cut

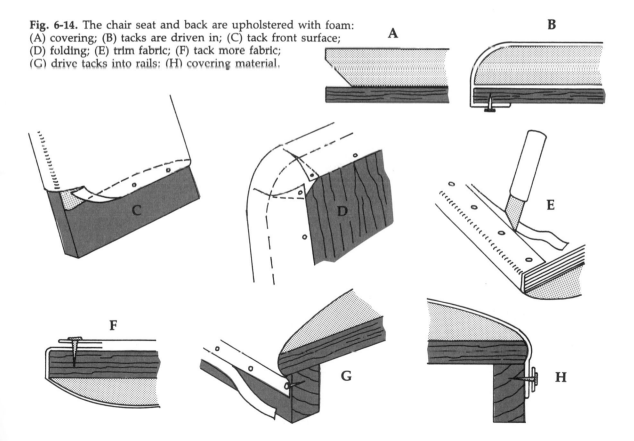

Fig. 6-14. The chair seat and back are upholstered with foam: (A) covering; (B) tacks are driven in; (C) tack front surface; (D) folding; (E) trim fabric; (F) tack more fabric; (G) drive tacks into rails; (H) covering material.

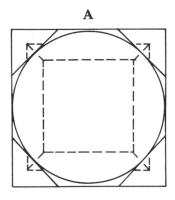

A

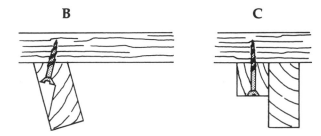

Fig. 6-15. The framework of the low chair can be made into a small table when it is no longer needed for a child: (A) top; (B) pocket screws; (C) screws through framework.

B   C

the covering diagonally across, leaving plenty of material so tension across the corners will tuck the covering over the filling and pull it down around the wood.

Trim the covering below the tacks. A decorative strip in tape form, called *gimp*, can be tacked over the cut edge, but a parallel strip of the covering material also makes a neat finish (FIG. 6-14H).

When the time comes to convert the chair to a table, remove the tray and back as well as the footrest (if it has not already been removed). Lever away the tacks holding the upholstery. A broad screwdriver is useful for this. Once a few tacks have been removed, it is usually possible to grip the covering material and jerk this away to remove the remaining tacks.

Holes can be filled with stopping and surfaces might need a fresh coat of varnish or other finish. If the seat (which is now to become a shelf) has been left with a poor surface, cover it with laminated plastic.

The top can be round, octagonal, or square (FIG. 6-15A). It may be slightly bigger than the area outlined by the feet, but not more than a few inches, or the table would be unstable.

Construction could be in any of the ways described for other tables. Plywood or particleboard could be edged and assembly will be simplest if the underside is level. Unless the chair has suffered misuse and is now unsteady, the absence of a front rail will not matter. If stiffening is necessary screw a crossbar to the tops of the front legs. Attach the top with pocket screws upward from the insides of the side rails and from the outside of the sloping back rail (FIG. 6-15B). Another way is to fix square strips around the insides of the framework and drive screws up through them (FIG. 6-15C).

FIRST CHAIR

This chair differs from the previous one by being more like an adult chair, but it is of a size to suite quite a small child, at first with a tray that can be swung up from its locked-down position. The tray can be removed when the child gets bigger and the chair will be suitable for more general purposes. You can also add feet to the legs to increase the height for a growing child or perhaps convert the chair into a rocker.

The necessary materials are found in TABLE 6-8. The basic chair is made of a close-grained hardwood, with plywood for the seat and the tray base. The back shown is not intended for upholstery, but the seat can be fitted with a loose cush-

Table 6-8. Materials List for a First Chair.

2 legs	1 × 22 × 2
2 legs	1¼ × 14 × 1¼
2 seat rails	2 × 12 × ¾
2 seat rails	2 × 15 × ¾
2 arms	1¼ × 14 × 1¼
2 back rails	2 × 15 × ¾
1 slat	4 × 8 × ½
2 slats	2½ × 8 × ½
1 seat	13 × 16 × ½ plywood
2 tray arms	1¼ × 20 × ¾
1 tray	9 × 20 × ½ plywood
1 tray frame	1 × 20 × ½
2 tray frames	1 × 9 × ½

ion or be padded in a similar way to that described for the previous chair (FIG. 6-14).

Start by making a full-size drawing of the side view (FIG. 6-16A). The front legs are 1¼ inches square. The back legs are 1¼ inches square as high as the seat, then the rear edge slopes back from there. The front edge continues upright as far as the arm position, where it also slopes back. This gives extra thickness for strength where the tray arms pivot. There is a full-size drawing of the front view (FIG. 6-16B), but as there is little shaping, it will probably be satisfactory to work from a small drawing.

Mark out the two back legs together and use them to mark the front legs, so all heights that should be the same will match (FIG. 6-17A).

Fig. 6-16. This first chair looks like a small version of an adult chair, with a tray that can be removed when it is no longer needed: (A) side view; (B) front view.

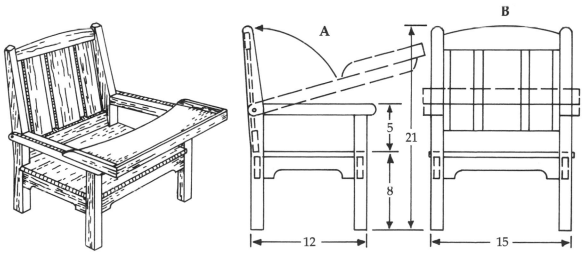

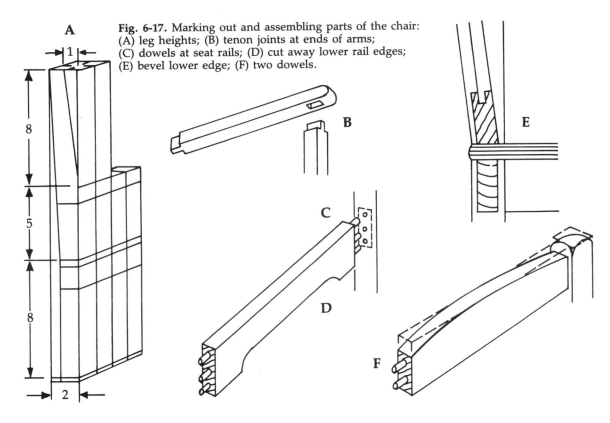

Fig. 6-17. Marking out and assembling parts of the chair: (A) leg heights; (B) tenon joints at ends of arms; (C) dowels at seat rails; (D) cut away lower rail edges; (E) bevel lower edge; (F) two dowels.

All of the joints can be dowelled for the main construction, although mortise and tenon joints at both ends of the arms would be stronger (FIG. 6-17B). If the seat rails are not tenoned, put three dowels at each position (FIG. 6-17C). Keep these rails deep to provide stiffness, but lighten their appearance by cutting away the lower edges (FIG. 6-17D).

Crosswise stiffness is provided by similar seat rails between front and rear pairs of legs. Round the lower edges, so there is nothing rough where the child's hands may reach. Then join two back rails with tenons or dowels. The bottom back rail rests against the plywood seat, so position it to allow for this and bevel its lower edge (FIG. 6-17E). The tops of the uprights are rounded in both directions and the top rail curved to join the uprights an inch down from the top, where two dowels at each end should be sufficient (FIG. 6-17F).

Fill the back space with three slats, with the center one 4 inches wide and the others 2½ inches wide. This allows spaces of about ¾ inch, which are safe amounts where small fingers may reach. Narrower gaps may pinch fingers, while larger ones might allow a hand to push through and become stuck.

The ends fit into the rails with short tenons (FIG. 6-18A). Mark their lengths together, with the distances between the shoulders the same as the distance between the rails on the uprights (FIG. 6-18B). Cut all joints before assembling any parts of the chair. The two back rails and their slats can be glued as a unit before the other parts. Check squareness by measuring diagonals and leave the assembly to set, so that the other parts are held squarely when they are assembled.

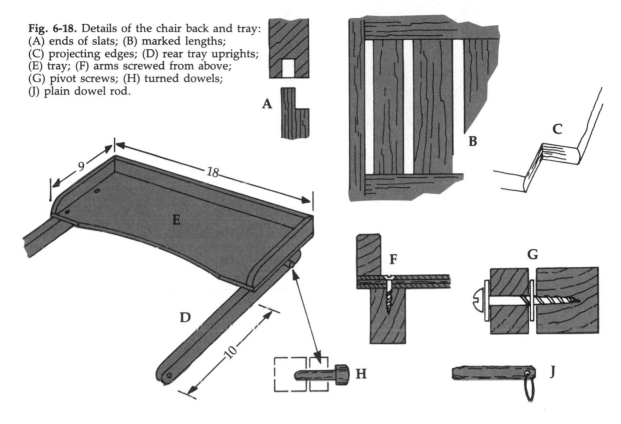

Fig. 6-18. Details of the chair back and tray: (A) ends of slats; (B) marked lengths; (C) projecting edges; (D) rear tray uprights; (E) tray; (F) arms screwed from above; (G) pivot screws; (H) turned dowels; (J) plain dowel rod.

Make up the two side assemblies. Join the front legs into the arms. For the strongest construction these are better glued, clamped, and left to set before continuing. If so, check that the diagonals measure the same on the square parts and make sure one side matches the other when put over it.

Before joining the sides with the crosswise parts, make the plywood seat, using the other parts to obtain its sizes. Notch it at the legs and round the projecting edges (FIG. 6-18C). Fit the seat at the same time as the crosswise parts are assembled. If the parts are pulled together with clamps, the plywood seat can be nailed or screwed to its rails, then the clamps removed, as the seat will hold the joints tight. If only one bar clamp is available, fastening the seat progressively will allow the clamp to be moved from one place to another.

Check squareness before the glue sets. Stand the chair on its legs on a known flat surface and stand back to see that it looks right from several directions.

The tray rests on the chair arms, but it is attached to tray arms that pivot on screws in the rear uprights (FIG. 6-18D). The size shown allows for the tray to swing over the top of the chair back and down to rest on the floor behind. If alterations are made to the chair sizes, check that the edge of the tray will clear the chair when it is swung up.

The tray is a piece of plywood framed on three sides (FIG. 6-18E). It can have a painted design or a decal or it can be surfaced with laminated plastic for easy cleaning. If it is made a little wider than the distance across the tray arms, they can be screwed from above (FIG. 6-18F).

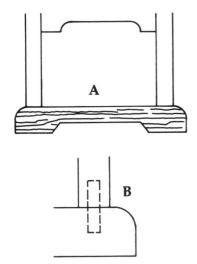

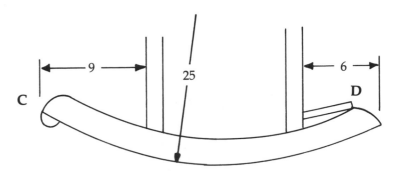

Fig. 6-19. The chair can have its height increased with feet or it can be made into a rocker: (A) feet; (B) feet attached to legs by dowels: (C) small blocks; (D) footrest.

The pivot screws look best if round headed and driven through washers, under the heads and between the wood surfaces (FIG. 6-18G). To hold the tray down, drill for dowels on each side. If a lathe is available they could be turned (FIG. 6-18H). Otherwise use plain dowel rod, with a cord loop through a hole for pulling (FIG. 6-18J). Sand the ends so they make a push fit. Ideally this will be tight enough for the child to be unable to withdraw them, while not being so tight that parent has difficulty removing them or pushing them in. Alternatively there could be metal catches.

The seat can be upholstered in the way described for the previous chair or you can tape a cushion to the seat.

If the chair height is to be increased later, you can affix blocks of wood to each leg, but it would be more stable to arrange feet across each side (FIG. 6-19A), attached to the legs with dowels (FIG. 6-19B).

The chair can be made into a small rocker in a similar way. Attach the two rocking pieces with dowels. The rocking pieces need not extend very far forward, but they should go far enough back to prevent the chair from being tilted so far that it tipped over backwards. Small blocks can act as stops (FIG. 6-19C). A footrest across the rockers will provide stiffness and give the child better control (FIG. 6-19D).

TABLE AND FORMS

If several children are to be grouped together for play, work or a meal, it is convenient to have a table with forms that can be pushed under it. A suitable design is based on the refectory table and matching forms that were used extensively in the baronial halls of feudal days in Europe. Having central supports at the ends of the table allows more knee room and there is less risk of a child knocking the table when getting in or out hurriedly.

The sizes shown are for a table for four children on two forms that should suit ages up to about 12 years old. If there is a large range of ages, one form could be made slightly lower than the other. The materials list is found in TABLE 6-9.

Table 6-9. Materials List for a Table and Form.

1 top	22 × 48 × ¾
2 top stiffeners	¾ × 48 × ¾
2 top stiffeners	2 × 22 × ¾
2 lips	1½ × 48 × ⅜
2 lips	1½ × 22 × ⅜
2 leg tops	3 × 21 × 1½
2 leg bottoms	3 × 21 × 1½
2 leg uprights	8 × 22 × 1
2 top rails	3 × 44 × 1
1 bottom rail	3 × 48 × 1
Each form:	
1 top	12 × 36 × ¾
2 top stiffeners	¾ × 36 × ¾
2 top stiffeners	1½ × 12 × ¾
2 lips	1½ × 36 × ⅜
2 lips	1½ × 12 × ⅜
2 leg tops	2 × 11 × 1 ¼
2 leg bottoms	2 × 11 × 1¼
2 leg uprights	6 × 10 × ⅞
2 top rails	2 × 33 × ¾
1 bottom rail	2 × 36 × ¾

The table legs are arranged fairly close to the ends of the top to give maximum length to forms that can be stowed underneath (FIG. 6-20). Also, if you give the top more overlap at the ends, then more children could sit on stools or chairs at the ends. If the top was not extended, the legs would interfere with the comfort of anyone sitting at an end. It might be possible to fit a flap or leaf to swing down at one or both ends and be held up with a hinged bracket, but anything adjustable on children's furniture is liable to be misused and cause possible accidents.

In earlier projects I suggested that tabletops should be made and fitted last, in this case it might be better to make the top first and use this as a guide to the sizes of other parts. The central part of the tabletop is a piece of plywood, blockboard, or particleboard, stiffened underneath and given a lipped edge (FIG. 6-21A). It could be faced with laminated plastic.

The stiffening is wider at the ends than the sides (FIG. 6-21B) and the leg assemblies are joined to these parts. The lipping strips are mitered at the corners to give a neat appearance, with the edges and corners rounded so there are no sharp edges where children will handle it (FIG. 6-21C).

Make up the top completely. In further work it will be used inverted, so protect its top surface by resting it on cloth or several layers of newspaper.

Build the legs up by fitting their top supports inside the stiffening. The traditional method of construction is with mortise and tenon joints top and bottom (FIG. 6-21D), but they can also be dowelled (FIG. 6-21E) or the top partly lapped and screwed (FIG. 6-21F). Lap the bottom into one side of a two-part foot, with a covering piece to make up the thickness (FIG. 6-21G). Cut away the undersides of the feet or add small pad pieces at the ends so the table stands firmly.

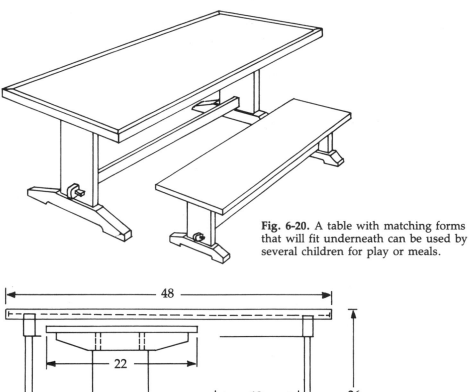

Fig. 6-20. A table with matching forms that will fit underneath can be used by several children for play or meals.

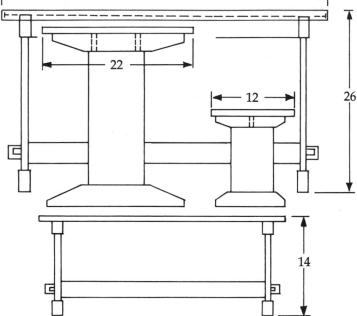

There should be two lengthwise rails or stretchers under the top and a single one at the bottom. Notch the top ones at their ends and strengthen the joints with glued blocks (FIG. 6-21H). In traditionally made refectory tables the bottom rail ends are taken through the legs and held with wedges (FIG. 6-21J). In children's furniture it would be unwise to have loose wedges, but the same method can be used, as it is a way of ensuring very rigid joints. Coat the wedges with glue when driving them in.

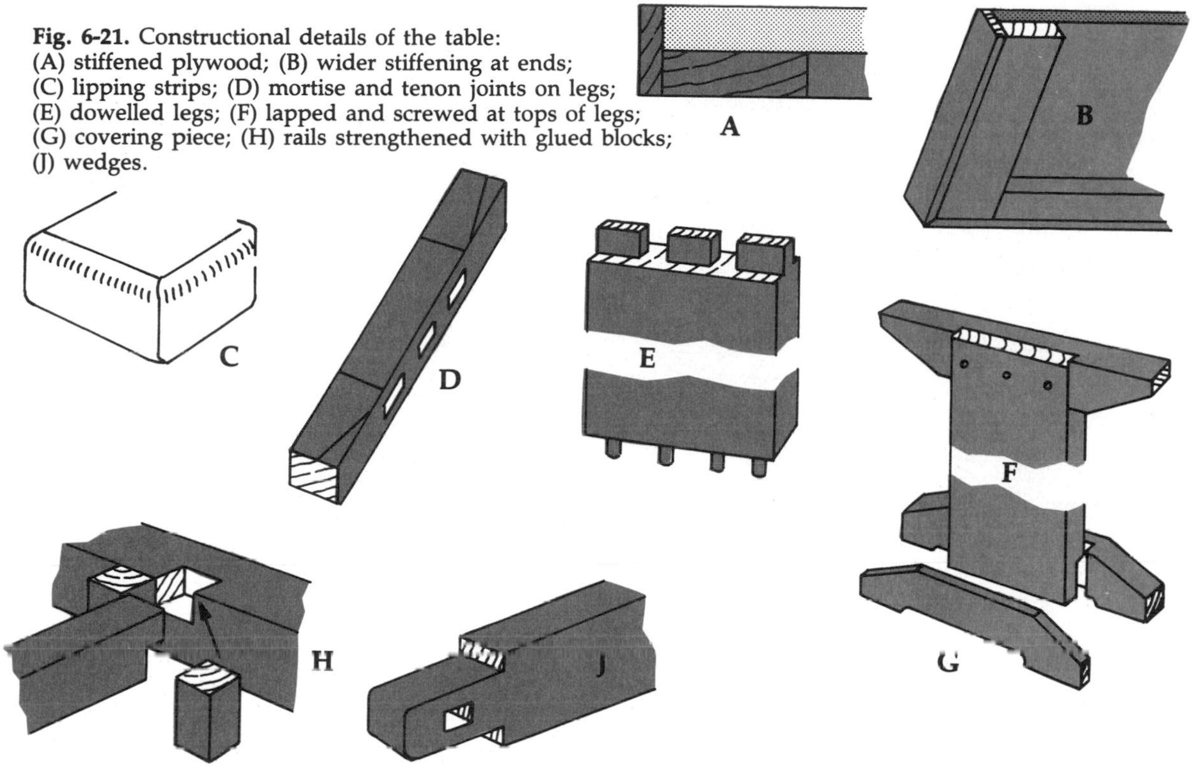

Fig. 6-21. Constructional details of the table:
(A) stiffened plywood; (B) wider stiffening at ends;
(C) lipping strips; (D) mortise and tenon joints on legs;
(E) dowelled legs; (F) lapped and screwed at tops of legs;
(G) covering piece; (H) rails strengthened with glued blocks;
(J) wedges.

Assemble the leg parts and place them inside the top to get the exact lengths to cut the rails. Make sure the length of the bottom rail will hold the legs upright when the table is finally assembled. Round the top edges of this rail where it is likely to be used as a footrest, possibly with bare feet.

The forms are made in almost the same way, except that the tops do not need laminated plastic surfaces and only one rail is required under the top (FIG. 6-22A). The overall length of a form should allow it to fit easily between the table legs and the feet should pass under the table rail. One form could be made so its legs are set in further from the ends so that they will pass inside the feet of the other if it is necessary to push the forms tightly under the table for storage. Different heights of seats will permit closer storage.

Next frame and lip a form top (FIG. 6-22B) and round its edges and corners well. The upright parts of the legs should be relatively wider to give stiffness, but otherwise are made in a similar way to those of the table. Join the central top rail in the same way as the table rails, using glued blocks (FIG. 6-22C) and wedging the bottom rail.

Join the tabletop to the legs with screws driven into the end stiffeners (FIG. 6-22D) and with pocket screws driven upward from the insides of the top rails. The single top rail of the form can have pocket screws driven from both sides (FIG. 6-22E).

Another method of fitting is to use metal plates, either the type sold as mirror plates or pieces of sheet steel made specially. One edge of the plate is let into

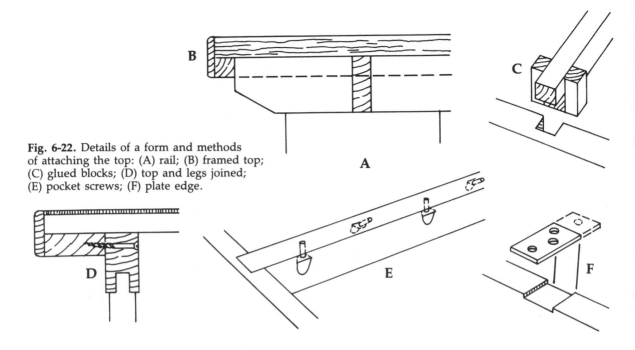

Fig. 6-22. Details of a form and methods of attaching the top: (A) rail; (B) framed top; (C) glued blocks; (D) top and legs joined; (E) pocket screws; (F) plate edge.

the rail or leg top (FIG. 6-22F) and a screw is driven upward through the projecting part into the top. A plate could be made to extend on both sides for use on rails.

NURSING CHAIR

For a mother who has to deal with all the requirements of a young baby, most normal chairs are not as convenient as they could be. What is needed is a firm seat, rather lower than normal and without arms or other obstructions. This chair might not be strictly a type of children's furniture, but it is for a child's benefit as well as for the comfort of his mother. It might have later uses for a child to sit or kneel on when an adult chair is still too high.

This chair has a seat of normal size, arranged a few inches lower than usual, with firm legs to make it as steady as possible. The materials can be found in TABLE 6-10. The seat and back are upholstered, but not enough to impair steadiness when dealing with a baby, as a heavily upholstered seat might. A drawer is provided under the seat, to hold the many small items that a nursing mother needs. As shown, it is intended for right hand use, but it could be made to open at the left. It could also be made double-ended, with a handle at each side, so it would slide either way. However, there is then the problem of keeping it in place, (which could be done with spring or ball catches). This would also reduce the chair strength slightly, although not enough to matter if joints are well made.

Although the chair is low and the legs are short, rails run between the back and front legs. Most strain on a chair comes in a front to back direction. If solid top rails were used at both sides and the drawer omitted, there would be enough stiffness without lower rails, but providing a drawer opening at one side reduces this stiffening effect and the lower rails compensate for it.

Table 6-10. Materials List for a Nursing Chair.

2 rear legs	$3\frac{1}{2} \times 30 \times 1\frac{1}{2}$	
2 front legs	$1\frac{1}{2} \times 13 \times 1\frac{1}{2}$	
2 cross rails	$6 \times 15 \times 1$	
1 side rail	$6 \times 15 \times 1$	
2 drawer rails	$1\frac{1}{2} \times 15 \times 1$	
2 bottom rails	$1\frac{1}{2} \times 18 \times \frac{3}{4}$	
1 back rail	$3 \times 15 \times 1$	
1 back rail	$2 \times 15 \times 1$	
4 drawer runners	$\frac{3}{4} \times 15 \times \frac{3}{4}$	
1 seat	$17 \times 17 \times \frac{1}{2}$ plywood	
1 back	$12 \times 17 \times \frac{1}{2}$ plywood	
2 back strips	$\frac{1}{2} \times 12 \times \frac{1}{2}$	
1 drawer front	$4 \times 14 \times 1$	
2 drawer sides	$4 \times 16 \times \frac{5}{8}$	
1 drawer back	$3\frac{1}{2} \times 14 \times \frac{5}{8}$	
1 drawer bottom	$14 \times 16 \times \frac{1}{4}$ plywood	

The entire structure of the chair could be dowelled or mortise and tenoned. The sizes in the material list are for dowelling and lengths of some parts should be increased if tenons are to be used. The only places where tenons are preferable to dowels in any case are the ends of the bottom rails. Material lengths allow for this.

As the back legs are the only shaped parts, there is no need for a full-size drawing of the chair. Mark out the two legs together (FIG. 6-23A). The tapers start from above and below the seat rail level. Front tapers are straight. At the back, shape the wood to a curve between the upper and lower slopes, but do not make the wood there narrower than 2½ inches.

With the outlines cut, mark on the positions of the seat rails and the lower rails on these legs and the front legs (FIG. 6-23B). Overall seat rail depths are the same at both sides, but at the drawer opening side there are two narrow rails instead of the one deep one at the other side (FIG. 6-23C). Leave the tops of the front legs a little too long until after joints have been prepared.

Mark on the two back legs where the back rails will come. Their front edges should be level with the sloping fronts of the legs (FIG. 6-24A). Crosswise seat rails have their inner surfaces level with the leg surfaces so they can act as drawer guides (FIG. 6-24B). The bottom rails are better arranged centrally at the legs (FIG. 6-24C). Leave their marking out until other parts are prepared and their lengths and angles can be checked.

The seat fits into rabbets in the rails, ¼ inch deep and ½ inch from the edge (FIG. 6-24D). The corners of the front legs are cut to match (FIG. 6-24E). To ensure accuracy, only partly cut away the leg tops and leave final trimming of these corner recesses until after the chair is assembled.

Temporarily clamp one side rail in position between the front and rear legs. Mark where the lower rail comes on the legs, if this has not already been done. From this mark the length and angles of the shoulders on the wood for the rail (FIG. 6-25A). Allow a further ¾ inch at each end for tenons. Cut these mortise and tenon joints for both sides of the chair.

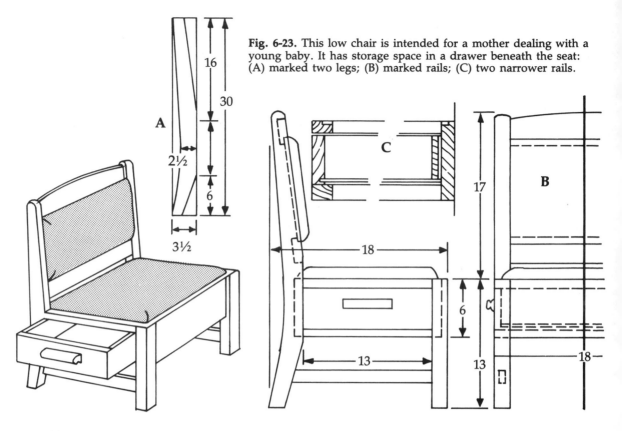

Fig. 6-23. This low chair is intended for a mother dealing with a young baby. It has storage space in a drawer beneath the seat: (A) marked two legs; (B) marked rails; (C) two narrower rails.

Rabbet the two back rails in a way similar to the seat rails and the ends should have three ⅜ inch dowels. The top rail should be wider to allow for curving the top edge. Also round the tops of the back legs.

Locate the dowels to miss the rabbet (FIG. 6-25B). Then mark and drill the back legs before assembling the chair sides (FIG. 6-24F). First assemble the side that has a solid seat rail. Assemble the other side over it to get both parts matching (FIG. 6-24G). Use a large try square to check that the front legs are upright in relation to the seat line.

Let the glue set, then clean off any surplus and make sure none has gotten into the dowel holes that make the joints the other way. If possible, stagger the dowels in the two directions so the holes do not cut into each other, but if the dowel holes one way cut into the dowels the other way slightly, it does not matter.

Assemble the two sides to each other with the crosswise back and seat rails. Pull the parts together with bar clamps. Check squareness by standing the chair on a flat surface while measuring diagonals across the seat position and across the back. Squareness of the seat part is particularly important if the drawer is to run smoothly.

Fit strips above and below the drawer position at back and front, making them wide enough for the drawer to run on and kick against (FIG. 6-25C).

Cut the drawer front to match the opening. Cut the wood for the drawer sides to slide easily between the runners and the kickers. Groove these parts to take

Fig. 6-24. Chair parts are doweled together:
(A) front edges of back legs; (B) crosswise seat rails;
(C) bottom rails; (D) seat fits into rabbets; (E) corners of front legs;
(F) marked back legs; (G) matching parts.

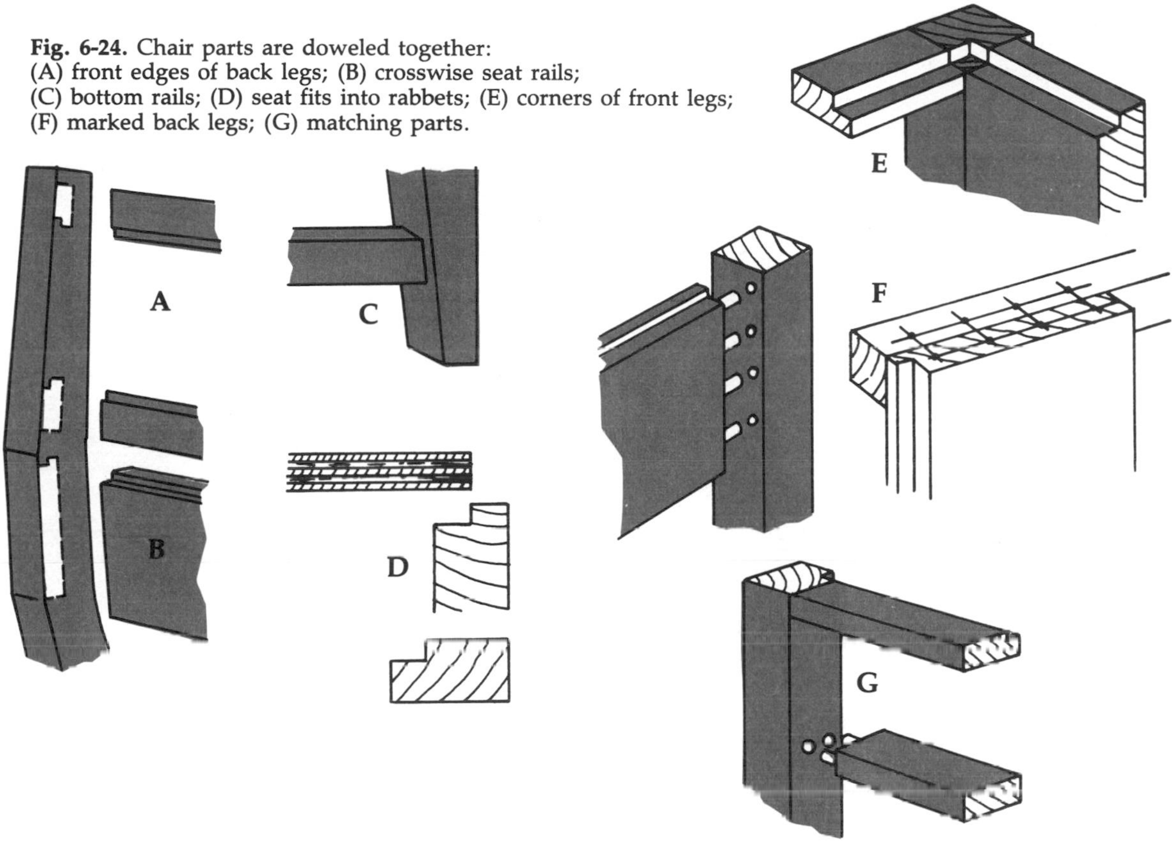

the plywood bottom. The drawer could be made with dovetails for the best traditional construction, but a simpler way is to rabbet the front for the sides that are screwed in. The back fits above the bottom groove in a dado which is also screwed (FIG. 6-25D).

Leave the drawer sides a little too long, so they can be trimmed to stop against the solid side rail when the front of the drawer is level with the rails at the other side. A metal or plastic handle could be used, but a wooden one screwed from the back is shown (FIG. 6-25E).

The seat is a piece of plywood that drops into the rabbets and is notched around the rear legs (FIG. 6-26A). You could drill a pattern of holes into it to allow air in and out as the seat filling expands and contracts when in use. The plywood should be a fairly tight fit after it has been upholstered so its first size should allow for the covering material that will wrap over the edges.

Covering can be over rubber or plastic foam in the way already described (FIG. 6-14). Keep the tacks far enough from the edge to be clear of the rabbets (FIG. 6-26B). Although the front corner fits into a right angle, take the sharpness off the plywood so it will not wear through the covering material. There is no need to cover the cut edges underneath with another piece of material.

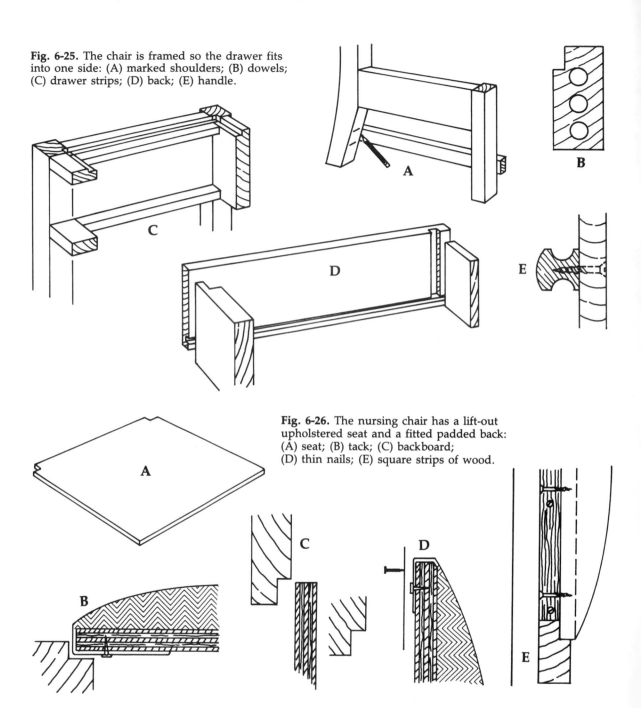

Fig. 6-25. The chair is framed so the drawer fits into one side: (A) marked shoulders; (B) dowels; (C) drawer strips; (D) back; (E) handle.

Fig. 6-26. The nursing chair has a lift-out upholstered seat and a fitted padded back: (A) seat; (B) tack; (C) backboard; (D) thin nails; (E) square strips of wood.

The backboard is also a piece of plywood that fits between the sides and into the rabbets in the rails (FIG. 6-26C). Cut it to a size that allows a tight fit after the upholstery covering material has been wrapped around. Although the seat can be lifted out, the upholstered back is fixed in place.

Cover the plywood in the same way as the seat, but as the rear surface will be visible, put more covering material on the back. If thin nails are used instead of tacks, they can come within the rabbets or under the fixing strips and be hidden (FIG. 6-26D).

Cut two square strips of wood to fit between the back rails. Screw them to the backboard and then to the legs after the board has been pressed into position (FIG. 6-26E). If reupholstery ever becomes necessary, they allow the back panel to be removed.

The woodwork should be painted, varnished, or polished before the upholstered parts are added, but remember to treat the strips that will attach the backboard in the same way. It will probably be best to make a trail assembly, then dismantle for wood finishing. The inner parts of drawers are usually left untreated.

HALF-LAPPED TABLE

A half-lapped table that can suit several purposes (FIG. 6-27). It can be painted all over in several bright colors and used as a play area for a child. A young child can stand or sit at a tall stool and spread toys around without much risk of many of them falling off. The child could also use coloring materials or clay. The table can also serve as a bench for constructional toys for him that might involve hammering parts together.

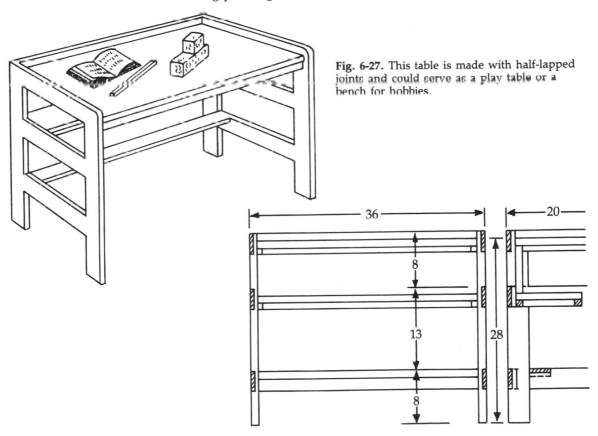

Fig. 6-27. This table is made with half-lapped joints and could serve as a play table or a bench for hobbies.

An older child might use the table as a bench for hobbies, such as assembling kits; making paper and card models; and other work involving the use of light tools, glue, and other workshop equipment. In this case the table might be left as bare wood or finished with stain and varnish. For a girl painting in a pastel shade might be best.

The table could be made as a desk or work table, to be used mainly for reading and writing. In that case, the framework can be made of a good hardwood, stained and varnished, or polished, with the panels forming the top. The back and shelf might be made of plastic-faced particleboard or veneered plywood in a light color contrasting with the surrounding darker wood.

The whole table is fairly light in weight and the method of construction uses wood of all the same section for the major parts. Nearly all the joints are the same type and size, so it is possible to set up equipment and prepare the cuts with very few alterations of settings. The suggested sizes (TABLE 6-11) can be altered to suit the child. Available space and the wood used for the framework could be larger or smaller sectioned than specified to suit stock sizes without having much effect on appearance or strength.

Table 6-11. Materials List for a Half-Lapped Table.

3 × 28 × 1	4 legs
3 × 20 × 1	3 end rails
3 × 36 × 1	3 long rails
20 × 36 × ¾	1 top
8 × 36 × ¾	1 shelf
8 × 36 × ¾	1 back
1½ × 36 × 1	1 top stiffener
1 × 36 × 1	1 shelf stiffener

The parts that make up the ends are joined with half-lap joints. Half is cut from the corners and where rails join the legs (FIG. 6-28A). With all the parts cut to length, use a table saw to first cut the shoulders, then remove the waste with the wood against the fence. Be sure to allow for the thickness of the saw cut and keep the cuts on the waste sides of the lines so the parts go together with the face sides level (FIG. 6-28B). One part of each joint can be cut, then a scrap piece of wood of the same section used to make an experimental cut representing the other part. This serves as a check to see that the joint will fit properly before cutting the second piece that will form part of the table.

If the joints have to be cut by hand, mark them all out together and do the same work on each joint as a complete stage, rather than work through all the cuts at one joint at a time. This way it is easier to get a uniform appearance. However, when making the final cuts on the second part of each joint, compare it with the part it has to fit and mark each pair of parts so they will be assembled together and not moved inadvertently elsewhere.

Whether you make joints by hand or table saw, work from face surfaces and keep these outward in the final assembly. The table is shown with all the horizontal parts lapped on the outsides of the uprights. Do not mix the pattern of joints. It would look odd if the joints on a leg had the horizontal parts outside at one position and inside at another.

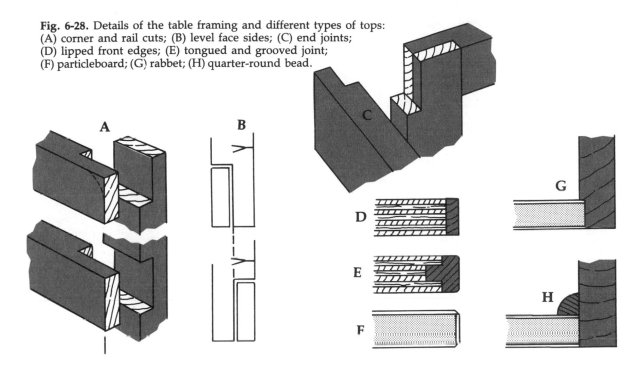

Fig. 6-28. Details of the table framing and different types of tops:
(A) corner and rail cuts; (B) level face sides; (C) end joints;
(D) lipped front edges; (E) tongued and grooved joint;
(F) particleboard; (G) rabbet; (H) quarter-round bead.

At the back lap the three rails into the legs and the bottom end rails, with the two top positions coming over the end joints (FIG. 6-28C). Although the leg parts could be cut away before their joints are made, it will be easier to get an accurate fit for the back rails if you assemble the ends first and cut the joint into them afterwards.

Select the material for the top, back and shelf. If you use plywood, the front edges should be lipped, either with a thin strip of wood glued and nailed on (FIG. 6-28D) or fitted with a tongued and grooved joint (FIG. 6-28E). If you use plastic-surfaced particleboard, you can probably buy it with its long edges as well as the surfaces covered (FIG. 6-28F). As only the front edges of the top and shelf are exposed, an edging strip can be ironed on if a cut edge has to be covered. A stock width of particleboard might suit the top and the table-sized adjusted to match, but if it has to be cut down, you can saw and plane the rear edge as well as the ends.

It should be satisfactory for the particleboard to butt against the border, but if the material is difficult to finish with a good edge, the border can be given a shallow rabbet to cover it (FIG. 6-28G) or a small quarter-round bead can be put over the joint (FIG. 6-28H).

Next, assemble an end (FIG. 6-29A). The joints are a feature in the finished appearance of the table, so do not try to hide them. Allow a little excess length on the horizontal parts, so their ends can be planed and sanded to match the leg edges.

Cut the top, back, and shelf. These must be exactly the same length and all the ends must be cut squarely. They settle the shape of the table and ensure rigidity by their close fit. The lengthwise rails have their lengths between shoulders marked from the top panel.

Half-Lapped Table   93

Fig. 6-29. How the table is put together:
(A) end; (B) top rail; (C) shelf rail; (D) bottom rail;
(E) glued block; (F) shelf rails; (G) screw heads;
(H) screws through end supports.

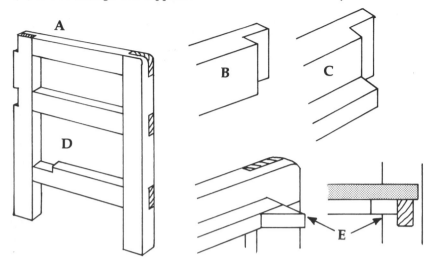
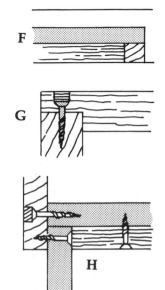

Half-lap the top rail into the end frames (FIG. 6-29B). The shelf rail is similar, but with a strip attached to support the shelf (FIG. 6-29C). Position the bottom rail on the end frame rail, at a height to use as a footrest (FIG. 6-29D).

Round the front top corners of the legs. Put supports in place for the top, but cut them back at the front to come inside a stiffening strip under the top. Be sure to strengthen each corner by gluing a block inside (FIG. 6-29E). Treat the shelf rails in a similar way (FIG. 6-29F). In both cases, make certain the supporting pieces at the front will fit closely and hide the end supporting strips.

When assembling, link the end assemblies with all the lengthwise rails. The joints can be glued and a few thin nails used, but it would be stronger and neater to use screws from the inside. Where the screw heads are hidden by other parts, they can be level with the surface, but elsewhere, as in the bottom rail, they should be counterbored and plugged (FIG. 6-29G). Glued blocks would provide further strength under those joints.

Put the shelf in position and screw upward through its supports. Put the back on the shelf and screw it to the two rails. Check that its top edge is level with the supports for the tabletop on the ends. Fix the top by screws through the back rail and upward through the end supports (FIG. 6-29H).

You should decide on the type of finish before final assembly. If you want a similar finish all over of paint or stain and varnish, all of the parts can be completely assembled. Even then, you should do some sanding and rounding of exposed parts, particularly rail edges and corners, as they are more accessible before assembly.

If you want a two-tone finish, leave the panels out until all the woodwork has been treated. This is important if plastic-surfaced particleboard is used alongside wood, so paint or stain does not run over. If you use paint or varnish, put masking tape on those areas, you wish to leave untouched.

EXTENDING CORNER TABLE

If space is limited or the full area of a tabletop is not always required, a table can fold or be fitted with leaves or flaps to allow it to be extended, but the common ways of doing this to many tables for adult use might not be suitable for children's furniture. This table is intended to be a plain rectangular shape for normal use, but a supported flap at one end can be pulled out to provide an extension at one side.

This table is particularly suitable for the corner of a room, or for typing, when it is possible to swing around to the typewriter on the extension without disturbing books and papers on the main table (FIG. 6-30). The slightly lower top is an advantage for most typewriters.

The extension is valuable when studying, as reference material can be spread on it while working on the main tabletop. The extension shown is at the right, but if it is more convenient for the room layout to have it at the other side, that's

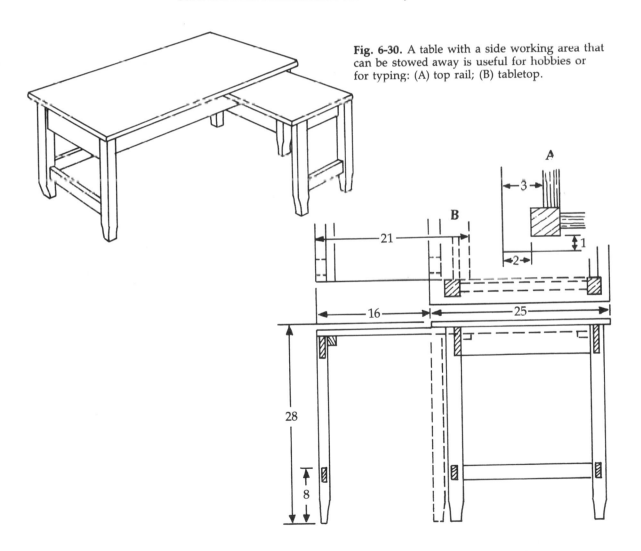

Fig. 6-30. A table with a side working area that can be stowed away is useful for hobbies or for typing: (A) top rail; (B) tabletop.

fine too. Although most people are right-handed, it makes little difference in practice which side a typewriter or reference book is located.

The materials needed for this project are listed in TABLE 6-12. The main table is like many plain tables, except the front rail is set back and the top overhangs more at the front. This allows the extension to slide in so its leg assembly does not project from the line of the front.

Table 6-12. Materials List for an Extending Corner Table.

4 legs	2 × 28 × 2
2 top rails	4 × 33 × 1
2 top rails	4 × 22 × 1
1 bottom rail	2 × 33 × 1
2 bottom rails	2 × 22 × 1
1 top	25 × 36 × ¾
2 drawer runners	2 × 22 × 1
Extension	
2 legs	2 × 27 × 1½
1 rail	3½ × 15 × 1
1 rail	2 × 15 × 1
1 top stiffener	1½ × 15 × 1½
1 top stop	2 × 15 × 1
1 top	15 × 21 × ¾
Magazine rack	
1 back	12 × 20 × ¼ plywood
2 sides	5 × 20 × ⅝
1 bottom	3 × 12 × ⅝
1 front	12 × 14 × ¼ plywood
3 slats	2 × 12 × ½
Folding drawing board	
1 top	20 × 20 × ¾ plywood
1 top strut	5 × 20 × ¾ plywood
Loose drawing board	
1 board	18 × 24 × ¾ plywood
2 battens	1½ × 18 × ¾
2 guides	2 × 24 × 1

The top of the table is made of thick plywood with a solid wood edging. The extension top does not have any framing and it should also be made of stout plywood with edging on the front and sides. Both parts would look best if finished with veneer on the top surface to match the wood used for framing. If it is a work surface rather than a desk, both surfaces can be covered with laminated plastic. If plastic-covered particleboard is chosen, the extension should be of a thicker grade so there is enough stiffness.

Mark out the table legs together. In FIG. 6-31A they are shown parallel, with the tapered lower corners which is a simple way of lightening appearance. If a lathe is available, the legs could be turned between the rail positions and below the bottom rails.

Arrange the top and bottom rails centrally at the two back corners and tenon or dowel them into the legs in the usual way. Set the top rail level with the inside surface of the leg (FIG. 6-30A) to give clearance to the extension legs in the stowed position. Prepare the rails and their joints, but do not assemble anything yet. Leave the preparation of the front rail and leg joint alongside where the extension will come, until the extension is prepared.

The extension top should fit closely under the tabletop, through a space cut in the front rail (FIG. 6-31B). The space should not have its edges rubbing on the extension top, as this will be controlled by the runners inside, but for the sake of appearance, do not cut the opening too big. Reduce the joint to the leg to suit (FIG. 6-31C).

With all the main table joints prepared, first assemble the ends, checking squareness and testing against each other in the usual way. Add the lengthwise rails and again check squareness while the table is standing on a level surface. Do not go any further with construction until the glue has set, but you can prepare the extension legs by checking their height against the top rail positions. Be sure to fit glides to the bottoms of the extension legs, so their thickness is allowed for when you finally trim the legs to length.

Arrange the rails on the extension so the bottom one is at the same height as those on the main table, and the lower edge of the top one matches the lower edge of the table front rail when the extension is closed (FIG. 6-31D). As there are no frames in the other direction to brace the extension legs, they should be firmly attached at the top with a block behind, but keep the total thickness less than the 3 inches—the tabletop will extend over the front rail (FIG. 6-31E). Screw and glue the parts together.

The extension top slides like a drawer under the tabletop. At the leg edge it runs in a guide fitted inside the top rail (FIG. 6-31F). At the other edge the runner is made wide enough to be screwed under the top (FIG. 6-31G). You can make both parts by cutting rabbets in solid wood or by joining pieces.

Arrange the tabletop to overhang the legs by about 1 inch on the back and ends, increasing this to 2 inches at the front (FIG. 6-30B). This gives a 3 inch clearance for the extension legs to be housed. Invert the table frame on the top and fix with pocket screws. Fit the runner at the leg edge and use the extension top as a guide to the location of the other runner when it is screwed to the top.

The front of the extension should fully retract without the rear edge hitting the back rail. When a satisfactory movement of the extension has been arranged, screw a stop strip under the extension rear edge to prevent it from pulling out (FIG. 6-31H). Do not glue it, in case the parts have to be dismantled later for a repair or alteration.

Try the action of the extension with the table standing on its legs. It is better for the extension legs to be slightly too short than slightly too long. If they are too long, the front of the table might have to be lifted when they are moved. If they are too short, the slight slope of the extension will not be noticeable.

You might want to include some modifications depending on the intended use of the table. A rack for magazines or other papers can be included on the extension legs (FIG. 6-32A). Fit the plywood back between the legs attach to the rails, either permanently or with keyhole slots hanging over roundhead screws to allow the rack to be lifted off. Similar racks can be added at either of the main table ends.

Fig. 6-31. Details of the construction of the table and its extending flap:
(A) tapered corners; (B) extension top; (C) leg joint; (D) closed extension;
(E) 3 inch extension; (F) top railguide; (G) under-the-top runner;
(H) extension stop sign.

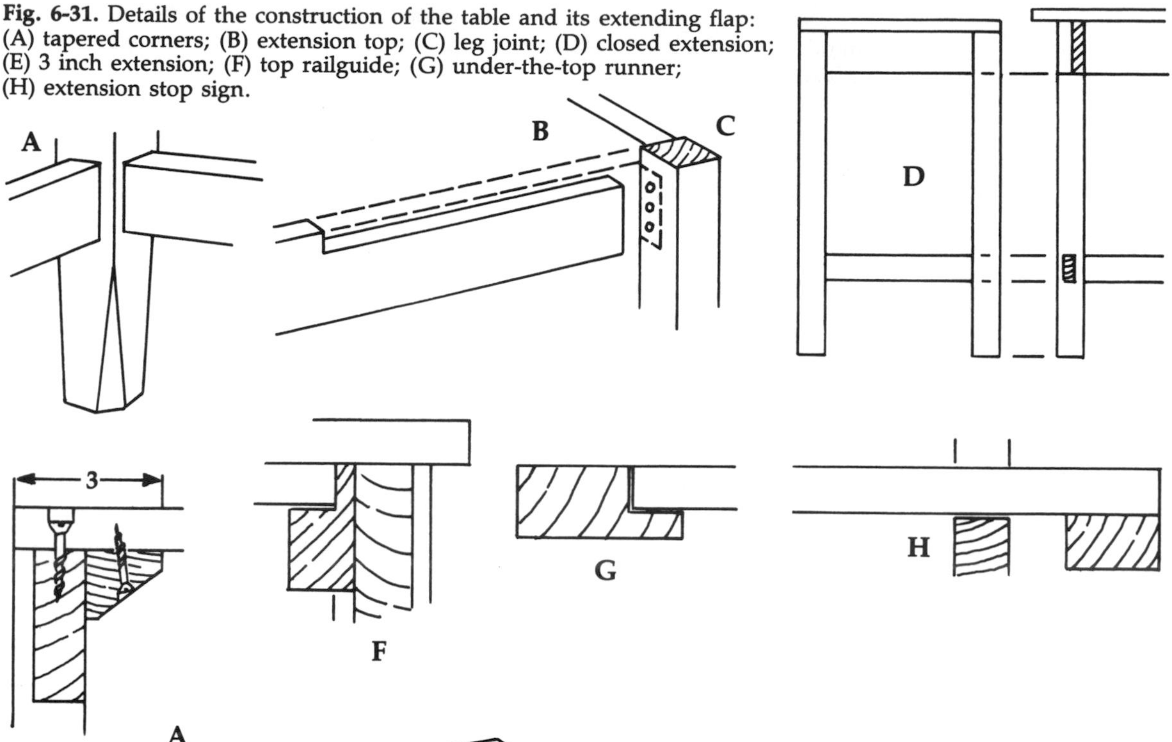

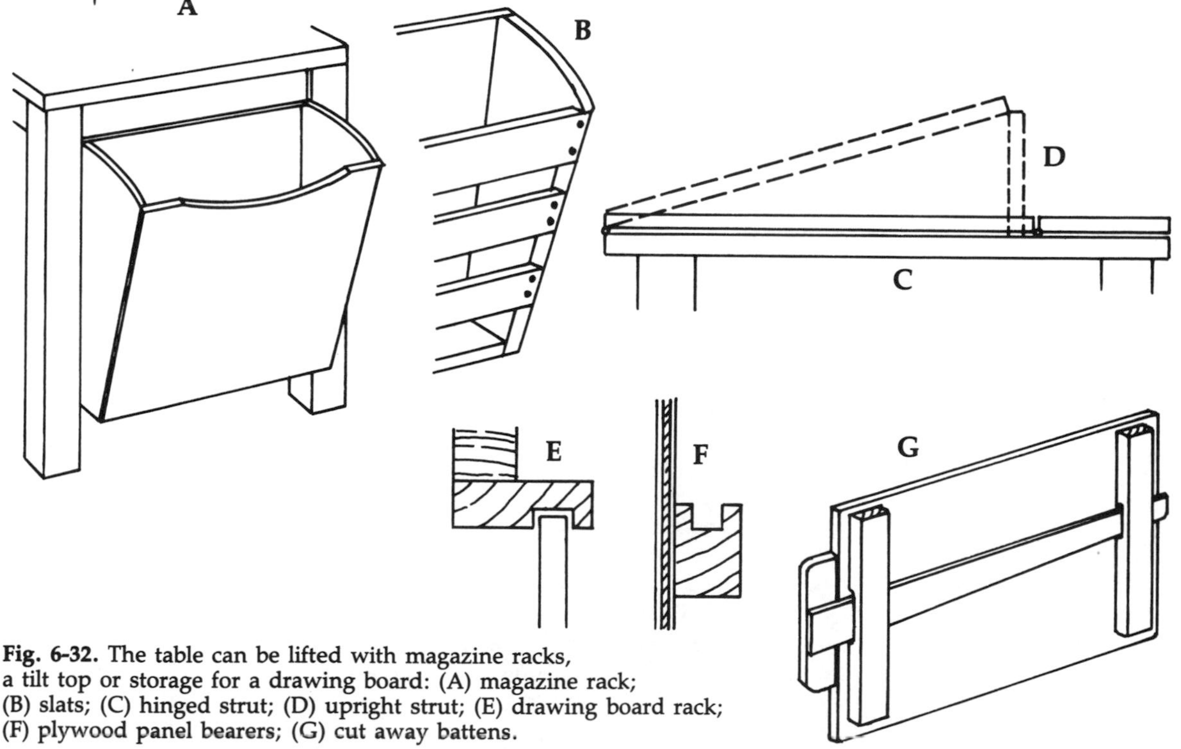

Fig. 6-32. The table can be lifted with magazine racks,
a tilt top or storage for a drawing board: (A) magazine rack;
(B) slats; (C) hinged strut; (D) upright strut; (E) drawing board rack;
(F) plywood panel bearers; (G) cut away battens.

Shape the sides so the top is wider than the bottom and the front is a complete enclosure. Or arrange slats across (FIG. 6-32B). Check sizes of the papers to be held, but allow plenty of space.

If the table is to be used for drawing, you should provide a sloping surface by hinging a piece of thick plywood at the front that is about as wide as the part of the table beside the extension.

At the back there should be a piece of similar plywood that makes up the table depth and acts as a strut. Hinge these parts together (FIG. 6-32C). For normal use, both pieces remain flat, but when a sloping board is needed, you can bring the rear hinged piece upright as a strut (FIG. 6-32D).

For some types of drawing, particularly if it is draftsmanship rather than artistry, it is better to have a loose drawing board to which the paper is fastened. Such a board can fit into a rack inside the end table legs (FIG. 6-32E). You can attach grooved pieces to the rails, although if you plan for the drawing board rack before the table is made, you can attach a plywood panel with bearers (FIG. 6-32F).

A drawing board can be a carefully squared piece of plywood, but it helps to have thin battens across to raise it off the table. If the table is to have a T square, the battens can be cut away so it stows through them (FIG. 6-32G) when the board is put away.

PLYWOOD UPHOLSTERED CHAIR

A child will find a plain or lightly upholstered chair uncomfortable after a short time and will become restless. An older child who has to sit for long periods studying or working at a desk needs to be comfortable if he is to continue without having to shift his position or get up to relieve developing aches. Traditional full upholstery was complicated, but with modern materials, attractive, comfortable padding is available with little skill or equipment.

This piece of furniture (FIG. 6-33) can be completed as a stool and would be suitable for a girl to use in front of her dressing table or mirror. With the back it makes a comfortable chair to sit at a table or desk. It would suit any of the tables already described, but it would be particularly suitable with the half-lapped table (FIG. 6-27). It can also be used independently in a child's bedroom.

TABLE 6-13 lists the necessary materials. The sizes given allow for an uncompressed seat height of 14 inches, which is an average height for a child. If you increase the height by 2 inches or 3 inches, the chair would suit an adult or teenager. The back assembly fits outside the stool, so it would be possible to make and use a stool, then add the back later.

The chair is of unit construction. The seat is an open box, which is upholstered (FIG. 6-33A). The back is a frame, which is also upholstered. Having these separate assemblies makes upholstery much easier than if they had to be dealt with as built-in parts of a chair. The legs are shaped pieces of plywood (FIG. 6-33B) that fit outside the upholstered seat, then the back frame is supported by two more pieces of plywood (FIG. 6-33C).

The plywood edges will be exposed, so they should be cut with a fine saw—either a bandsaw or saber saw if possible—then the edges smoothed and sanded so nothing breaks out and spoils the appearance. You should round all of these edges, but there is no need to make the sections semicircular, although that could be done if you prefer. This would be fairly simple to do with a powered spindle shaper, although difficult to do neatly by hand.

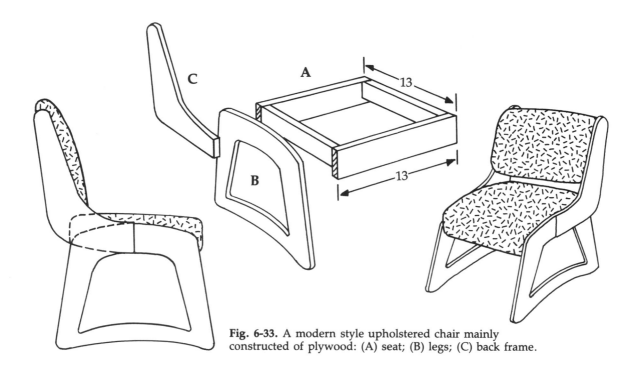

Fig. 6-33. A modern style upholstered chair mainly constructed of plywood: (A) seat; (B) legs; (C) back frame.

Table 6-13. Materials List for a Plywood Upholstered Chair.

2 seat frames	3 × 13 × ¾
2 seat frames	2 × 13 × ¾
2 back frames	1½ × 14½ × ¾
2 back frames	1½ × 10 × ¾
2 legs	13 × 17 × ¾ plywood
2 backs	11 × 15 × ¾ plywood

Start by making the seat box. The ends should be narrower than the back and front, so that they will not show below the legs (FIG. 6-35A). None of the box will show in the finished chair, so you need not use high quality wood.

Screw corners and reinforce with glued blocks (FIG. 6-35B), or tongue the narrow pieces into the others (FIG. 6-35C). Dovetails can also be used. This might be a good practice piece for a beginner since joints that don't turn out as good as they should will not show.

The back frame is better half-lapped (FIG. 6-35D). The size allows for ¾-inch-thick plywood legs. If you use a different thickness, alter the frame accordingly. Both seat and back frame cam should have their inner edges toward the rounded upholstery (FIG. 6-35E), but otherwise the edges are better if left square.

The legs have closed bottoms for rigidity as there is no other lower framing. Do not omit the bottom cross pieces as the legs would then be too flexible. The sizes (FIG. 6-34B) give the sape a straight-line pattern, which is then rounded. If you have a suitable saw to take a double thickness, the two parts can be temporarily

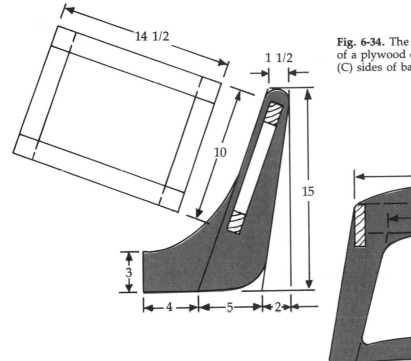

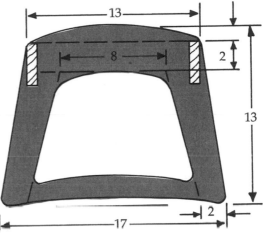

Fig. 6-34. The main shapes of the parts of a plywood chair: (A) seat; (B) leg sizes; (C) sides of back.

nailed together and cut in one process. Otherwise, do final shaping and checking together.

The side of the back (FIG. 6-34C) will overlap the legs up to their middle. Draw the straight-line shape first and add the rounding. These parts and the legs are visible woodwork, so get the edges and surfaces to a good finish, before starting assembly.

Assemble the parts after upholstering with screws. Some of the holes can also be made at this stage. As much as possible, screw heads should be hidden, but where they must enter from an outer surface, the pattern of plugs in counterbored holes might be regarded as a decorative feature you give the wood a clear finish. A painted finish would hide them in any case.

Put screw holes in a zigzag pattern in the ends of the seat box for the screws that will go through the upholstery into the legs (FIG. 6-35F). There can be some screws from the leg into the box, with those in the rear half hidden by the back parts, but it would be better to have longer screws through the back parts as well. Drill a zigzag pattern of counterbored holes in the back parts (Fig. 6-35G). Drill smaller holes in the legs to match, which will later be continued into the box for longer screws (Fig. 6-35H).

The back frame is screwed from outside in counterbored holes, their plugs can supplement the pattern made by the plugs lower down, but screws can also be driven from inside the frame after upholstering. Prepare the holes for whichever method is to be used.

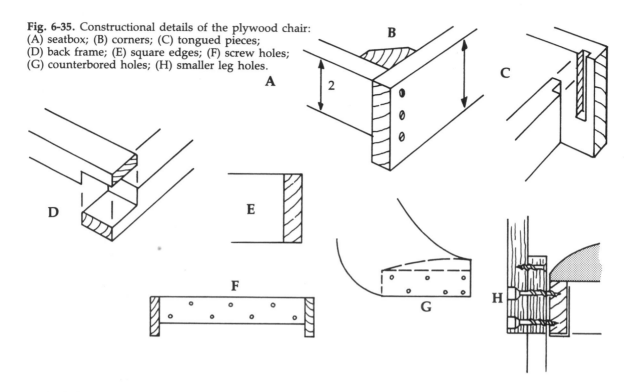

Fig. 6-35. Constructional details of the plywood chair: (A) seatbox; (B) corners; (C) tongued pieces; (D) back frame; (E) square edges; (F) screw holes; (G) counterbored holes; (H) smaller leg holes.

Upholstering starts with rubber-type webbing. With the usual width of about 2 inches, you can obtain sufficient springing with three pieces back to front and two across for the seat (FIG. 6-36A), while three from top to bottom should be sufficient for the back (FIG. 6-36B). Attach the webbing by tacking. (Often special metal attachments are used along with rubber webbing in larger work, but tacking is simple and satisfactory in this chair.)

Position the webbing and take one end under the box edge. Most of this webbing is strong enough tacked through one thickness (FIG. 6-36C), but if there is any tendency for the tacks to pull or tear, tack a single thickness and double back for another row of tacks (FIG. 6-36D). Do this with the three back-to-front on the seat first.

As the webbing is elastic, it is important to get the same tension in each piece. How much tension to allow will depend on the particular webbing you use, but a piece should be quite taut. However, allow for the further tightening of the crosswise pieces. Slackness will cause the finished seat to sag too much. Pencil where the edge of the wood comes on an unstretched piece and decide on the amount of tension that seems satisfactory, then pencil where this comes. If you repeat marks at the same distances apart on the other pieces of webbing, the pieces can all be pulled to the same tension.

It will probably be possible to get sufficient tension by hand pulling, but use a strainer if one is available. An alternative is a short length of wood, which can lever the webbing (FIG. 6-36E). Tack the second ends in the same way as the first. In the other direction, weave the pieces over and under. Treat the back frame similarly, although there are no crosswise pieces.

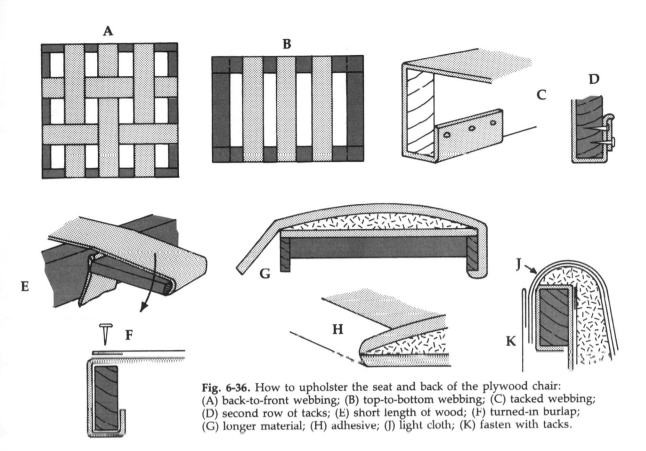

Fig. 6-36. How to upholster the seat and back of the plywood chair:
(A) back-to-front webbing; (B) top-to-bottom webbing; (C) tacked webbing;
(D) second row of tacks; (E) short length of wood; (F) turned-in burlap;
(G) longer material; (H) adhesive; (J) light cloth; (K) fasten with tacks.

Cover the webbing with cloth. Traditionally burlap was used, but any piece of cloth, tacked around the edges, with a turn-in to hide fraying will suffice (FIG. 6-36F).

There are several types of padding that can go over this. It is possible to buy shaped rubber or plastic cushion pieces that are already shaped in section. If you can find a suitable one of these you can put it in position and cover, with no other work needed. You can also use a thick piece of foam, cut around the edge and pulled to a curve as described for a plain seat (FIG. 6-14). The method that follows is adaptable to any size and suitable for the back and seat.

The top and bottom of the padding is plastic foam sheet about ⅜ inches thick. This should compress enough at the edges and there should be no need for tapering the thickness. Between these pieces, use particles of foam, which are sold in bulk as pillow fillings. Cut one piece of sheet foam to about the size of the seat box and place over the cloth and webbing. The other piece should be as wide as the seat, but long enough to wrap around at back and front (FIG. 6-36G).

To help the padding assembly stay in place, fasten a strip of cloth with adhesive along one side to hold the top and bottom together (FIG. 6-36H). Put the foam particles in place and draw the top foam sheet over the back and front of the box, so you can judge the evenness of the doming of the seat. A length of wood can be used through the open side to regulate the foam particles.

When the section is satisfactory, draw down the other side with more cloth and adhesive. In the other direction draw the foam over the box edges, where it can be held with a few tacks and the edge trimmed.

In traditional methods of upholstery, horsehair and fibers were used and there was a risk of ends pushing through the weave of covering material. It was common to first cover with a tightly woven linen to prevent this. Although this is unnecessary with foam padding, a first covering of light cloth does help to get a good shape to the filling before the outer covering is put on. This is optional, but there could be a layer of light cloth under the covering that will be seen (FIG. 6-36J).

At the side of both parts, only the webbing and the covering go over the edge, so the surface against the wood will be flat. The padding is kept on the surface. Using cloth held to the sheet foam with adhesive helps keep the padding in place, but check that none is pulled over the edges when tensioning and fastening the cloth.

There is no need to put anything under the seat to hide the webbing, but at the chair back, use a piece of the covering material over the back frame. Turn the edges under and fasten with tacks (FIG. 6-36K). Nails with decorative head can be used.

Mark where the completed seat will meet with the legs and check the second legs by sighting across the first so that both sets match and the seat will be level. Test on a flat surface before driving all screws. The screws should be as tight as possible—maximum leverage in tightening can be achieved by using a screwdriver bit in a brace. Mark both leg tops the same to get the back mounted symmetrically. Choose screws that go almost through the seat box as well as the plywood leg.

BOOKRACK TABLE

This is a desk or work table with a drawer and with book shelves at each end, as well as a back assembly that prevents things from falling off and can hold a row of books as well as a row of small items (FIG. 6-37). The materials list is found in TABLE 6-14. The whole piece of furniture has hints of colonial design, although it does not follow exactly any furniture of that period.

In its basic form the table might be finished as a desk for study or drawing. It can also be made more like a bench, with the back part fitted with racks and hooks for tools. The bookcase ends can be given doors, so more tools and equipment could be stored there.

Original colonial furniture of similar appearance was used for personal toilet purposes, with a bowl and ewer. Those features might not be needed today, but the desk can also be used as a side table in a bedroom, possibly with a painted finish.

The front and back of the table are made of plywood, with the back extended upward for the above-table assembly. If you want a table without anything above its top, cut off the back plywood at the same level as the front piece and arrange the top so that it overlaps the legs by the same amount all around.

Because these pieces of plywood affect other sizes mark at least one of them out first (FIG. 6-38A). The plywood pieces should fit between the legs, but overlap other parts (FIG. 6-37A).

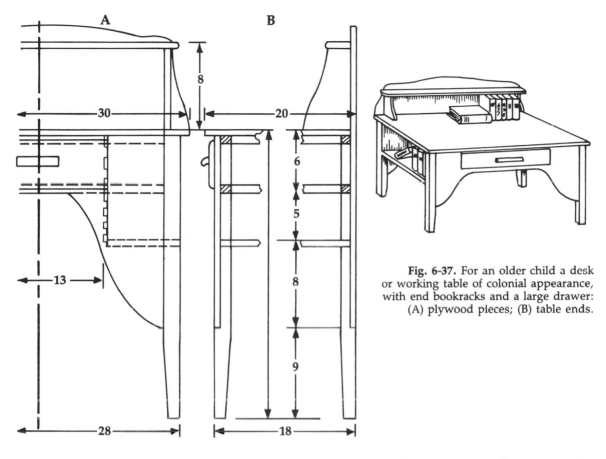

Fig. 6-37. For an older child a desk or working table of colonial appearance, with end bookracks and a large drawer: (A) plywood pieces; (B) table ends.

From the tabletop down the shapes are the same, but the front is cut out for the drawer (FIG. 6-38B) and the back goes up to make the shaped upper part (FIG. 6-38C). Use the marked-out plywood as the drawing for getting sizes of other parts for front and back.

In the other direction the table shown is 20 inches wide, which is a reasonable proportion in relation to length and height. If the table is made much narrower it would have to be positioned against a wall to ensure stability. At the size shown the table can stand free with little risk of being knocked over.

The legs should be square and parallel to below where the plywood reaches, and the outer corners left straight. The inner surfaces, however, should taper slightly (FIG. 6-38D).

At the top, tenon or dowel rails above and below the drawer level (FIG. 6-38E). There should only be top rails across the end.

At the bookrack level the shelf will be supported by strips of wood underneath and attached to the plywood. It might be sufficient to notch the shelf around at each leg, but it would be better to notch the leg. This could be a stopped dado, but it is simpler to make a tapered dado, so the exposed edge finishes cleanly (FIG. 6-38F).

Table 6-14. Materials List for a Bookrack Table.

4 legs	1½ × 28 × 1½
4 rails	1 × 28 × ¾
2 rails	1½ × 18 × ¾
back	29 × 30 × ½ plywood
1 front	19 × 25 × ½ plywood
4 drawer guides	1½ × 18 × ¾
4 drawer guides	¾ × 18 × ¾
1 back shelf	3 × 30 × ⅝
2 back shelf supports	5 × 8 × ⅝
2 shelves	7 × 18 × ⅝
2 rack backs	11 × 18 × ⅛ hardboard
4 rack sides	7 × 11 × ⅛ hardboard
1 top	20 × 30 × ¾
1 drawer front	4 × 13 × ⅝
1 false drawer front	5 × 14 × ½
2 drawer sides	4 × 18 × ½
1 drawer back	3½ × 13 × ½
1 drawer bottom	13 × 18 × ¼ plywood

Prepare the end rails and assemble the two table ends, so that they are square and match each other (FIG. 6-37B). Make the four lengthwise rails. They could be full width at the ends, but for a smoother inside to each bookrack, allow for a piece of ⅛ inch plywood or hardboard to be let in (FIG. 6-38G). These lines fit into the two rails and against a strip of wood on the shelf.

The shelves are pieces of solid wood, which should be stiff enough without supports under their fronts, but if thinner wood seems likely to sag you can fit the front edge into a rabbet in a deeper stiffener across the fronts.

The back of each rack is a piece of hardboard or plywood, nailed or screwed to the shelf. It should present a smooth surface toward the books, supported at both long rail levels by pieces that also form drawer runners and kickers (FIG. 6-39A). They can be notched into the long rails with half-lap joints. Take care that their positions allow for the back thickness, so that it is vertical against the shelf (FIG. 6-39B).

Drill the top rails for screws that will be driven upward into the top. Spacing at about 6-inch intervals should be satisfactory, but use extra screws near the corners.

Have all the parts prepared before any further assembly. Fit the lengthwise rails, pull the joints tight and fit the plywood back and front, using pins that will be set below the surface. Be sure the edge joints to the legs are as tight as possible.

Put strips of wood in the angles below the shelf level (FIG. 6-39C). Do all of this before any glue has started to set, so the whole table can be carefully squared and left to stabilize as a unit.

Next, enter the shelves from the inside and glue and pin them to the supporting strips. Cut the bookrack backs to fit between the front and back panels. Notch them around the lengthwise rails. They can be left standing a little too high for levelling later. Put these pieces in place and fit the guides for the drawers

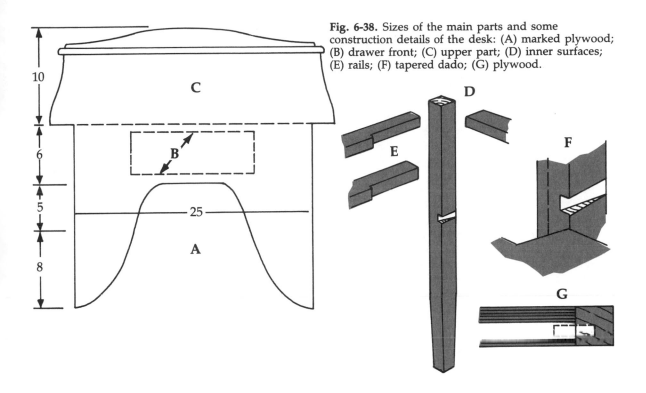

Fig. 6-38. Sizes of the main parts and some construction details of the desk: (A) marked plywood; (B) drawer front; (C) upper part; (D) inner surfaces; (E) rails; (F) tapered dado; (G) plywood.

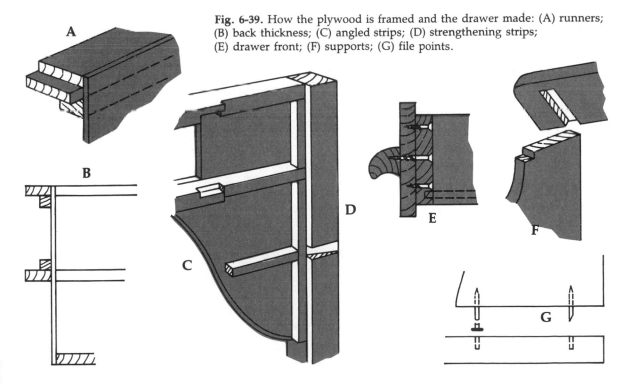

Fig. 6-39. How the plywood is framed and the drawer made: (A) runners; (B) back thickness; (C) angled strips; (D) strengthening strips; (E) drawer front; (F) supports; (G) file points.

that come behind them. Glue as well as pin all joints and include strengthening strips in the joints that are not otherwise supported (FIG. 6-39D).

Now the whole table is framed up except for the top. Plane the top surface level. In any construction that involves plywood coming edgewise, it is always a good idea to try to get the solid wood parts as true as possible, but leave plywood projecting slightly for planing level later.

Make the drawer before fitting the tabletop. It could be made in any of the ways already described, but since it will have a false front that overlaps the opening, there is no need to use front joints hidden behind the normal front surface. You could use through dovetails, rabbets, or even directly screw the sides into the front.

Adjust the side lengths so the drawer, without the false front, will slide in slightly too far. Then when the false front is added, it will act as a stop before the drawer hits the back of the table.

The false front can be solid wood, although if you want a clear finish, you can use a piece of the same plywood used for the table front, to provide a match. Another attractive alternative is a drawer front that is lighter or darker for contrast. In any case, the drawer front should be about ½ inch bigger all around. Its edges could be molded or left square with the sharpness taken off the angles. Fit it with glue and screws from inside (FIG. 6-39E). If the handle is also attached with screws from inside, that will further strengthen the joint.

Before fitting the top to the table, do any sanding, glue removal, and other finishing of any accessible inner surfaces. The top overhangs the ends and front, but at the back it comes close against the rising back plywood. Besides screwing up through the table rails, you can put some screws through the back. Those screws should be counterbored and plugged if that side will be visible. If the back will be against a wall, they may be merely countersunk.

Attach the back shelf and its supports by screwing through the plywood. If the supports are let into the shelf, screws there can be avoided (FIG. 6-39F). The bottoms of the supports can be let into the tabletop in a similar way.

If the top is plywood, cutting neat dados is difficult, as there is a risk of the surface veneers splintering. It would be better to use dowels or screws upward through the tabletop.

Another simple joint is a form of reverse nailing. Drive two stout nails into the support with about ½ inch projecting. Cut off the heads and file points on what is left (FIG. 6-39G). Put a support in position and press it to mark where these points will come. Drill undersize holes at these places, then glue the wood surfaces and tap the support into close contact. The nails act like metal dowels to reinforce the glue to prevent sideways movements.

If the table is to be used mainly for writing or drawing and its use is liable to change, finishing in the simple way shown might be best. If it is to have definite permanent uses, some other modification can be made. More supports can be added to hold books at the ends only, while a strip between them would keep pens, pencils, and drawing instruments out of the way (FIG. 6-40A).

If the desk is to be used for painting with water colors or other liquids is to be frequent, holes can be made to hold jars or bottles (FIG. 6-40B) with plywood fitted below. The drawer could be given compartments to store supplies. Even for general writing use it is helpful to arrange a front rack for small things (FIG. 6-40C) or a sliding tray (FIG. 6-40D).

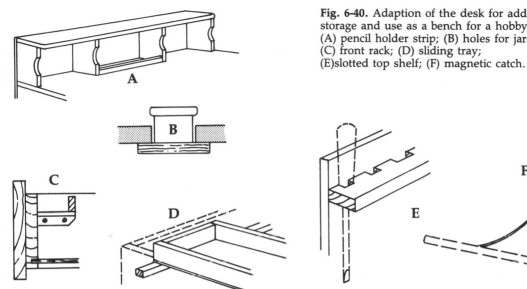

Fig. 6-40. Adaption of the desk for additional storage and use as a bench for a hobby: (A) pencil holder strip; (B) holes for jars; (C) front rack; (D) sliding tray; (E)slotted top shelf; (F) magnetic catch.

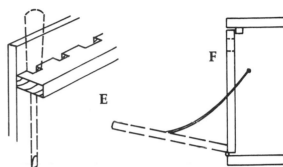

If the table is to be used more as a bench for a hobby, racks could be put along the back for tools. The top shelf could be slotted before putting in place, to hold tools such as screwdrivers, files, chisels, and squares (FIG. 6-40E).

If the bookracks would be more useful as storage compartments, they can be fitted with doors. For easy access when working on top, they are best hinged along their bottoms. A simple door can be a piece of thick plywood with a finger hole at the top, instead of a handle, that closes against a stop with a spring or magnetic catch (FIG. 6-40F).

The door can be allowed to swing down out of the way, but if it would be better for it to stop horizontally, include a folding strut, or just a piece of cord. It might also be convenient to put tools in spring clips on the insides of the doors, so that they swing out when the doors are opened.

PIANO STOOL

This is an upholstered stool with a box top. Although described as a piano stool, it would also make a suitable seat for use at a child's table. The box will hold a large amount of sheet music, but it can also be used for toys, books, and the many small items that a child accumulates.

The height shown in FIG. 6-41 will suit a child playing a piano. It might be lowered an inch or so for use at a table. In any case, the actual sitting height is affected by the thickness of upholstery used on the top. The necessary materials are found in TABLE 6-15.

The legs are splayed in both directions to give stability and an attractive appearance. This arrangement forms the outline of part of a cone. If arranged with much spread, the actual cross section of legs will no longer have right-angled corners. With only the small amount of spread shown here, the difference between the theoretically correct cross-sectional angle and a right angle is so slight that it can be ignored.

Fig. 6-41. A piano stool with an upholstered top and a storage box.

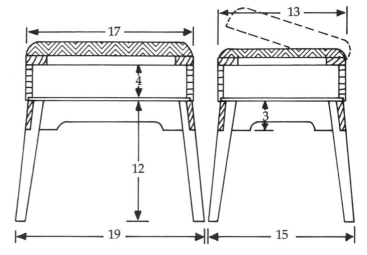

Table 6-15. Materials List for a Piano Stool.

2 box sides	4 × 17 × ⅝
2 box ends	4 × 13 × ⅝
1 box bottom	13 × 17 × ¼ plywood
2 lid frames	1½ × 17 × ⅝
2 lid frames	1½ × 13 × ⅝
1 lid base	13 × 17 × ¼ plywood
4 legs	1½ × 13 × 1½
2 rails	3 × 16 × ⅝
3 rails	3 × 12 × ⅝

The stool is made in two parts. The box, with its hinged lid, is one unit and the legs and framework another, like the main parts of a small table. The units are screwed together so that they can be disassembled if alterations or repairs are required later.

The box can be made with any of the usual corner joints. The most expert way would be with concealed dovetails, or through dovetails, but simpler rabbeted or dado joints are acceptable. The plywood bottom fits into a rabbet (FIG. 6-42A) and the corner joints should be arranged to hide this. Normal corner joints should be strong enough, but if reinforcing is needed, you can glue in triangular blocks (FIG. 6-42B).

The lid is framed. The corner joints will be hidden by the covering material, so they can be simple half-laps, glued and screwed (FIG. 6-42C), open mortise and tenon, or even bridle joints (FIG. 6-42D).

The finished lid has to match the box outline. To allow for slight differences, make the lid a little too big and plane the edges to match the box after it has been made. Mark the box and lid so the parts come together the same way each time.

The lid can be upholstered on an open frame with webbing, but the lid shown is a piece of thin plywood that is drilled with a few ventilation holes to let air in and out (FIG. 6-42E).

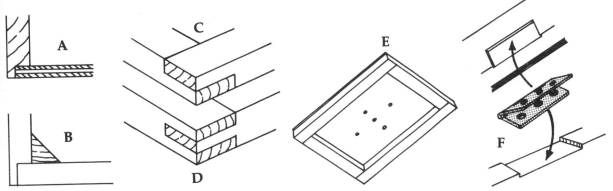

Fig. 6-42. Details of the top of the piano stool: (A) plywood bottom; (B) triangular blocks; (C) corner joints; (D) bridle joints; (E) lid; (F) hinges.

For the neatest appearance the hinges should be let into both parts (FIG. 6-42F). If you use hinges with flaps as wide as the box thickness, it is easier to cut recesses straight across than to make them stopped. Let the hinge flaps in slightly less than their thickness, so there will be a slight gap between the wood surfaces and the lid will close fully without binding. I also suggest fitting a strut to prevent the lid from going past a vertical position when it is opened. Make a temporary assembly with hinges and strut to test their action, then remove them until the wooden parts have been finished.

The legs should taper, from 1½ inches to 1 inch square in their length, without the parallel square top for rail joints that is used in some tables. For convenience leave some spare wood at the top so that the leg can be held in a vise while you are planing the taper. The excess can then be cut (FIG. 6-43A). It might be possible to make all the legs from one long parallel piece and cut them off as each is shaped, or each leg could be made from a piece of wood that is a few inches too long.

Draw one corner of the stool full-size (FIG. 6-43B). This view is the same in both directions, so it will serve as a guide when marking rails both ways. The box should overhang by ⅜ inch all around. Its lower edge is rounded.

The outer surfaces of the rails should be level with the leg surfaces and can be joined with barefaced tenons or dowels (FIG. 6-43C). The upper edge of each rail must be bevelled slightly. This could be done in advance, but it will be simpler to cut the tops of the legs correctly after the joints have been prepared. Have the rails stand a little too high and plane them after assembly.

Reduce the rails in width to give a lighter appearance. A simple outline is shown in FIG. 6-41, but several other shapes are possible (FIG. 6-43D). To ensure an exact match at each corner, make a template for the outline (FIG. 6-43E). As hands will be put under the stool to lift it, round the edges and remove any sharpness from the angular parts in the design.

The box is attached by screwing downward from inside. It might be possible to screw directly into the rails with slightly angled holes, but it will be stronger to screw into blocks in each corner and a rail across the center (FIG. 6-43F).

Screw and glue the corner blocks. The center rail is tenoned or doweled into the outer rails, so it has to be included when the other parts are glued and clamped.

The bottoms of the legs might not matter if they are cut square and the sharpness is taken off the corners. However, to get true surfaces on the bottoms,

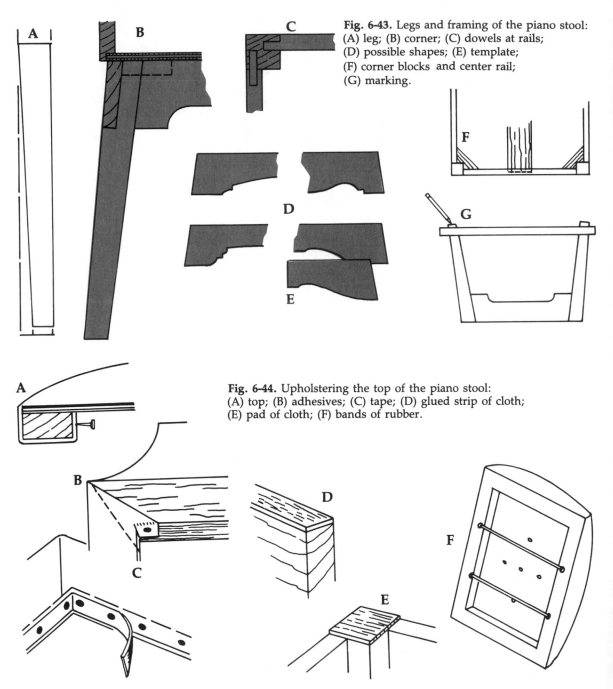

Fig. 6-43. Legs and framing of the piano stool: (A) leg; (B) corner; (C) dowels at rails; (D) possible shapes; (E) template; (F) corner blocks and center rail; (G) marking.

Fig. 6-44. Upholstering the top of the piano stool: (A) top; (B) adhesives; (C) tape; (D) glued strip of cloth; (E) pad of cloth; (F) bands of rubber.

leave trimming to length until after assembly, then mark where the cuts have to come on all outer surfaces with a straightedge parallel with the top (FIG. 6-43G).

The top can be upholstered with a rubber or foam pad and the covering material taken into the center recess for tacking (FIG. 6-44A). At the corners there will be surplus material to dispose of. If the material is light and flexible, you can fold it under without causing much bulk, but in most cases it is best to cut away so there is an overlap that can be held with adhesives (FIG. 6-44B).

You can also add a piece of gimp or tape added to make a neater finish inside (FIG. 6-44C). Also the covering material closing on to a wood surface might become worn. For the best finish glue a strip of thick cloth around the edge of the box (FIG. 6-44D). This reduces wear and noise. A simpler alternative is to glue a pad of cloth on the top of each front leg. This keeps the lid covering away from direct contact with the wood (FIG. 6-44E).

The recess in the lid can be used as extra storage space for papers by putting a few bands of stout rubber between screws (FIG. 6-44F). These must be arranged far enough in from the edges to be clear of the box when the lid is closed. How the box is finished depends on what furniture it has to match, but whatever treatment you choose outside, a lightly colored painted surface looks good inside the box.

LADDERBACK CHAIR

Chairs with slats across the back, which are the reason for the special name, were popular pieces of colonial furniture. Some had plain wood or upholstered seats, but the majority were made with a seat woven from a rope made of straw or other fibrous material. The most durable were made of the dried tough rushes, sedges, and other plants that grow at the water's edge. This particular type of seat became known as rush pattern (FIG. 6-45). The materials list is found in TABLE 6-16.

Anyone with a lathe might want to make chairs, but many lathes do not have a sufficient capacity between centers to make the back legs of an adult chair. The common limit is about 30 inches. For a child's chair, however, the back legs can be within this limit and it is possible to make a reproduction chair of attractive appearance that includes all the traditional features in a slightly smaller size.

This chair should suit a child between 6 and 10 years (FIG. 6-45A). The back

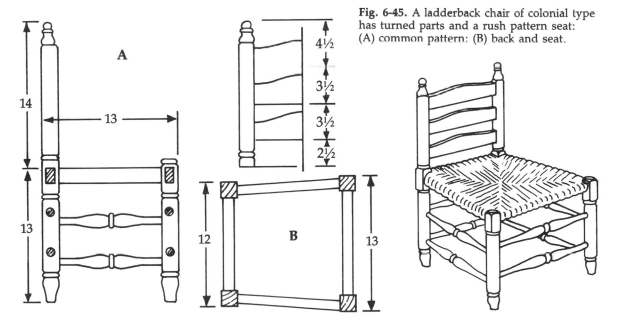

Fig. 6-45. A ladderback chair of colonial type has turned parts and a rush pattern seat: (A) common pattern: (B) back and seat.

Table 6-16. Materials List for a Ladderback Chair.

2 legs	1½ × 27 × 1½
2 legs	1½ × 14 × 1½
3 rails	1½ × 12 × 1
1 rail	1½ × 11 × 1
6 rails	1½ × 12 × 1½
2 rails	1½ × 11 × 1½
3 slats	3 × 11 × ½

is upright, there are double rails in each direction, and the rush pattern seat is wider at the front than the back (FIG. 6-45B). Although the chair might look more complicated than some of the other chairs described, construction is fairly simple if taken a step at a time.

The wood you choose for the legs should be properly seasoned and free from defects. The back legs are quite long in relation to their thickness and it is important that they are absolutely straight when mounted in the lathe and will not warp after turning. Some chairs of this type have fully turned legs, but with this chair, the wood is left square at all the seat joints for strength and ease of accurate cutting.

Prepare the wood for the back legs a little too long and mark the limits of the square parts before mounting in the lathe. It will be helpful to prepare a *rod* with the main sizes on a piece of scrap wood (FIG. 6-46A). This can be held close to the wood and positions marked from it. Turn the wood round and parallel each side of the square part. Cut in with the point of the chisel at the ends of the square part and turn beads there (FIG. 6-46B).

At the top end, turn the finial (FIG. 6-46C) but do not reduce the waste end so much that the wood is weakened at this stage. Do all the other turning before completing the knob and cutting off. Turn the foot (FIG. 6-46D). Leave cutting into the center until other turning has been finished, then make the end slightly hollow so the leg will stand firmly.

Locating rungs and slats will be easier if some pencilling is done before cutting off the ends of the leg and removing the wood from the lathe. While the wood is rotating, hold a pencil on the toolrest to mark the positions of rung holes (FIG. 6-46E) and the tops and bottoms of the slat joints.

Have the toolrest exactly at lathe center height. Hold the wood with one of the flat surfaces horizontal. It would be best if the lathe headstock is locked, but otherwise the wood can be held by hand. Draw a pencil along the wood to make a lengthwise line where the centers of holes and joints will come (FIG. 6-46F). Move the wood through a right angle so the next flat surface is horizontal and mark the rung holes the other way (FIG. 6-46G).

When turning and marking the other back leg, check it against the first leg as well as the marked rod. As the rung holes are staggered, make sure the second leg is a pair to the first and not marked with the hole positions the same way.

Deal with the front legs in a similar way (FIG. 6-47A). Lengths can be marked from the same rod as used for the back leg; cut down if its excess length would foul the headstock. Be sure to get a good finish to the tops of the beads above the square parts, as these are prominent on the finished chair.

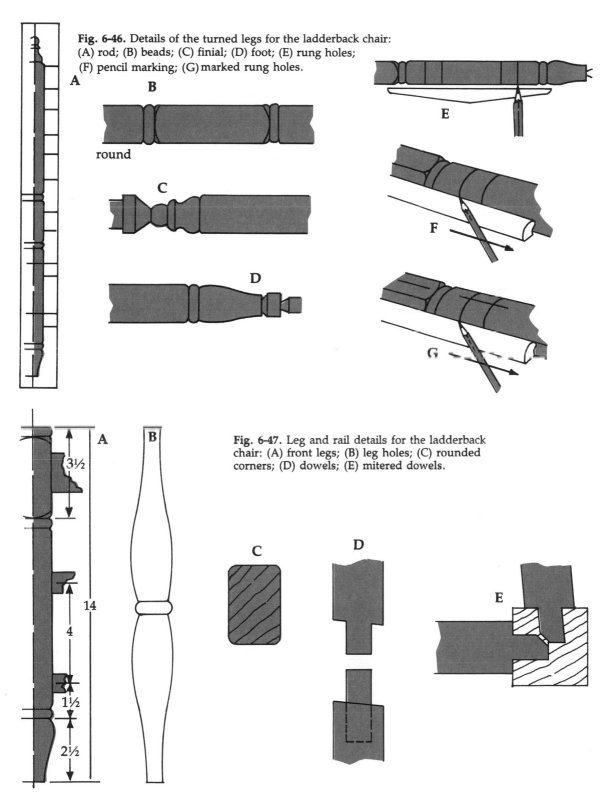

Fig. 6-46. Details of the turned legs for the ladderback chair: (A) rod; (B) beads; (C) finial; (D) foot; (E) rung holes; (F) pencil marking; (G) marked rung holes.

A

B

round

C

D

E

F

G

Fig. 6-47. Leg and rail details for the ladderback chair: (A) front legs; (B) leg holes; (C) rounded corners; (D) dowels; (E) mitered dowels.

A

B

C

D

E

3½

14

4

1½

2½

The rails should be turned with central beads and ends that taper to make a tight fit in the leg holes (FIG. 6-47B). Drill a hole with the bit that will be used in a thin piece of wood, so this can be used to test the ends of the rails in the lathe at the tailstock end. Calipers will have to be used at the other end.

Make the ends parallel or with a very slight taper. This allows some adjustment by moving the rail in and out of its hole during assembly. Allow sufficient length for rails to go about halfway through the legs. The side and front rails should all be the same length and the back two shorter.

Rails can be turned a little too long and sawn to matching lengths later, but do this at each end so the beads remain central. Be careful to keep maximum diameters the same. Turn the central beads first after making the wood round and check for a uniform size here with calipers. If there are slight differences in the sweep of the curves to the ends, they will not be as noticeable as errors in the diameters.

The corners of the four seat rails should be rounded (FIG. 6-47C) and joined to the legs with tenons or dowels (FIG. 6-47D). There is not much taper in the sides, but for closest joints, draw the plan view (FIg. 6-45B) and cut the ends of the side rails to the angles obtained from this. Tenons or dowels can be taken far enough into the legs so they are mitered (FIG. 6-47E).

The back slats are quite thin and the only satisfactory end joints are barefaced mortise and tenons (FIG. 6-48A). Curve the edges in crosssection and cut down the widths enough to allow the joints to have square edges (FIG. 6-48B).

Assemble the back of the chair first. The slats and the seat rail will set the width. Pull these joints tight by clamping. The turned rails will probably settle in their correct positions without difficulty, but check that the beads come centrally between legs. The rail joints can be secured against movement before the glue has set by thin nails driven from what will be the inside of the chair (FIG. 6-48C).

Next, assemble the front in the same way. Be careful that the feet are not pulled in too far. Check that the front assembly has the legs upright by testing over the back assembly. The seat and lower rails back to front should present no difficulty in assembling, but make a check of diagonals across the seat while the chair is standing level. If necessary, put a board across the seat with a weight on it to hold the whole assembly true while the glue sets.

The chair will probably be sufficiently strong enough to stand up to use by a child without further strengthening, but wooden angle brackets in the corners of the seat rails can be added if desired and will be hidden by the seat.

Use a triangular piece about ¾ inches thick with its corner cut away to clear the leg, then drill screw holes diagonally toward the corner (FIG. 6-48D) so that

Fig. 6-48. Joints in the back and seat of the ladderback chair:
(A) back slats; (B) square edges: (C) inside of chair; (D) screw holes.

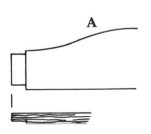
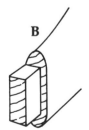
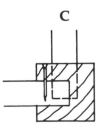
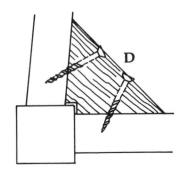

A   B   C   D

as they are tightened, the wood is pulled toward the corner. The bracket serves as a brace between the rails and should not be a close fit on the leg.

A traditional seat made from rushes, grasses, or other fibrous natural materials was worked while twisting these things into ropes as weaving progressed. It is better today to use a prepared rope; it is easier to work, stronger, and more durable. You could use any ordinary rope, but there are ropes of plastic and other materials sold especially for this purpose. One material is *seagrass*, an imported rope available in many colors.

The color of most of the original materials was gray/green, but for a child's chair a brighter color might be chosen. There is not much room for variations in design, but it is possible to have one color in the corners and another in the main body of the seat pattern.

A good idea is to first make a few shuttles or spools on which to wind the rope (FIG. 6-49A). They can be quite rough. Use a smoothly pointed stick with its higher part left square (FIG. 6-49B).

The pattern looks the same above and below. Inside there are strands which go across the seat and do not show at what joint the work is finished. *Joins* should come in these parts. Start near the middle of a rail, by knotting the rope end and driving in tack (FIG. 6-49C).

Take the shuttle of line over the far rail, underneath and up through the middle of the seat. Go back over the adjoining rail and up the center again (FIG. 6-49D). This is one continuous action. The seat is made by continuing it enough times to fill the space. The parts that show in the completed seat are the wraps around the rails. Get them close to the leg. Hold the line tight at that leg, go to the next corner and do the same actions (FIG. 6-49E). Pull the line tight between the corners and get it tight around the second leg before moving on to the third corner.

After the fourth corner, make the next turns around the first corner inside the first turns, and so on around the seat. As the seat is narrower at the back, you would fill up that rail with turns before the other rails. To correct this take

Fig. 6-49. The method of working a rush pattern seat; (A) spools; (B) pointed stick; (C) knotting rope end; (D) shuttle line; (E) pulling line; (F) keep taking the line around; (G) push turns; (H) seat.

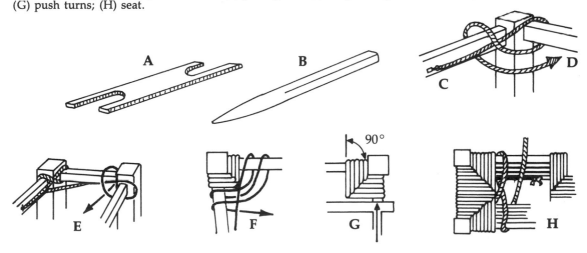

the line twice around each front corner at about every fourth time around the seat (FIG. 6-49F) until the spaces of bare wood left exposed on front and back rails are the same.

Be sure to keep a good tension on the lines at all times. If you have to join in a new piece, knot it tightly in one of the parts going across the seat. Watch that the corners are kept square. Use the square edge of the pointed stick to push the turns close together along the rails (FIG. 6-49G). Also use it or a straightedge to see that the pattern is kept straight across. As the pattern progresses, be careful of turns riding over each other at the angle in the inner corner of each part.

As the pattern fills up, use the pointed stick to open the center so the end of the rope can be pushed through. At this stage you will have to use a long end of line as there is no space left to pass the shuttle. Try to get in as many turns as possible to make a tight pattern. If opposite sides fill up, while there is still space on the other rails, take the line up and down with a figure eight action between them. This would have to be done in any case on a seat that is longer one way than the other (FIG. 6-49H). Finish by tacking through the rope under a rail and push the end inside from below.

In traditional chairs with the covering material twisted into rope as covering progressed, it was common to pad between the top and bottom by pushing oddments of the covering material into the spaces that develop as the pattern is worked. But in a chair of this size there is no need to do this, providing you keep sufficient tension on the rope at all stages. In use, the center of the seat will sag slightly, but if it is tight to begin with, this will not be excessive and will improve comfort and appearance.

7

Storage Units

THE MAJORITY OF CHILDREN are untidy if left to their own devices. They have to be trained to look after things, put them away after use, and realize the advantages of being orderly with their toys, books, and clothes. It is difficult to do this if there are insufficient or unsatisfactory storage places provided. This applies no matter what the age, but the type of storage units provided might change as a child gets older.

Fortunately there is not such a need to scale storage equipment to the size of the child and many items can be used at all ages with some adaption. They might even go on to other uses in adult life. The youngest child needs storage space for a lot of toys, while older children will want to accommodate books and hobby materials.

Not all of the storage items will be used only by the child. Parents might want to put some things away out of reach, so they can control their uses. The youngest child should have some place to put toys—perhaps a box or trolley that can be moved from place to place. Parents may have to follow up and assist in the early stages, but if the storage place is there, it is the first step in a training in tidiness.

Storage equipment should be as space-saving as possible. There will have to be some things that have a place in the center of the room and some can be portable, but many units are better if made to stand against a wall or be fixed to it.

Also many things can be made that do not take up floor space—the hanging or built-in racks, shelves, and cupboards. They serve a purpose without reducing play or work space on the floor. Combined units are also handy. A bookcase that is the upper part of a cabinet with drawers and shelves should be more compact than having these facilities in separate items.

Some of the tables described in Chapter 6 also have storage capacity and it is a good idea when furnishing a small room to try to arrange storage space in furniture that is primarily for other purposes. Additional storage items will have to be fitted into the layout of the room. Besides the portable and freestanding items, the walls should be looked at and units planned to get as much of the child's miscellaneous collection of equipment as possible off the ground. This applies to clothing as well as toys and books.

SHELF UNITS

Hanging bookshelves form the basic concept of wall furniture, although they can support many other things besides books. Books in quantity can be surprisingly heavy, so do not use too thin a section of wood. A slim shelf that seems adequate when first loaded with books might develop a sag after a few months.

Do not expect a shelf to carry a heavy load over too long a span. Long bookshelves should have intermediate supports. The designs can also include divisions or a change in depth so a long span is broken, providing strength intermediately as well as having a pleasing appearance (FIGS. 7-1 through 7-4). They can be symmetrical (FIG. 7-1A) or asymmetrical (FIG. 7-1B).

DIVIDED BOOKSHELF

The basic design, from which most others develop, has two shelves between uprights (FIG. 7-1C). For a materials list, see TABLE 7-1. The shelves can rest on battens (FIG. 7-1D) or, better yet, joined with stopped dados (FIG. 7-1E). In both cases something has to be done about rigidity and hanging. This is most simply done by nailing on a plywood back (FIG. 7-1F), which is then screwed to the wall.

Another way is to leave most of the back open, but put a stiffener under the top shelf (FIG. 7-1G) and screw to the wall through that. Shelves with open backs allow things put on them to mark the wall, so it is better to give the unit its own back. Although plywood or hardboard will enclose the back, they do not always

Fig. 7-1. Shelf units can be in many forms and be used for books and other things. Construction can be with nails or dado joints: (A) symmetrical; (B) asymmetrical; (C) two shelves; (D) battens; (E) stopped dados; (F) plywood back; (G) stiffener.

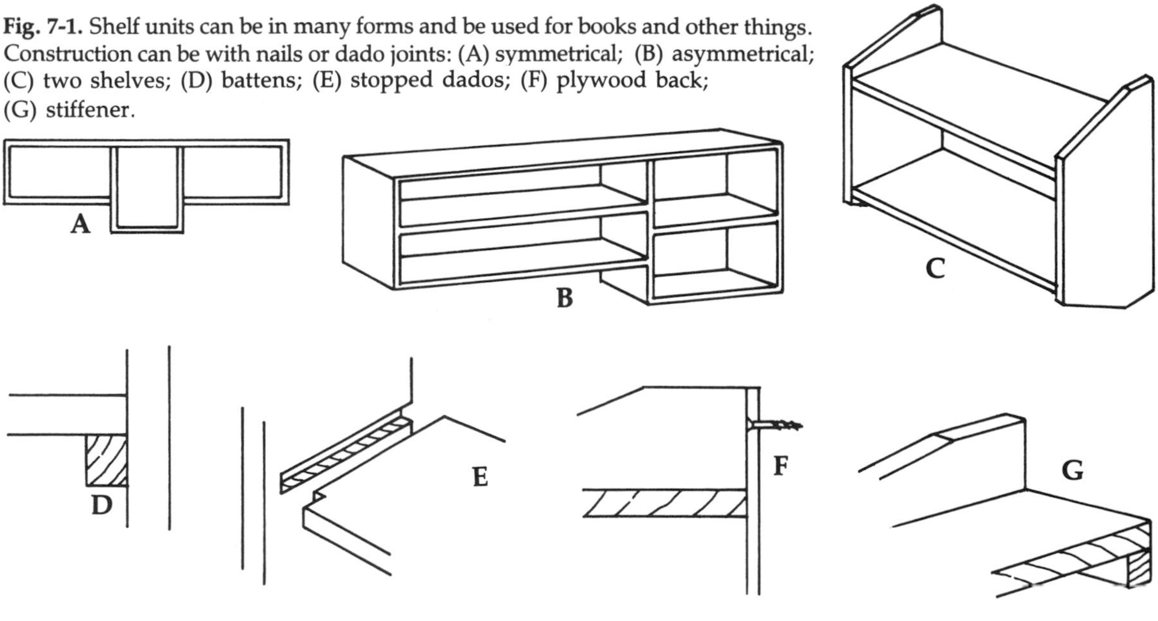

Table 7-1. Materials List for a Divided Bookshelf.

2 uprights	6 × 13 × ⅝
1 upright	6 × 12 × ⅝
1 shelf	6 × 30 × ⅝
1 shelf	6 × 20 × ⅝
1 shelf	6 × 10 × ⅝
1 rail	⅝ × 20 dowel rod

fasten securely into the wall, so it is better to have solid wood above the top shelf for screwing and plywood behind the other parts.

BOOKSHELVES

There are many kinds of shelves—three of which are suggested (FIG. 7-2A). For a materials list, see TABLE 7-2. There can be straight slopes on the ends, but curves can be carried around the top and back. The bottoms of the sides could have similar curves, but the bookcase will eventually stand on a floor or table, feet can be cut on the bottom. If you use curves at the top and bottom, you can improve appearance by hollowing the front edges between shelves, but the sides would serve their purpose just as well with straight edges.

Rabbet the sides to take the plywood back (FIGS. 7-2B and 7-2C). Then make the shelves to match. The solid wood above the top shelf has to be let in deeper, so cut the rabbet further there to accommodate it (FIG. 7-2D).

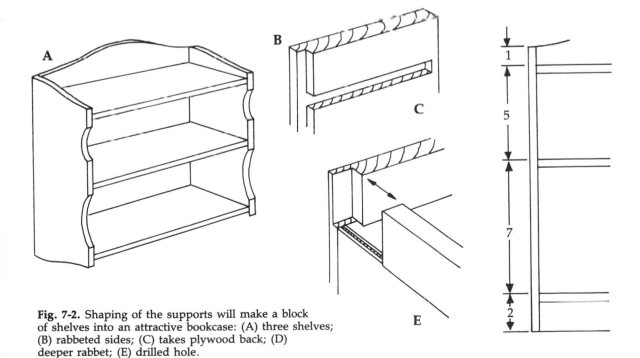

Fig. 7-2. Shaping of the supports will make a block of shelves into an attractive bookcase: (A) three shelves; (B) rabbeted sides; (C) takes plywood back; (D) deeper rabbet; (E) drilled hole.

Table 7-2. Materials List for Bookshelves.

2 ends	5 × 15 × ⅝
3 shelves	5 × 15 × ⅝
1 top	2½ × 15 × ⅝
1 back	14 × 15 × ¼ plywood

Next, shape and round the edges. Drill holes for screws upward into the top piece through the rear edge of the top shelf and then drill holes in that piece for screwing to the wall (FIG. 7-2E). The dado joints can be strengthened by screwing diagonally upward from below.

WALL FITMENT

To break up the shelf lengths of a long bookcase, you can change the depth to suit different size books (FIG. 7-3A). The number of changes made will depend on the overall length and the number of different size books. For very wide books or magazines laid flat, the shelves can project forward from the uprights. For the neatest joints then the dados can be cut through and the shelf end allowed to overlap (FIG. 7-3B). For a complete materials list, see TABLE 7-3.

Table 7-3. Materials List for a Wall Fitment.

1 shelf	6 × 41 × ⅝
1 shelf	6 × 12 × ⅝
1 shelf	6 × 14 × ⅝
2 uprights	6 × 7 × ⅝
2 uprights	6 × 8 × ⅝
1 rail	2 × 26 × ⅝

The sides can also project below the bottom shelf. In this case, dado joints can be used. It would be better if the side did not go below the shelf level, there has to be a stronger joint to take the load. A through dovetail is best (FIG. 7-3C).

The stepped arrangement, if taken below, can be adapted to another use. There can be a rail, made from a piece of dowel rod, fitted into holes, (FIG. 7-3D) to serve as a rack for ties, belts and other items of clothing.

A part of the rack can be fitted with a door and the enclosed space arranged above or below the bookshelves. It might be at one end or could be between open shelves.

The simplest door is a piece of thick plywood cut to fit over the surrounding edges (FIG. 7-3E), with hinges behind one edge and a fastener that fits into the other side. Another door fits inside the frame. It could be similar plywood, or framed with thinner plywood in a plowed groove (FIG. 7-3F). This might be also a good place for a mirror fitted into rabbeted wood (FIG. 7-3G).

In the common bookcase assembly, the shelves are supported by the ends. It is possible to make an assembly with one or more shelves, since the strength members and upright divisions are dependent on them. In the example (FIG. 7-4A) there is a main shelf, which can be hung from the wall with metal mirror plates

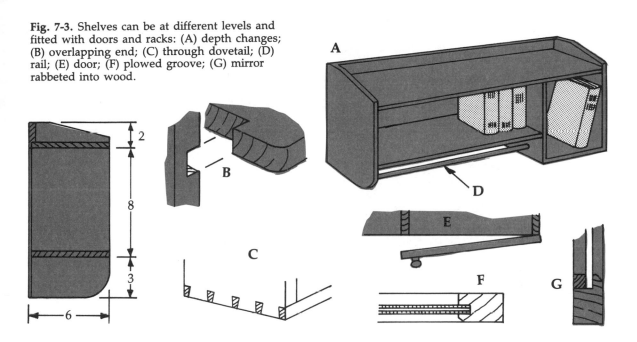

Fig. 7-3. Shelves can be at different levels and fitted with doors and racks: (A) depth changes; (B) overlapping end; (C) through dovetail; (D) rail; (E) door; (F) plowed groove; (G) mirror rabbeted into wood.

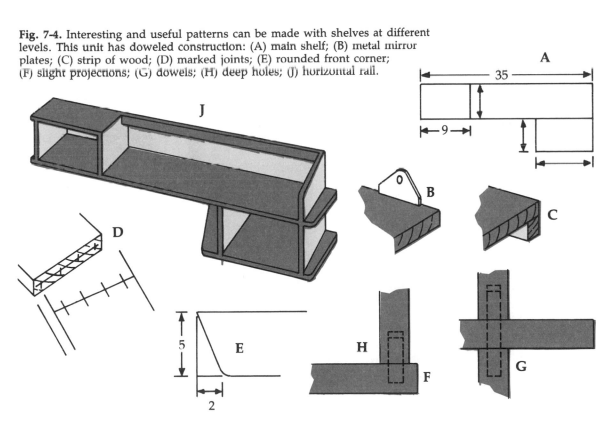

Fig. 7-4. Interesting and useful patterns can be made with shelves at different levels. This unit has doweled construction: (A) main shelf; (B) metal mirror plates; (C) strip of wood; (D) marked joints; (E) rounded front corner; (F) slight projections; (G) dowels; (H) deep holes; (J) horizontal rail.

(FIG. 7-4B), or there can be a strip of wood under the rear edge (FIG. 7-4C) to take screws into the wall.

The other parts are joined with dowels. Four dowels $\frac{5}{16}$ inch or $\frac{3}{8}$ inch diameter in each joint should be strong enough. Cut the ends of the wood accurately and mark the joints together (FIG. 7-4D) or use a dowel jig. Cut the shelf ends and other exposed ends at a slope with a rounded front corner (FIG. 7-4E). Use a template to get them all the same, or cut one end and use that as a template at the other places. Where the ends are cut squarely, they could come level with the part joining, but they are shown with slight projections (FIG. 7-4F). Although they appear square, take off all sharpness before assembly.

At the end where there are uprights above and below the shelf, take dowels right through (FIG. 7-4G). Elsewhere put the dowels about three-quarters of the way through the shelf. Be sure to make the holes in the uprights slightly too deep (FIG. 7-4H) so the joint can be squeezed tight with a clamp.

A horizontal rail behind the top space (FIG. 7-4J) will strengthen the assembly and provide another place for screws to the wall. For a child who collects small, decorative animal figures, the extending parts might be taken a little further to provide space for displaying them.

CHEST

This chest is a storage box that might have uses for keeping together the toys of a young child, but it is intended to be more suitable for an older boy or girl (FIGS. 7-5 and 7-5A). Boy or Girl Scouts would find the box very convenient for storing the ropes and other equipment needed for their many activities. It would also be handy for packing some of the equipment needed for camping, or for a treehouse or a den in the yard. It can easily be brought into the home for storage. The chest would also be suitable for tools, fishing gear, and other outdoor activity items. The top is a suitable height for a makeshift seat. It might also be used as a table by children sitting on the ground.

TABLE 7-4 lists the necessary materials. The main parts are plywood, but instead of being framed on the inside in the more common way, all of the framing is outside and can be regarded as a design feature. This makes for a very simple method of construction. You can use fitted joints in some places, but a nailed construction will be satisfactory. With all framing outside, the interior remains smooth. Without any fittings or projections, the inside of the box could be used like the oldtime blanket chest for storing clothing, bed linen, and the like. A child might want to fill the chest with dolls' clothing and other soft items. Also, a sliding tray is shown that can be lifted out for those little children's treasures that might get lost amongst the bigger things. The end handles allow two children to drag or carry their chest.

Sizes can be schemed to cut from an available plywood panel, but the sizes shown (FIG. 7-5) are based on end panels 12 inches square and side panels 12 × 24 inches. All of the external framing is $\frac{3}{4}$-inch-square strips. The box plywood shown is $\frac{1}{4}$ inch thick, but if thinner plywood is available, the chest could be lightened by using it. The lid is a single unframed piece of $\frac{1}{2}$-inch plywood. It would be unwise to reduce this, as anything less might distort it.

Start by making the two ends (FIG. 7-6A). Miter the corners and glue and nail the strips through the plywood. Cut the two plywood sides to the same depth as the ends (FIG. 7-6B) and attach their stiffening pieces in the same way (FIG. 7-6C),

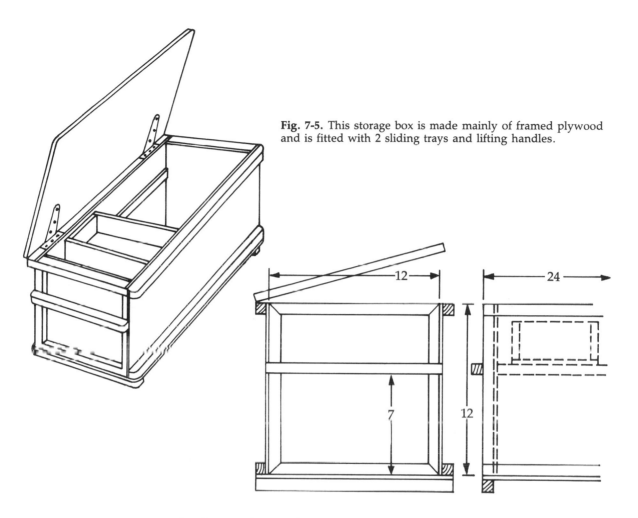

Fig. 7-5. This storage box is made mainly of framed plywood and is fitted with 2 sliding trays and lifting handles.

but keep nails away from the end overlaps. The stiffening pieces might be left on too long for trimming after assembly.

Glue and nail the plywood sides to the ends. The best joints at the corners are made with ¼-inch dowels, which should be long enough to go through the miters into the top and bottom end pieces (FIG. 7-6D). Nail and glue on the bottom plywood (FIG. 7-6E). Trim the stiffening pieces and round their corners (FIG. 7-6F), except at the top rear corners where the lid will be fitted.

The bottom is raised off the ground with strips across the ends. A simple way of attaching them would be to locate them far enough in from the ends for nails to be driven downward from inside (FIG. 7-7A), but the completed box (FIG. 7-5) is shown with them level at the ends. They can be fastened there with screws driven upward and deeply countersunk or counterbored and plugged (FIG. 7-7B). Then round the corners to match the other parts.

The tray is a nailed box (FIG. 7-7C), although the corners could be made with dovetails or other joints. Do not make the box too narrow, as a very narrow box might pull askew and be difficult to slide. A plain box might be easy for an adult

Table 7-4. Materials List for a Chest.

2 ends	12 × 12 × ¼ plywood
8 end frames	¾ × 12 × ¾
2 sides	12 × 24 × ¼ plywood
4 side frames	¾ × ¾
1 bottom	14 × 26 × ¼ plywood
2 feet	¾ × 14 × ¾
1 lid	14 × 26 × ½ plywood
2 handles	¾ × 14 × ¾
2 runners	¾ × 24 × ⅜
2 box sides	3 × 12 × ½
2 box ends	3 × 6 × ½
1 box bottom	6 × 12 × ¼ plywood

to grasp and lift out, but for a child, include finger holes for lifting (FIG. 7-7D). The runners need not be very thick—one of the ¾-inch strips cut down the center will make both.

One type of handle that would appeal to a child might be a rope loop through a drilled block of wood at each end (FIG. 7-7E). Or there could be a strip of wood across, either screwed or dowelled at the ends (FIG. 7-7F). Round the parts that will be held and locate any type of handle above the center of the end.

The lid is a piece of plywood that matches the outline of the top of the box. To get a close fit, leave it too big and trim the ends and front after the back edge has been hinged.

Fig. 7-6. Constructional details of the box. Stiffened sides are fitted to framed plywood ends: (A) ends; (B) sides; (C) stiffening pieces; (D) end pieces; (E) bottom plywood; (F) rounded corners.

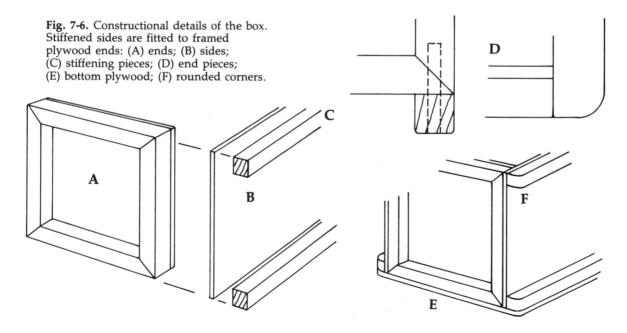

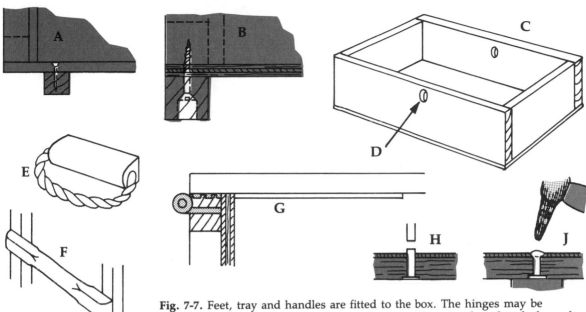

Fig. 7-7. Feet, tray and handles are fitted to the box. The hinges may be riveted to the lid for extra security: (A) bottom; (B) counterbored and plugged; (C) tray, (D) finger holes, (E) rope loop, (F) strip of wood, (G) lid clearance, (H) countersinks; (J) cross peen hammer.

You could use ordinary hinges let into the box edge and lid, but T or strap hinges provide a stronger fastening to the wide, thin lid. The long arm goes on the surface of the lid, but the other part should be let into the box edge enough to allow the lid to close with only slight clearance (FIG. 7-7G).

Screws might hold well enough in the plywood, but a more secure way of fastening is to rivet the hinges. This can be done with stout nails of about the same size as the holes in the hinge, put through drilled holes in the plywood and cut off so enough projects to hammer into the countersinks of the hinges (FIG. 7-7H). Support the nail head on an iron block and use a ball- or cross-peen hammer to spread the cut end (FIG. 7-7J).

PARTICLEBOARD CABINET

Particleboard, available in uniform widths and thicknesses, with little risk of warping or twisting, has many attractions, particularly when it is covered during its manufacture with a plastic coating that can be in one color or finished to simulate wood grain. Some is available with real wood veneers, but for children's furniture the plastic covering is better able to stand up to the anticipated rough treatment.

One problem with covered particleboard is that the things made with it must be rather angular, as it is impossible to shape contours and hide the rather unattractive particleboard core that is exposed during cutting. The angular shape is acceptable for many items and much modern adult furniture is made with this material.

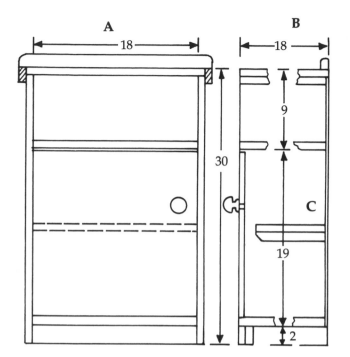

A

18

B

18

30

9

19

C

2

Fig. 7-8. A cabinet with shelf and door can be made of particleboard and used at a bedside: (A) wood with particleboard; (B) sizes.

Since edges and corners cannot be rounded much, the corners of furniture made with this material have angles that could hurt a child unless something was done to protect them. Coupled with this is the rather clinical appearance of the plain colors and the severe outlines (FIG. 7-8).

The cabinet shown is made with wood and particleboard (FIG. 7-8A). For a complete materials list, see TABLE 7-5. The wood covers the angles that might hurt a child and breaks up the shape for a more pleasing appearance, which can be accentuated by finishing the wood in a contrasting color. A wooden knob to the door complements the effect, although another type of handle can also be used. A strip wooden handle would match the other woodwork.

Covered particleboard is available in lengths with the parallel edges, as well as both surfaces, covered. As much as possible, a design should be arranged to

Table 7-5. Materials List for a Particleboard Cabinet.

2 sides	18 × 30 × ⅝ particleboard
1 top	18 × 20 × ⅝ particleboard
2 shelves	18 × 19 × ⅝ particleboard
1 door	18 × 19 × ⅝ particleboard
1 plinth	2 × 19 × ⅝ particleboard or wood
1 top	1½ × 21 × ⅝ wood
2 tops	1½ × 18 × ⅝ wood
1 back	19 × 30 × ⅛ hardboard or plywood
Joint covers from 8	½ × 19 × ½ wood
1 shelf, optional	15 × 19 × ⅝ particleboard

make use of the stock widths, but if edges have to be cut and they will be visible in the finished job, matching plastic veneer with self-adhesive glue can be ironed on.

The cabinet provides a top at table height, a shelf under it, and storage space behind a door below that. It could stand anywhere in a room and be used for many things. The top would make a hygienic surface for a young cook to prepare food. The cabinet would also be useful beside a bed.

The sizes of this cabinet are based on a stock width of 18 inches (FIG. 7-8B). The two sides, the door, and the top use this width unaltered. The two shelves are reduced in width to allow for the thickness of a hardboard back. Similar cabinets can be made in other sizes by relating the dimensions to another stock width.

If you want to avoid cutting down the door width, the width between the sides has to be sufficient to allow clearance for the hinges at one side and about the same for free movement at the other side. The hinges are of the thin flush type, in which one leaf fits into the other and there is no need to let either part into the particleboard (FIG. 7-9A). This requirement settles the lengths of the shelves. Cut them to finish at this length. Allow a little for careful planing and get the ends as square as possible in width and thickness. Cut enough off the back edge to allow for the thickness of the back material.

Make the two sides, making sure the top is long enough to overlap them (FIG. 7-9B). Mark where the shelves are to come on the sides. This is best done with a pencil so the lines are easily rubbed off later.

Fig. 7-9. Particleboard parts are joined with screws or dowels, or by using strips of wood inside: (A) leaf; (B) sides; (C) plastic plugs; (D) glue, (E) plastic blocks; (F) a cross joint; (G) blocks.

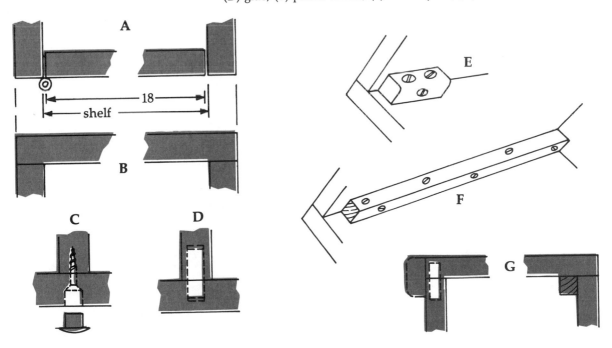

There are three ways the shelves could be joined. Screws can be counterbored and covered with matching plastic plugs (FIG. 7-9C). Dowels can be fitted into the ends of the shelves, then glued into holes in the sides with clamps (FIG. 7-9D). Make sure there is some excess length in the holes for surplus glue and to prevent the dowels from bottoming (FIG. 7-9D). Dowels or screws should be at about 3-inch intervals across the width.

Another way is to use the prepared plastic blocks screwed into the angle at intervals (FIG. 7-9E). Pieces of wood can be used in the same way across a joint (FIG. 7-9F). Their ends may act as door stops.

If you want to avoid holes on the top surface, the cabinet top is best fastened with dowels or blocks underneath (FIG. 7-9G). Although the ends of the particleboard core show at this stage, they will be covered with wood later, so there is no need to iron on any edging pieces.

At the bottom there should be a plinth set back between the sides. It could be matching particleboard. If cut from a wide piece, the part cut beside it would make an internal shelf on battens (FIG. 7-8C). The plinth could then be wood to match the top edges. Attachment by plugging screws through the sides or by screwing blocks of wood inside both ways (FIG. 7-10A).

When all these parts have been asssembled, the hardboard back is added. Carefully square it, as one of its purposes is to hold the cabinet in shape. Then screw or nail this back to the shelves, but at the sides and top there should be strips of wood screwed to the particleboard (FIG. 7-10B). Attach the back with glue and either small screws or fine nails. While driving nails, hold an iron block against the wood strip to prevent the other screws from being strained.

Next, make the door. Allow enough clearance at the top and bottom to iron on edge strips. Use a finely set plane to remove sharpness on all exposed edges of the door and the cabinet, but keep the cuts very light. Attach the hinges and the knob or handle. You might want to fit a magnetic catch. If the joint strips

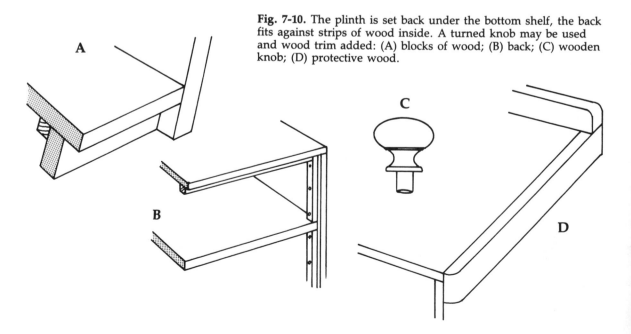

Fig. 7-10. The plinth is set back under the bottom shelf, the back fits against strips of wood inside. A turned knob may be used and wood trim added: (A) blocks of wood; (B) back; (C) wooden knob; (D) protective wood.

do not serve as a door stop, fit a short strip of wood to the side to stop the door from going in too far. If you have a wooden knob made on a lathe, make a dowel end to glue in a hole (FIG. 7-10C).

The protective wood at the top goes along the sides and a piece at the top to prevent things from falling over the back (FIG. 7-10D). The sides of the wood against the particleboard should be flat and smooth, but all other edges and corners should be thoroughly rounded.

Prepare the wood parts with holes drilled for plugged screws. Do most of the sanding necessary before screwing in place. When the plugs over the screws have been levelled, use masking tape on all adjoining particleboard surfaces, then finish the wood. It can be stained and given a gloss or matt varnish finish. No treatment is needed for the surfaced particleboard, except to wipe it clean with a damp cloth.

STORAGE CABINET

This is intended to be a spacious cabinet a child can put many things into at the end of the day (FIG. 7-11). It would also be of use to an older child, who needs space for sports equipment, camping gear, game items, and similar bulky items. The upper part is a broad shelf into which magazines and books can be put. There would also be room for a tape recorder, typewriter and other broad and shallow items.

The cabinet makes a perfect partner to the chest of drawers (FIG. 7-15), which is of comparable size and a similar overall appearance. The two could be used in a bedroom for storing clothing, bedding, and things besides toys and activity equipment. This materials list is found in TABLE 7-6.

There are several possible ways of making both pieces of furniture. Solid wood throughout would be expensive and heavy, and getting suitable boards might be impossible. Therefore, the main parts can be made of thick plywood or surfaced

Fig. 7-11. A storage cabinet, made by traditional methods has ample storage space for large things and a broad shelf for sports equipment, tape recorders and similar things.

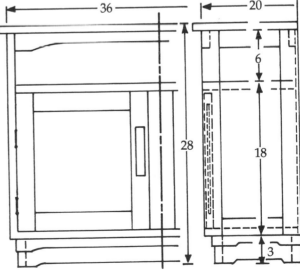

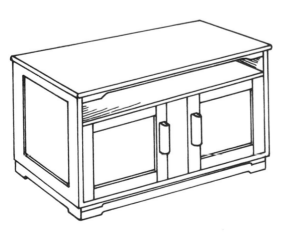

Table 7-6. Materials List for a Storage Cabinet.

4 end frames	1 × 24 × 2
4 end frames	1 × 19 × 2
2 top rails	1 × 36 × 2
2 shelf rails	1 × 35 × 2
2 shelf rails	1 × 20 × 2
2 bottom rails	1 × 35 × 2
2 bottom rails	1 × 20 × 2
1 door divider	1 × 18 × 3
2 top frames	1 × 38 × 2
2 top frames	1 × 21 × 2
4 door frames	1 × 18 × 2
4 door frames	1 × 16 × 2
2 door handles	1 × 6 × 1 ¼
2 plinths	1 × 36 × 3
2 plinths	1 × 20 × 3
2 end panels	19 × 23 × ¼ plywood
1 shelf panel	19 × 34 × ¼ plywood
1 bottom panel	19 × 34 × ¼ plywood
1 top panel	19 × 34 × ⅜ plywood
2 door panels	15 × 17 × ¼ plywood
1 back	24 × 36 × ¼ plywood

particleboard. The cabinet shown is intended to be made with thinner plywood panels framed around. This traditional way should appeal to the enthusiastic woodworker as the framed construction involves some simple joint cutting. Also it would be possible to use dowels in some joints where tenons are shown, but tenons are more appropriate to paneled work. Making furniture in this way results in light, rigid assemblies.

There is no need for the plywood and solid wood to match if the finished cabinet will be painted, but for a clear finish, plywood with surface veneer to match the surrounding wood will look best. If stain is to be used, it might be possible to make the ordinary plywood match the solid wood, but allow for the fact that plywood is more absorbent and may finish a darker color than the surrounding frame.

Nearly all the framing is 1 × 2-inch section and the plywood panels that do not take a load can be ¼ inch. The top should be thicker and so should the bottom if it is anticipated that heavy things will be put on it. The cabinet is made as a unit that is supported on a separately made plinth.

The frames for the ends and doors are plowed to take the plywood panels (FIG. 7-12A). The frame for the top is rabbeted deep enough for the thicker top panel (FIG. 7-12B), while the shelf and bottom need shallower rabbets (FIG. 7-12C). The pieces at the back of the end frames have rabbets for the back panel (FIG. 7-12D). Where the back passes over the shelf and bottom they are cut back to suit and there are no rabbets to cut. All of these parts should be prepared, slightly overlength, before starting the actual construction. Wood to make the handles could also be prepared in advance (FIG. 7-12E).

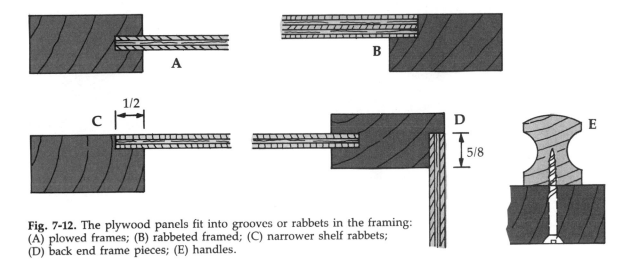

Fig. 7-12. The plywood panels fit into grooves or rabbets in the framing: (A) plowed frames; (B) rabbeted framed; (C) narrower shelf rabbets; (D) back end frame pieces; (E) handles.

The end frames (FIG. 7-13A) have mortise and tenon joints at the corners. The tenons are cut back to the bottoms of the grooves and haunched to the groove depths. The horizontal parts have the tenons (FIG. 7-13B). The mortises should be about 1 inch deep.

At the upper corners are rails under the top, both tenoned into the ends (FIG. 7-13C). The back piece is kept the full depth, but the front one is shaped and rounded (FIG. 7-13D).

At shelf level the front and back pieces should have tenons into the ends (FIG. 7-13E). The shelf itself is made up with the lengthwise pieces mortised to take the tenons on the end parts. The tenons are shouldered to the rabbet line and need not be haunched (FIG. 7-13F).

The bottom is made in a similar way to the shelf, except that it meets solid wood in the full width instead of the plywood panel and pocket screws from below can supplement the corner tenons (FIg. 7-13G). Check both shelf and bottom for width so they assemble level with the depth of the back rabbet.

The divider between the doors joins the bottom and shelf with barefaced tenons, so the front surfaces are level (FIG. 7-13H). Be careful to get the distance between shoulders exactly the same as the distance between the joints on the ends, so the shelf is not distorted. Any deflection of its front edge would be very obvious in the finished cabinet.

The first parts to assemble should be the ends. If the plywood panels are carefully squared, the ends should make up without difficulty, but check one end over the other. Pull the joints together with bar clamps, but if you drive a nail through the tenon before releasing the clamp, there is no need to wait until the glue has set. This can be done from inside where the nail head will not show in the finished cabinet.

It will probably be best to make up the frames for the shelf and bottom before adding their plywood. Joints can then be clamped tightly and the plywood trimmed to size afterwards. Slightly bevelling the plywood edge as it is planed will ensure a tight fit, so the under side goes easily into the rabbet and the top fits closely. Glue these panels in, but also use thin nails or pins as necessary. Punch them below the surface and cover them with stopping.

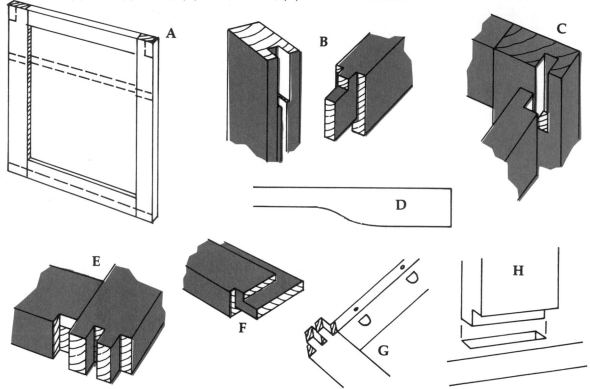

Fig. 7-13. Different types of mortise and tenon joints are used between parts of the cabinet: (A) end frames; (B) horizontal parts; (C) upper corners; (D) front piece; (E) shelf; (F) tenons; (G) corner tenons; (H) level front surfaces.

Remove surplus glue and do any sanding necessary to parts that will be difficult to reach after assembly. Check that meeting surfaces will match. Have the back panel ready, but oversize slightly. Assemble the carcass by putting the door divider in place, then join the bottom and shelf as well as the two top rails between the ends.

Check squareness by measuring diagonals, but before leaving the assembly to set, cut the back panel to size, while keeping its corners right angles. Fit it with glue and nails at about 3-inch intervals. Check squareness from above and leave the glue to set while the assembly is standing on a level surface. Put weights on a board across the top if there is any tendency to spring out of shape.

The top is made up like the shelf, with similar joints at the corners, but it overhangs the carcass by 1 inch at ends and front. If the plywood panel needs additional support, you can add intermediate cross members (FIG. 7-14A).

Round the edges and the front corners. The top can be attached to the carcass by any of the methods described for tables. There can be pocket screws upward at the ends and front. A strip of wood inside the back rail will take screws (FIG. 7-14B). If there are intermediate cross members, similar screwed strips can be used inside the front rail at these places.

Frame the doors in the same way as the cabinet ends. They finish level with the fronts of their frames and should be an easy fit in their openings. Hinge in

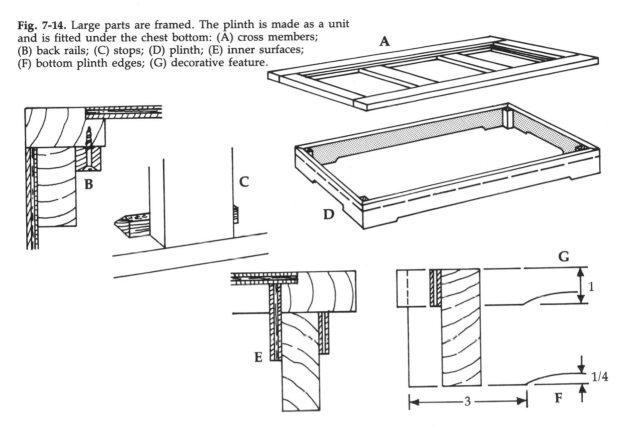

Fig. 7-14. Large parts are framed. The plinth is made as a unit and is fitted under the chest bottom: (A) cross members; (B) back rails; (C) stops; (D) plinth; (E) inner surfaces; (F) bottom plinth edges; (G) decorative feature.

the usual way and attach the handles with screws from inside. Strips extending behind the top and bottom of the door divider will act as stops (FIG. 7-14C). Fit ball or magnetic catches.

The plinth is made like an open box with mitered corners (FIG. 7-14D). Blocks inside can be screwed or dowelled as well as glued. The plinth sizes are best obtained directly from the cabinet bottom, as the plinth should be 1 inch in from the ends and front and there might have been slight variations from the intended size during making. The inner surfaces come level and this allows attaching with pieces of plywood (FIG. 7-14E).

The bottom edges of the plinth can be left straight, but they are shown cut away ¼ inch except at the corners (FIG. 7-14F). This helps to make the cabinet stand firm if there is any unevenness in the floor. A decorative feature could be narrow pieces of plywood put around the front and ends, with similar profiles (FIG. 7-14G). They could be painted or stained in contrast to the main color scheme.

CHEST OF DRAWERS

There are some things that are better kept in drawers than in a cabinet and this item is intended to be a companion piece to the cabinet (FIG. 7-11). The two can be used together as a matched pair.

The arrangement shown has two narrow drawers at the top and two deep full width ones below (FIG. 7-15). This arrangement could be modified to have all

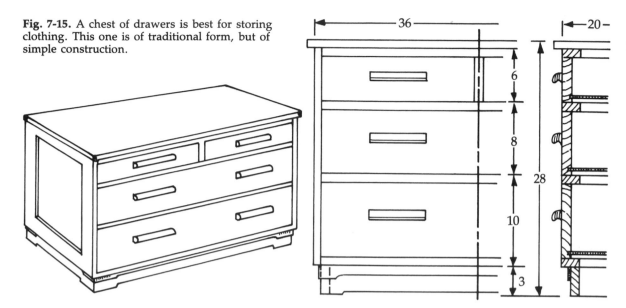

Fig. 7-15. A chest of drawers is best for storing clothing. This one is of traditional form, but of simple construction.

the drawers full width or the lower part could be divided to take three drawers instead of two. The overall sizes are the same as for the cabinet and much of the body construction is the same. See TABLE 7-7 for a complete materials list.

The supports for the drawers are made in a similar way to the shelf in the cabinet, but without the plywood panel. This applies to the frame under the top as well as to the part under the bottom drawer.

Start by making the two ends, and then mark on them where the drawer rails will come (FIG. 7-16A). At these places put strips to thicken the panels and form drawer guides. These should be level with the framing and extend behind the rails (FIG. 7-16B). The drawer guides allow the ends of the drawer rail frames to be made straight across at all positions, instead of having to be shaped into the panels as in the cabinet shelf. They will also take pocket screwing from below at each position, as suggested for the cabinet bottom.

Each drawer rail frame is made up by simple mortise and tenon joints (FIG. 7-16C), as there are no plywood panels to be fitted. Then the long members extend to make tenons into the ends (FIG. 7-16D). It would be possible to substitute dowels for tenons in both directions (FIG. 7-16E). The top and bottom surfaces of these drawer rail frames act as runners and kickers for the drawers, so be careful that the joining surfaces are level at the corners.

The divider between the top drawers is best made as a frame in a similar way. Front and back uprights are tenoned into the rails (FIG. 7-16F). The other pieces act as drawer guides.

The back of the chest is a piece of plywood set into rabbets in the ends and screwed to the back parts of the rail frames. A drawer pushed back hard might put a heavy load on the plywood, so screws are preferable to nails at the joints. However, front stops (described later) should remove most of the risk of hitting the back.

Make up all the rail frames and check that they match. Prepare the divider and fit between the two top frames. Assemble all the frames to the ends, check squareness, and add the back plywood.

Table 7-7. Materials List for a Chest of Drawers.

4 end frames	1 × 24 × 2
4 end frames	1 × 19 × 2
8 rails	1 × 35 × 2
8 rails	1 × 20 × 2
2 dividers	1 × 20 × 2
2 dividers	1 × 6 × 2
2 plinths	1 × 36 × 3
2 plinths	1 × 20 × 3
2 top frames	1 × 38 × 2
2 top frames	1 × 21 × 2
2 end panels	19 × 23 × ¼ plywood
1 top panel	19 × 34 × ⅜ plywood
1 back	24 × 36 × ¼ plywood
2 drawer fronts	5 × 18 × 1
1 drawer front	7 × 34 × 1
1 drawer front	8 × 34 × 1
6 handles	1 × 6 × 1¼
4 drawer sides	5 × 20 × ⅝
2 drawer sides	8 × 20 × ⅝
2 drawer sides	8 × 20 × ⅝
2 drawer backs	4½ × 18 × ⅝
1 drawer back	6½ × 34 × ⅝
1 drawer back	7½ × 34 × ⅝
2 drawer bottoms	18 × 20 × ¼ plywood
2 drawer bottoms	20 × 34 × ¼ plywood

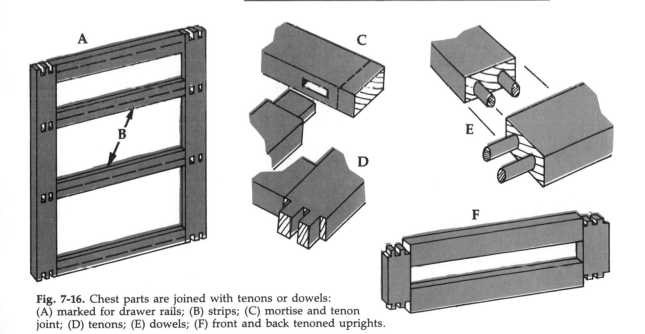

Fig. 7-16. Chest parts are joined with tenons or dowels: (A) marked for drawer rails; (B) strips; (C) mortise and tenon joint; (D) tenons; (E) dowels; (F) front and back tenoned uprights.

Fig. 7-17. Drawers may be solid wood or plywood, with wooden handles and stops on the front rails: (A) strips under plywood bottom; (B) wide rubber stripping; (C) front stops: (D) handle.

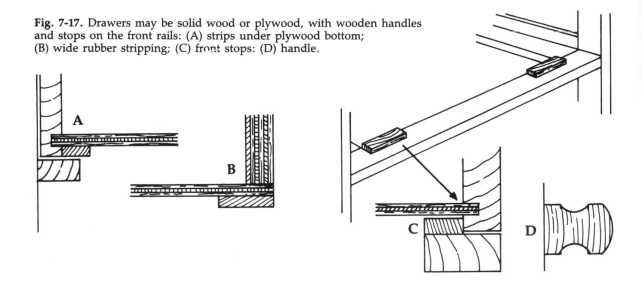

The plinth is exactly the same as that for the cabinet. Make it and attach it at this stage.

The drawers can be made in any of the ways already described. The fronts should be wood that matches the rest of the chest, but softwoods could be used for the inner parts. Sides and backs could be ½-inch plywood instead of the slightly thicker solid wood specified.

A heavily loaded drawer puts heavy friction on the meeting surfaces, so make these as wide as possible to reduce wear. Strips under the plywood bottom can be extended to overlap the runners (FIG. 7-17A). If you use ½-inch plywood for the sides, cutting a groove for the bottom might not be satisfactory. A simple way of dealing with this is to fasten the bottom under sides of reduced depth and put a wide rubbing strip under that (FIG. 7-17B).

The drawer fronts should close level with the front of the chest. With drawers of this size it is better to arrange stops at the front than to rely on the ends of the drawer sides hitting the back of the chest. Stops a few inches long can be put at two or three places across each front rail that comes under a drawer. Make them as thick as they can be and still clear the drawer bottom. Arrange the front edge of each stop so it brings the drawer to a halt in the right position (FIG. 7-17C). It might be wise to screw the stops on dry at first so their positions can be corrected if necessary, then apply glue and join them permanently.

Drawer handles could be metal or plastic if desired and need not match the cabinet exactly but the handles should be similar to those on the cabinet doors. They could be of symmetrical section (FIG. 7-12E) or they could be modified to look almost the same, but with a deeper groove on the underside (FIG. 7-17D).

The chest top is the same as that for the cabinet and it can be screwed upward through the top frame all around. Leave final fitting of the top until all drawers are fitted and found to work satisfactorily, as it is easier to check on their operation without the top.

COMBINED UNIT

Although separate items of furniture allow various arrangements in a room and it is possible to move one piece elsewhere without affecting other things, there are places where one piece of furniture combining several functions might be preferred. This applies where space is small, as a combined unit will normally take up less than several units of the same total capacity.

It is also a good idea when a child is expected to restrict his activities and toys or hobby material to a particular place. If the storage space is all in one piece of furniture, there can be no doubt where things have to be put.

The design shown (FIGS. 7-18 and 7-19) is just a suggestion. There are many possible variations. The sizes given should bring everything within the reach of a child aged about 8 years or older. (For a complete material list, see TABLE 7-8.) There is a main body and a front divided down the center so there are three drawers at one side and a door at the other. Both halves could have doors or there could be drawers in both halves or long drawers across the width. The top of the chest is intended to be a work surface, but at the back there is a bookshelf unit that is screwed on and could be removed. The unit is shown with one high shelf so there could be large books below it or space for large toys or construction kits. Closer shelves could be fitted and the back might be extended upwards with more shelves—to room height if desired. Consider how the furniture will be moved, but if the bookcase part can be taken off, it should be possible to move the parts through any doorway and around bends in staircases.

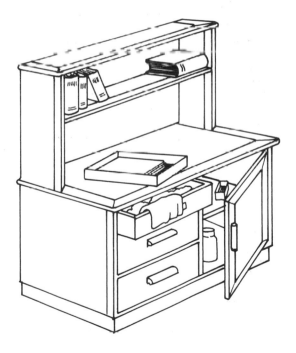

Fig. 7-18. A combined unit gets the functions of many separate pieces of furniture into a small space and gives a child a center for his play and hobbies.

Fig. 7-19. Suggested sizes for the combined unit.

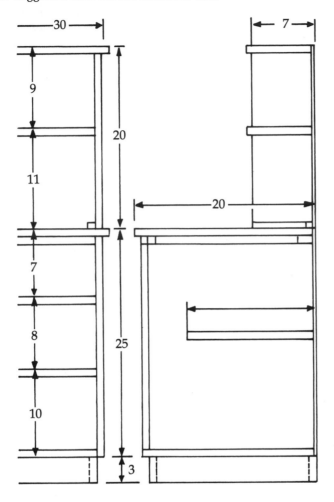

All of the major construction is intended to be in ¾-inch plywood, with exposed edges lipped with solid wood. Plow a groove in the plywood and make a tongue in a piece of solid wood to fit in it (FIG. 7-20A). If the solid wood is made slightly too thick, it can be planed to match after gluing. Miter any corners that are exposed (FIG. 7-20B).

The lipping could be treated as a decorative feature by making it in a wood that contrasts with the plywood. A dark rim to light colored plywood looks attractive and is complementary to the otherwise rather severe lines of the design.

Prepare the pieces of plywood that have to be lipped first. The top of the bookcase and the top of the chest should be lipped at fronts and ends. All other parts that show their edges to the front, including the bookshelf, the chest bottom and its division as well as its ends, should be lipped on those edges.

The rail under the top, the drawer dividers and other narrow parts can be solid wood. The door and drawer fronts would look attractive lipped all around, especially if the furniture is expected to have long use and is given a clear finish.

Table 7-8. Materials List for a Combined Unit.

2 ends	18	×	25	×	¾	plywood
2 ends	2	×	25	×	¾	
1 divider	18	×	25	×	¾	plywood
1 divider	2	×	25	×	¾	
1 chest top	19	×	30	×	¾	plywood
1 chest top	2	×	32	×	¾	
1 chest top	2	×	20	×	¾	
1 bottom	18	×	30	×	¾	plywood
1 bottom	2	×	30	×	¾	
2 top frames	2	×	30	×	¾	
2 top frames	1	×	19	×	¾	
4 drawer dividers	2	×	14	×	¾	
4 drawer dividers	1	×	19	×	¾	
1 shelf	14	×	19	×	¾	plywood
2 shelf battens	1½	×	14	×	¾	
2 plinths	3	×	28	×	¾	
2 plinths	3	×	19	×	¾	
1 door	14	×	23	×	¾	plywood
2 doors	2	×	15	×	¾	
2 doors	2	×	24	×	¾	
1 drawer front	9¼	×	14	×	¾	
1 drawer front	7¼	×	14	×	¾	
1 drawer front	5½	×	14	×	¾	
1 drawer back	8½	×	14	×	½	
1 drawer back	6½	×	14	×	½	
1 drawer back	4¾	×	14	×	½	
2 drawer sides	9¼	×	19	×	½	
2 drawer sides	7¼	×	19	×	½	
2 drawer sides	5½	×	19	×	½	
3 drawer bottoms	14	×	19	×	¼	plywood
4 handles from 1	1	×	24	×	1¼	
2 bookcase sides	6	×	20	×	¾	plywood
2 bookcase sides	2	×	20	×	¾	
1 bookcase top	7	×	30	×	¾	plywood
1 bookcase top	2	×	30	×	¾	
2 bookcase tops	2	×	8	×	¾	
1 shelf	7	×	30	×	¾	plywood
1 shelf	2	×	30	×	¾	
Bookcase joint from 1	¾	×	44	×	¾	

For a painted finish the whole piece of furniture could be made with the plywood edges uncovered. If care is taken to avoid tearing out the edges and they are sanded, a few coats of paint will disguise the exposed plys.

As plywood does not take well to many of the usual joints for solid wood, it is better to use screws with their heads sunk by counterboring, then plugged in many of the main joints. There are, however, some places where dowels are more appropriate.

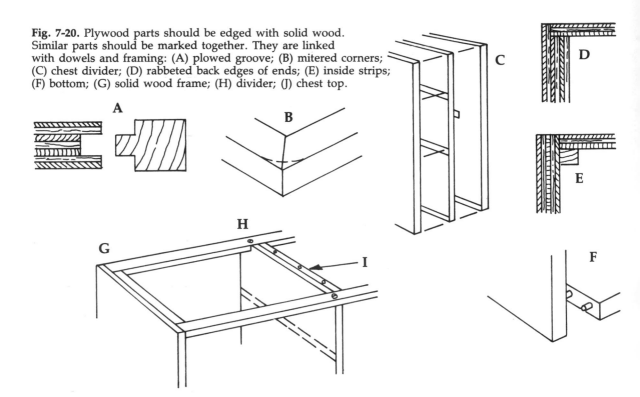

Fig. 7-20. Plywood parts should be edged with solid wood. Similar parts should be marked together. They are linked with dowels and framing: (A) plowed groove; (B) mitered corners; (C) chest divider; (D) rabbeted back edges of ends; (E) inside strips; (F) bottom; (G) solid wood frame; (H) divider; (J) chest top.

The chest divider and the two ends can be marked out together to get overall sizes and spacings correct (FIG. 7-20C). Cut the divider to length and mark one side of one for the drawer dividers and the other side for the shelf. The back edges of the ends should be rabbeted (FIG. 7-20D), but if there is a risk of the plywood breaking out, there can be strips inside for the plywood chest back (FIG. 7-20E).

The bottom goes right across and fits between the ends, either with screws or dowels (FIG. 7-20F). Under the top there is a solid wood frame of the same size, with its corners dowelled and its ends screwed to the chest ends (FIG. 7-20G). The divider is screwed upward through the bottom and downward through the top frame (FIG. 7-20H) with a strip across it on the side away from the drawers for screwing upward into the chest top (FIG. 7-20I).

The drawer dividers are made up as frames, similar to the top frame, but fitting between the end and the chest divider (FIG. 7-21A). Be careful that corners are square, the runner parts are screwed at right angles to the front, and spaces between them are parallel (FIG. 7-21B). If a shelf is to be provided, it can rest on bearers, so it can be removed (FIG. 7-21C). The door can be hinged at either side, but unless there is a special reason for doing otherwise it is most convenient to have its handle near the center of the chest.

The back is a piece of thin plywood. Although the bookcase part will hide its edge if taken over the chest top, it is probably better to rabbet the top, so the back plywood will not show if the chest is ever used without the bookcase (FIG. 7-21D).

The plinth comes level with the back, but is set in about ¾ inch at ends and front (FIG. 7-21). Back corners can lap, but the front corners should be mitered.

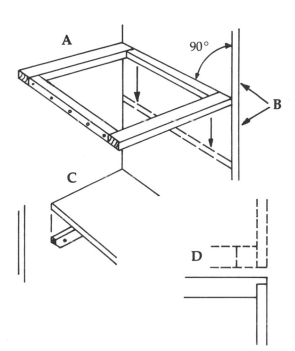

A

90°

B

C

D

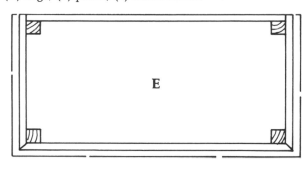

Fig. 7-21. Assemble parts squarely.
Fit the plinth with screwed blocks:
(A) dividers; (B) parallel spaces; (C) shelf;
(D) edge; (E) plinth; (F) inside blocks.

E

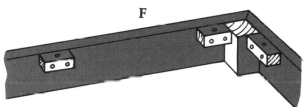

F

All four corners can be strengthened with blocks glued inside. Attach the plinth with screws upward through blocks inside (FIG. 7-21F).

The drawers can be made in any of the ways already described. If their fronts are solid wood, dovetails will be the best joints. Otherwise a screwed lap joint can be used. Fit stops to the front drawer rails. Choose or make drawer and door handles that match.

Next, make the two ends of the bookcase. Like the ends of the chest they should have rabbets for the back (FIG. 7-22A). The top could also be rabbeted, but as it is above the line of sight, it would not matter if the back plywood went over it (FIG. 7-22B). The top projects at the ends and front and it can be attached to the sides with screws or dowels (FIG. 7-22C). There could be shallow dados through only one or two plys to give a positive location (FIG. 7-22D), but there would still have to be dowels or screws.

For the shelf joints I suggest you make dados to resist the downward load, along with dowels or screws (FIG. 7-22E). If the front of the shelf projects the same amount as the top it can cover the dado ends (FIG. 7-22F). At the bottom of the bookcase arrange strips around the inside of the ends and back for screwing into the chest top. (FIG. 7-22G).

This completes the basic construction, but there are some possible modifications. For instance, there could be intermediate uprights in the bookcase to prevent partial rows of books from falling over (FIG. 7-23A). One or more drawers could be slung below the shelf for small items. The drawer can run on hooked pieces which are hidden by an overlapping front (FIG. 7-23B).

In addition, there could be racks at the back of the lower part of the bookcase for tools, paint brushes, and similar things. One rack could go the whole width

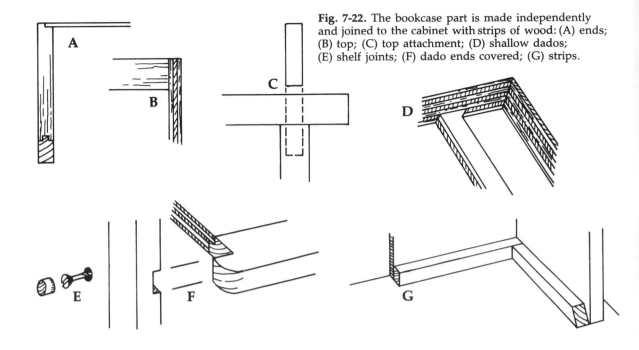

Fig. 7-22. The bookcase part is made independently and joined to the cabinet with strips of wood: (A) ends; (B) top; (C) top attachment; (D) shallow dados; (E) shelf joints; (F) dado ends covered; (G) strips.

and be pierced with holes and slots (FIG. 7-23C). If it is attached by screwing through the back, it can be removed if alterations are needed.

The inside of the door can be another place for racks. Tools could have their fitted rack (FIG. 7-23D) or spring clips can be used. Another type of rack would hold flat papers, like sheet music or thin booklets (FIG. 7-23E). Coiled cord or loops of ribbon could hang from pegs. These could be pieces of dowel rod angled upward (FIG. 7-23F). Screw hooks would be better driven into a batten than directly into the door because then anything hanging would be kept clear of the door.

It is also possible to fit racks at one or both ends of the chest. There could be a rack for magazines and other flat papers. Its front might be a piece of plywood or several strips of wood (FIG. 7-24A). Another end fitting could be a towel rail, made with a thick dowel rod supported in holes in blocks screwed to the chest (FIG. 7-24B). Such a rack could be doubled with lighter dowel rods into staggered holes (FIG. 7-24C).

A board for drawing or modelling could be stored on battens so it rests like a lid inside one of the drawers (FIG. 7-24D). A sliding tray or pencil rack, as described for some desks, could be fitted inside a drawer. A rack for a drawing board could go on one end.

In any place where something is to hang or fit into racks, it is a good idea to either draw the outline of it or paint its shape in a different color, so it is possible to see when the thing is not in place and the pattern there shows the child which way it has to be replaced.

There could be a mirror fitted inside the back of the bookcase, particularly for a girl making clothes for herself or her dolls.

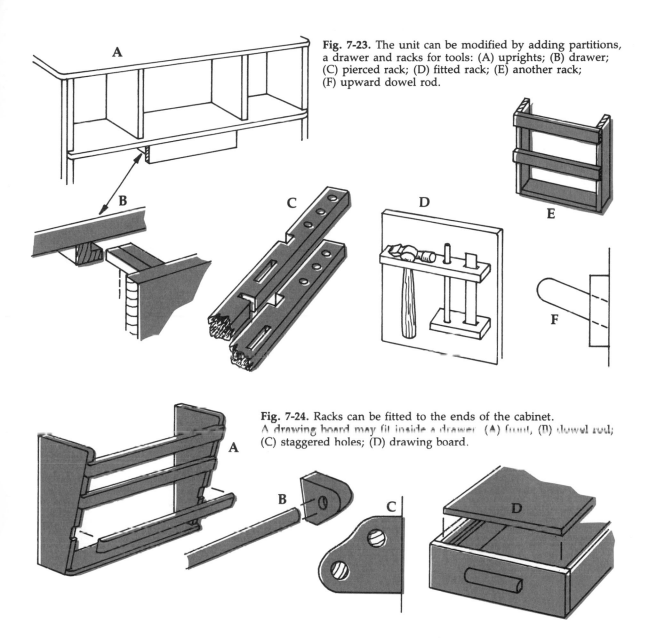

Fig. 7-23. The unit can be modified by adding partitions, a drawer and racks for tools: (A) uprights; (B) drawer; (C) pierced rack; (D) fitted rack; (E) another rack; (F) upward dowel rod.

Fig. 7-24. Racks can be fitted to the ends of the cabinet. A drawing board may fit inside a drawer. (A) front; (B) dowel rod; (C) staggered holes; (D) drawing board.

SMALL CHEST OF DRAWERS

This chest is intended for use where space is limited (FIG. 7-25). It could stand beside a bed in a small room and be used for a child's clothes, while the top will hold a bedside lamp and many other things. The three drawers increase in depth toward the bottom. Besides looking better than three drawers of equal depth, this arrangement encourages larger and heavier things to be put low, where they assist stability. There is enough clearance below the bottom drawer to allow floor cleaning without moving the chest.

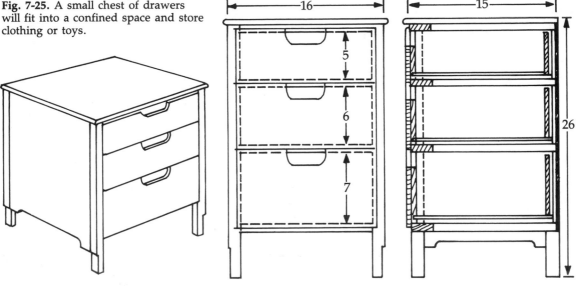

Fig. 7-25. A small chest of drawers will fit into a confined space and store clothing or toys.

Table 7-9. Materials List for a Small Chest of Drawers.

4 legs	1¼ × 26 × 1¼
5 rails	2 × 15 × ⅝
8 rails	2 × 16 × ⅝
1 top	16 × 18 × ⅝
1 drawer front	5 × 15 × ⅝
1 drawer front	5½ × 16 × ½
1 drawer front	6 × 15 × ⅝
1 drawer front	6½ × 16 × ½
1 drawer front	7 × 15 × ⅝
1 drawer front	7½ × 16 × ½
1 drawer back	4 × 15 × ½
1 drawer back	5 × 15 × ½
1 drawer back	6 × 15 × ½
2 drawer sides	5 × 15 × ½
2 drawer sides	6 × 15 × ½
2 drawer sides	7 × 15 × ½
6 drawer guides	1 × 15 × 1
2 sides	15 × 23 × ¼ plywood
1 back	15 × 22 × ¼ plywood
3 drawer bottoms	15 × 15 × ¼ plywood

The method of construction shown uses conventional joints. The materials list is found in TABLE 7-9. Dowels might be substituted in some places.

The back and side panels are thin plywood level with the leg surfaces. For a painted finish it does not matter if the surface colors match, but for a clear finish the side plywood veneer could match the solid wood. Or there would be an interesting effect if their colors were very different. The top could be plywood, either untreated around the edges or with lipping. It could be veneered or plastic-covered particleboard.

Start by marking all four legs together (FIG. 7-26A). Mark where the drawer dividers come on all legs, but only cut joints in the front legs. At the back legs, notch and screw the dresser runners. Cut rabbets for the plywood (FIG. 7-26B).

The plywood panels do not continue below the bottom rails. If facilities are available for making stopped rabbets, they can be stopped there and let the legs continue the full square to the floor. As the chest normally stands against a wall, rabbets cut in the easier way right through would not show on the backs of the rear legs. At the sides a rabbet cut the full length can be disguised by reducing the thickness of the bottom part of the leg (FIG. 7-26C).

The front rails are all the same. The simplest way to prepare them to take tenons in the side rails is to plow grooves in the whole length (FIG. 7-26D). The unwanted parts of the grooves will not show in the finished chest. At the front corners, each rail should have a tenon into the leg. Notch around each as far as the side rabbet (FIG. 7-26E). The top mortise is open, but the others are the normal closed form. The important rail measurements are between the shoulders at the front. Mark all the rails together and cut these lines with a knife.

At the top there is a rear rail joined to the rear legs in the same way as at the front, but in this small chest there is no need for back drawer rails at the other positions. Instead, each side rail has a tenon into the lowered groove in its front rail and is shouldered to fit the inside back leg as far as the rabbet, with a piece extending over the back leg for screwing (FIG. 7-26F).

Fig. 7-26. Mark out legs together. Let plywood into rabbets and join parts with mortise and tenon joints: (A) marking four legs; (B) cut rabbets; (C) thinner bottom part of leg; (D) grooved front rails; (E) tenoned rail; (F) extending back leg piece.

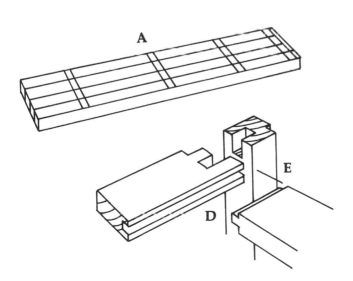
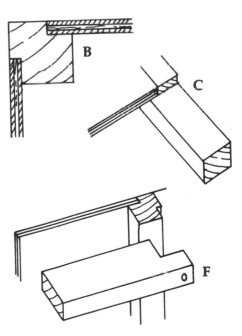

With all the parts prepared, make up the front by gluing and clamping the drawer rails to the legs, while checking squareness. Join the top rail to the rear legs and fit the back plywood. Check that this assembly matches the front. Leave the glue to set.

Join the back and front with the drawer runners and rails. Clamp the parts together and add the side plywood panels. Check squareness when viewed from above. Fit the drawer guides (FIG. 7-27A). Get their inner surfaces level with the inner surfaces of the legs, so the drawers will slide smoothly and not meet any uneven joints.

The drawers shown are made with dovetails (FIG. 7-27B), but any of the simpler methods could be used. The false fronts will act as stops, so the drawers should be made so they do not quite reach the plywood back. Drawer backs are kept below the top edges of the sides and come above the plywood bottom, which slides in plowed grooves (FIG. 7-27C).

Make each drawer complete except for its false front. Try it in position and make any adjustments needed. The three false fronts should make one pattern, meeting closely and with their edges level. All edges overlapping legs should be round, as should the top edge of the top drawer and the bottom edge of the bottom drawer. Where the drawers meet, however, leave the edges square, with no more clearance than is needed for easy movement (FIG. 7-27D).

You could fit ordinary handles to the drawers, but those shown have cutouts that allow a hand to enter and grip the drawer front. The false front could have

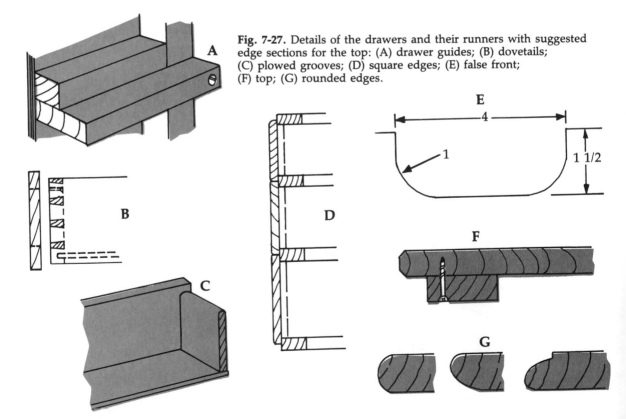

Fig. 7-27. Details of the drawers and their runners with suggested edge sections for the top: (A) drawer guides; (B) dovetails; (C) plowed grooves; (D) square edges; (E) false front; (F) top; (G) rounded edges.

its cutout shaped before attaching to the drawer (FIG. 7-27E), then the inner front shaped to match. Round the hollow in section and take off any sharp corners.

The chest top overhangs at the sides and front and is attached with screws upward through the top frame (FIG. 7-27F). Sharpness should be removed from corners and the edges could be rounded or molded (FIG. 7-27G).

TILT BOX

A young child is more likely to put things away in a box with an opening at the top than he is to use drawers or open a door. This unit should appeal to him since besides being a box with a lid at the center, there are tilt bins at the sides which he can draw out to put things in. Then they drop back under their own weight (FIGS. 7-28 and 7-29). It is a simple enough mechanism for the child to appreciate, as there are no knobs to turn nor levers to operate. TABLE 7-10 offers a complete materials list.

Construction is almost entirely in ½-inch plywood. With good quality plywood it will probably be sufficient to glue edges and join them with thin screws. If it is a type of plywood that tends to split when screws are driven edgewise, you can fit strips of wood around the angles in the box section to provide enough stiffening for the whole unit.

The main body is made with two spacers fitted between the sides and attached to a bottom, with all of these parts simple rectangles (FIG. 7-30A). There should be a strip across the top of each spacer to take the lifting lid (FIG. 7-30B) and similar pieces go around the other internal angles if necessary (FIG. 7-30C).

Make the plinth below the bottom out of 1-inch-square strips, mitered at the corners, and attach them by screwing down through the box bottom (FIG. 7-30D).

Each bin pivots on two screws or bolts. It's a good idea to make a full-size drawing of one end of the box and a bin to get the shape of the bin sides (FIG. 7-31A). Locate the center on which the bin will pivot and draw a curve for the top edge, using the pivot point as the center for compass. The stop that limits the movement of the bin is a piece of dowel rod drilled to take a fixing screw (FIG. 7-31B). Mark where this is to come and draw further curves for the slot (FIG. 7-31C). It might be sufficient to use wood screws, but a small bolt and nut would be better able to stand up to frequent use (FIG. 7-31D).

Fig. 7-28. A box with a central compartment and tilting end boxes may be finished brightly to please the child or given a finish to match other furniture.

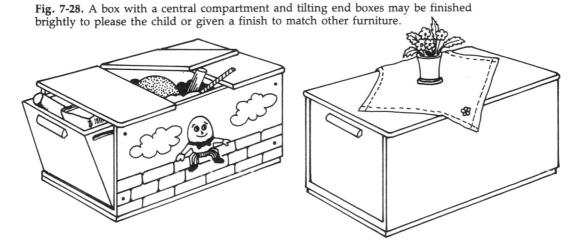

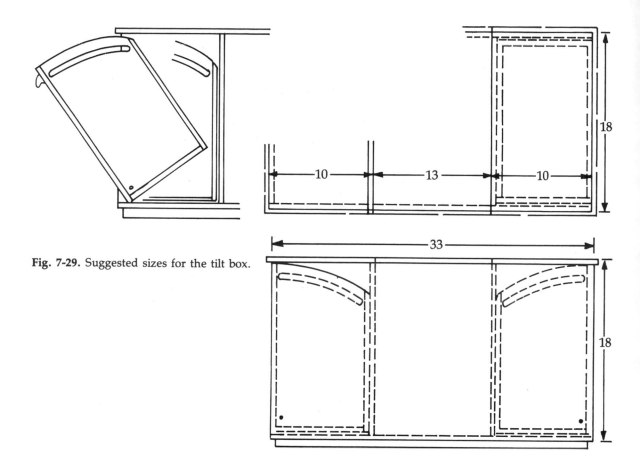

Fig. 7-29. Suggested sizes for the tilt box.

Table 7-10. Materials List for a Tilt Box.

2 sides	18 × 33 × ½ plywood
2 dividers	17 × 18 × ½ plywood
1 bottom	18 × 33 × ½ plywood
2 plinths	1 × 32 × 1
2 plinths	1 × 17 × 1
1 top	13 × 20 × ½ plywood
2 tops	11 × 20 × ½ plywood
2 top bearers	½ × 18 × ½
4 bin sides	9 × 16 × ½ plywood
2 bin fronts	16 × 17 × ½ plywood
2 bin backs	14 × 17 × ½ plywood
2 bin bottoms	9 × 17 × ½ plywood
2 handles	1 × 6 × 1 ¼

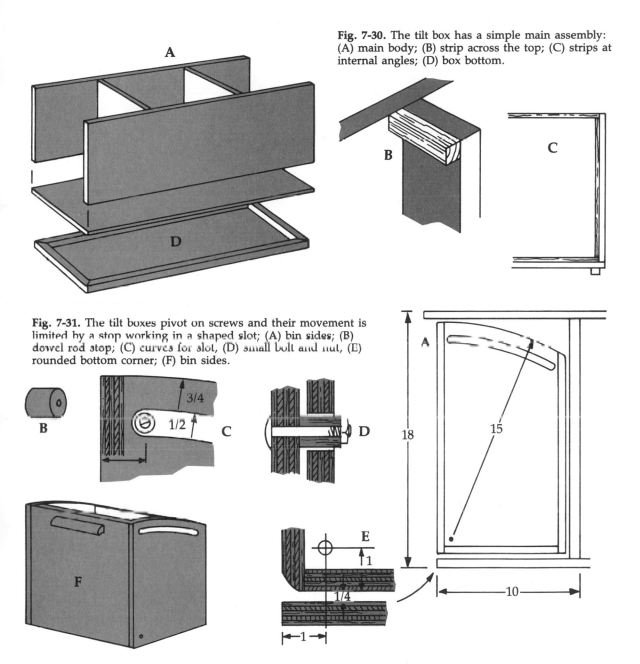

Fig. 7-30. The tilt box has a simple main assembly: (A) main body; (B) strip across the top; (C) strips at internal angles; (D) box bottom.

Fig. 7-31. The tilt boxes pivot on screws and their movement is limited by a stop working in a shaped slot; (A) bin sides; (B) dowel rod stop; (C) curves for slot, (D) small bolt and nut, (E) rounded bottom corner; (F) bin sides.

At the bottom there will have to be about ¼-inch clearance and the bottom corner of the front of the bin should be rounded slightly (FIG. 7 31E). Mark the position of the pivot and stop on one actual side. Make one bin side and try its action with awls pushed through these points.

If the trial assembly functions satisfactorily, make the other bin sides and the parts to fit between them (FIG. 7-31F). Drill through for ³⁄₁₆-inch bolts at the pivot and stop positions. Make wooden handles or fit metal or plastic drawer pulls near the tops of the bins. Assemble to check the correct action, then disassemble for painting.

The top is in three parts. If you want the grain to show through the final finish, cut these parts from one piece so the grain matches. Then fasten down the two end sections permanently. The central piece fits between them. It could have a frame on the underside to fit in the opening so it can be lifted away completely, but it will probably be better to hinge it at one side, or put hinges on the surface between it and one end section so it will swing flat on to the end. If it is hinged at one side, use a strut or a cord to stop it from swinging past upright.

The top should overhang a small amount all around. Allow a little for final trimming, then assemble the three parts of the top together and trim the edges to match. They could be molded, but it should be sufficient to round the corners and take the sharpness off the edges.

This piece of furniture is probably best finished by painting in bright colors for a young child to use. However, it is the sort of thing that might have uses for other items besides toys when the child gets older, so a matching furniture finish might be more appropriate, although the first bright colors could be painted over later with something less boisterous.

8

Bedroom Furniture

THE YOUNGEST CHILD spends more than half of his or her time in bed. Even an adult spends about one third of his life in bed, so a bedroom is a very important part of a home. In many homes the bedroom is also the only reasonably private place where a child can get away from others. In this case, the bedroom becomes a playroom or activity room, as well as somewhere to sleep.

In a tightly packed house, particularly with several children, there might be a need for a room that is convertible, with beds to stack or rearrange so as much space as possible is available for daytime activities. If the room is shared by two children, there can be some furniture of use to both of them. However, a child appreciates having his own things and there should be items that each can call his own. This is particularly important when there is a wide age difference.

In most homes the children's rooms are small. This means that scaling down furniture to suit the smaller user will also help to economize space. It is also worthwhile to think about ways of making dual-purpose furniture, either convertible for second uses or items that combine two functions at the same time and take up less space than separate items.

One possibility is to have the main items along one wall, with storage for adult reach above that intended for the child, and a dresser and chest arranged between the taller items. Much depends on the window disposition and the arrangement of artificial light. Drawer space under a bed also helps to avoid wasted space.

Bunk beds are good savers of floor space and the arrangement usually appeals to the children concerned, although making the beds every day might not be as simple as with independent beds.

If you plan bedroom furniture that allows for the child's growth, you will avoid trouble later on. A wardrobe might be made high enough for later use, but a lower rail for hanging smaller clothes can temporarily be put across and moved up as the clothing gets longer. Things like dressers can be made to suit a taller child with a stool provided for the younger child at first, but if you add a mirror that can have its angle adjusted, one dresser height can accommodate children over quite a large age range.

Beds are not as easy to adjust to size. A crib or cot for example is not needed for long. Sometimes the arrival of a child causes the parents to build a most elaborate crib that only gets a brief period of use. If one will be needed for other children or it is to be passed to parents of another new child, the work might be justified, but in many cases it would be better to make a simple crib that could be disassembled when no longer needed. It can also be made to fold, so that it can be stored and brought out occasionally for a visitor with a baby.

It is best to make a bed large enough to be of use for several years. If space permits it can even be made long enough for an adult, so it will serve as a spare bed for anyone.

If you only need to make one piece of furniture to be used with the existing furniture, planning it is quite simple. Needs and available space will be the main considerations. If you intend to fill an otherwise empty room, it is worthwhile to draw a plan to scale, then cut pieces of cardboard to the same scale to represent the furniture. These can then be moved around and different positions tried. Check that the room door can swing open without touching furniture and that there will be sufficient access past furniture. The space between furniture near the entryway of a room should not be less than the width of the doorway. If projections a short distance into the room cause a narrowing of space, a child running in or out might knock against them.

Another consideration is light. Light from the window should not be blocked. It is particularly important that light should fall on the dresser area and it would be wrong to put a wardrobe or tall chest so it casts a shadow there. Artificial light can often be moved around to suit, but it will be less trouble to make use of existing light.

Another consideration is heating or cooling. If air is to circulate, nothing should be done to obstruct or deflect it and make it less effective. If heating is by a radiator, there is no use arranging something too close to it since it will absorb the heat instead of letting it spread into the room.

The floor plan and its cardboard outline models will provide most of the information needed on possible sizes of things and where to place them, but make allowances for windows and other wall openings or attachments. A chest can be made to come as high as the bottom of a window, yet it would be a nuisance if a few inches higher. When you make your own furniture, variations like this can be allowed for, but buying ready-made furniture means having to accept it as it is, even if it is not quite the size you wish.

Avoid packing a room too tightly. A child needs plenty of floor space. There are certain essential items of furniture, but it is possible to design them so they make the best use of space and leave as much open area as possible. As much as possible, put furniture around the wall, where it is less dangerous than anything free-standing near the center of the floor. Mirrors can be particularly hazardous, especially if they are adjustable. It should not be possible for a child to get behind them and there should be enough of the furniture's surface projecting in front of them to offer protection.

A child might spend some time in a bedroom due to illness, so the needs of a child confined to bed should be considered. The headboard could include racks for books and enough side table area for toys and other things to be within reach. Some sort of bed tray to stand over the child's legs would be worth having and either this or a separate item could serve as a book support. There might also be a support to go behind pillows to make sitting in bed more comfortable. Anything that makes staying in bed more endurable will benefit the parents as well as the sick child.

It is probably best to avoid electrical appliances that the child can touch. If there are built-in electric lights or other fittings, they should be of the type where an inquisitive child cannot meddle with them and open anything where there would be a risk of electric shock. If there is a light over a mirror it is better if placed high and switched on with a cord than where a child might remove a lamp or uncover a switch.

Bedroom furniture does not have to be quite as utilitarian as storage boxes and chests. The first requirement is to make the thing functional, but it can also be good looking. It is no use making something that looks attractive, but does not do its job properly. A child will not appreciate furniture that is of an unusual design but will not do what he wants it to. If he is to put things away, he is most likely to do so if the action is simple. If the furniture has to be opened in a particular way because of its special design, or things can only be hung in a certain manner or sequence, those clothes or other things are going to find a place on the floor. Functionalism is of prime importance. Decoration only comes second.

For very young children bright colors and painted designs on furniture are especially appropriate. Certainly something like the surfaces of a crib can be given bright decorations with decals and pictures of nursery rhyme and cartoon characters. However, this phase does not last long; therefore, it is not such a good idea to decorate things like dressers, wardrobes, and beds. It is probably best to make such items out of plain wood, with stain and varnish or a polish finish. If a good wood is finished in this way, the result is long-lasting furniture that will be of use to a child past the stage of nursery rhyme pictures.

Even if a good wood is not used, the painted finish can be more subdued. Bright wallpaper and gaily colored cloths and bed covers can serve the moment and then be changed to something more appropriate for an older child. The furniture underneath always remains unaltered.

The examples given in this chapter show a large range of styles and constructions. Although each individual item is complete, it is possible to combine parts of one piece of furniture with another, or just use ideas from another. I suggest you look through the whole chapter first, noting ideas, even if the object immediately in mind appears to be taken care of by one design. There may be particular facets of another design that could be incorporated to enhance functionalism.

CRIB

This crib or cot is of simple construction and is made to fold (FIG. 8-1). The support for the mattress lifts out and the ends fold inward (FIG. 8-1A) so the back and front come close together. Length and height remain the same, but the assembly

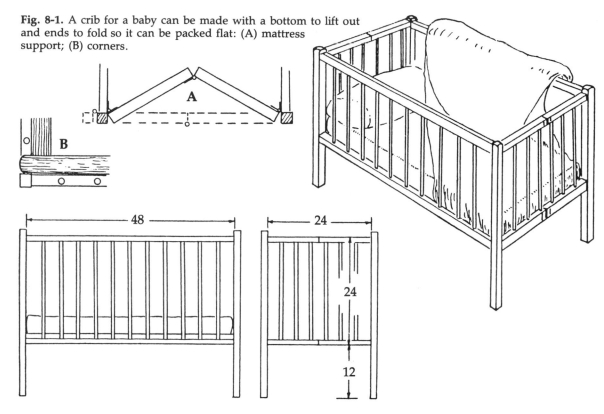

Fig. 8-1. A crib for a baby can be made with a bottom to lift out and ends to fold so it can be packed flat: (A) mattress support; (B) corners.

reduced to just a few inches thick. When the bottom is in place the frame is locked and there is no risk of accidental folding.

Sizes depend on the mattress you chose before starting on the woodwork. There are several sizes and thicknesses available. Most are about 48 inches long, but widths can be from 18 inches upward. The crib shown is intended for a mattress 48 × 24 inches. If you choose a thin mattress, there must be some springing in the support, but if it is 3 inches or more in thickness the mattress itself provides all the springing a baby needs and the support below it need not be flexible.

It is still advisable, however, to make it open for hygienic reasons and to allow air in and out of the mattress when it compresses or expands. Rubber or plastic foam is the usual interior material for this type of mattress. Also, measure the mattress carefully as dimensions might vary by an inch or so from those specified. Adjust the size you make the woodwork accordingly. The materials list is found in TABLE 8-1.

The sections of wood specified are fairly light so the whole crib is easy to move and store when not in use. These sections suit straight-grained hardwood, but if there is any doubt whether the wood is strong enough or holding its shape, they can be increased slightly. The rungs are pieces of ½-inch-diameter dowel rods. Standard 48-inch lengths will cut economically. If overall sizes are altered, allow for the dowel centers to be not more than 4 inches apart. The number of rungs along the sides do not matter, but at the ends there should be an even number of rungs to allow for folding in the middle.

Table 8-1. Materials List for a Crib.

4 legs	$1\frac{1}{4} \times 36 \times 1\frac{1}{4}$
4 rails	$1\frac{1}{4} \times 50 \times 1$
4 rails	$1\frac{1}{4} \times 26 \times 1$
2 bottoms	$2 \times 50 \times \frac{3}{4}$
2 bottoms	$2 \times 24 \times \frac{3}{4}$
34 rungs	$\frac{1}{2} \times 24$ dowel rods
1 bottom	$24 \times 48 \times \frac{1}{4}$ plywood
or 11 bottom slats	$2 \times 24 \times \frac{1}{2}$

Mark out the four legs (FIG. 8-2A) and four long rails (FIG. 8-2B). The strongest corner joints are mortise and tenons (FIG. 8-2C), as the sections of wood are not large enough to allow a good spacing of dowels and the only satisfactory arrangement would be dowels diagonally (FIG. 8-2D). With this arrangement, however, it is possible to get the rail out of square in relation to the leg if there are slight errors in the setting out.

Mark the rung positions on the rails together and drill slightly deeper than the dowels are expected to go. For accuracy this should be done on a drill press, with its depth stop limiting each hole. For freehand drilling, have an assistant watching that the drill is entering upright and use a depth gauge on the drill bit. Round the top rails and take the sharpness off their lower edges (FIG. 8-2E). The bottom rails need not be rounded, but make sure there are no sharp edges.

Round the edges of the legs between the joints and round the outer corners full length. The tops shall project a short distance above the top rails. This is done for strength in the joints. Also, the corners can hold things hung on them when the parent is attending to the baby. Next round the ends and glue the sides. Thin

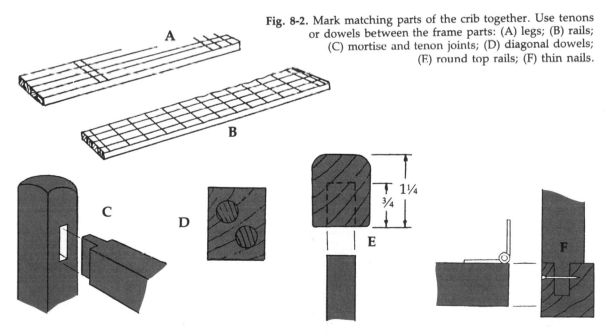

Fig. 8-2. Mark matching parts of the crib together. Use tenons or dowels between the frame parts: (A) legs; (B) rails; (C) mortise and tenon joints; (D) diagonal dowels; (E) round top rails; (F) thin nails.

$1\frac{1}{4}$

$\frac{3}{4}$

A

B

C

D

E

F

nails can be driven through the tenons from inside to hold the joints close without clamps (FIG. 8-2F). Check squareness and see that the opposite sides match.

The rails for the ends are made like the side rails and will be simplest to make with each in one piece, to be separated after the rungs have been secured (FIG. 8-3A). It is important that the spacing between the end rails is exactly the same as between the side rails. Use temporary pieces as stops during assembly (FIG. 8-3B). Thin nails through the corner dowel joints can be used to stop movement while glue is setting.

The mattress support at the bottom has sides long enough to rest on the lower end rails and cross pieces that hold the sides close to the legs (FIG. 8-1B). Be sure to make this bottom loose enough so that it is no trouble to remove. It is the closeness of the lengthwise pieces to the legs and the closeness of the cross pieces to the end dowels that ensure rigidity in use. Assemble the ends to the sides with their hinges, so the sizes of the bottom can be obtained from these parts arranged in position.

Next, tenon or dowel the corners of the bottom (FIG. 8-3C). Then round the projecting ends of the side pieces (FIG. 8-3D).

The simplest support for the mattress is a piece of plywood or hardboard nailed to the frame. Be sure to include a pattern of holes for ventilation. They could be ½ inch or larger and arranged at about 4 inch centers all over the sheet (FIG. 8-3E). You could also use pegboard of the type perforated with closely spaced

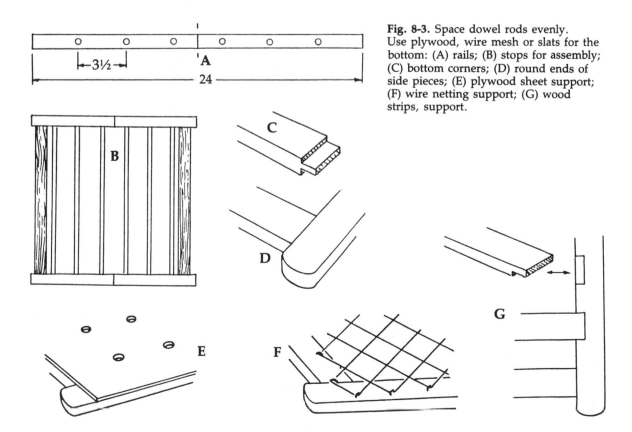

Fig. 8-3. Space dowel rods evenly. Use plywood, wire mesh or slats for the bottom: (A) rails; (B) stops for assembly; (C) bottom corners; (D) round ends of side pieces; (E) plywood sheet support; (F) wire netting support; (G) wood strips, support.

small holes. A very different type of bottom could be made of wire netting of the chicken wire or fence type, held on to the frame with staples (FIG. 8-3F).

Another type of support can be made by placing wood strips across (FIG. 8-3G). These can be quite light so they allow a little springing. Spaces between should not be much more than the widths of the strips for proper support.

Next, put the hinges on the surfaces of the wood (FIG. 8-2F). Check for sharp edges and round any corners by filing. Check that the screws go fully into the countersinks and there is no roughness left from a slipping screwdriver.

This is probably not the sort of furniture for varied colors, since there are no broad areas for decoration and it will probably be best to rely on a varnish finish. Any color to attract the child can be provided by toys hanging from the rails.

PANELED CRIB

This crib is a more substantial and permanent piece of furniture than the previous one (FIG. 8-4). As shown, it is a similar size, but its ends are completely closed and the sides have broad slats instead of round rungs. One side is arranged so the top half swings down for easier access to the bed and the child. The crib cannot be folded nor taken apart, but the bottom can be taken out for cleaning.

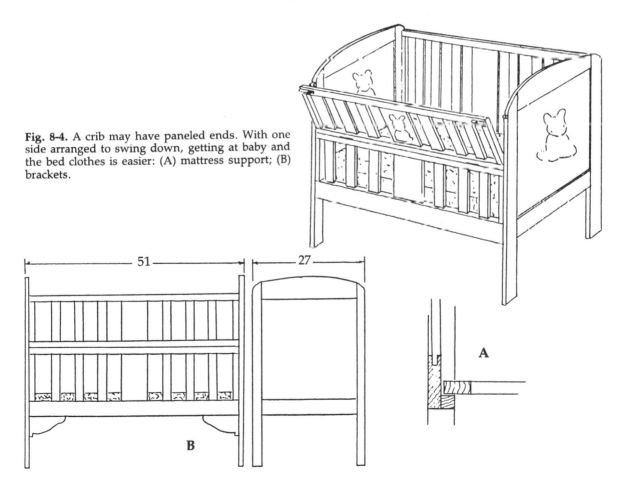

Fig. 8-4. A crib may have paneled ends. With one side arranged to swing down, getting at baby and the bed clothes is easier: (A) mattress support; (B) brackets.

As with the other crib, you should get the mattress before starting construction, to ensure a good fit. The sizes given are intended for a mattress 24 × 48 inches and if you use rubber webbing on the bottom support, it could be a thin one. A complete materials list can be found in TABLE 8-2.

Table 8-2. Materials List for a Paneled Crib.

4 legs	2 × 42 × 1
2 end rails	6 × 25 × 1
2 end rails	4 × 25 × 1
2 end panels	25 × 25 × ¼ plywood
4 rails	2 × 52 × 1
2 rails	4 × 52 × 1
2 slats	6 × 12 × ⅝
1 slat	6 × 25 × ⅝
12 slats	1½ × 12 × ⅝
6 slats	1½ × 25 × ⅝
2 bottom supports	1 × 49 × 1
2 bottom supports	1 × 25 × 1
2 mattress supports	2 × 49 × 1
2 mattress supports	2 × 25 × 1
4 brackets	4 × 8 × 1

The ends have plywood panels. All other parts are solid wood. If you want a clear finish, the plywood should have veneers that match the other wood, but for a painted finish its coloring does not matter. The central slats at the sides and the large areas of paneling at the ends could be decorated with decals. An overall painted finish is probably the best choice for most situations.

Start by making the two ends. Lay out the legs to show the positions of lengthwise parts. (FIG. 8-5A). The bottom side rails and the bottom end rails are the same size and their bottom edges should be level. The top edge of the mattress support should be at the center of these rails (FIG. 8-4A). The crib could be made with drop sides on both sides, but as the crib will usually be put against a wall, the back can have a rigid side with full length slats and only the front will be divided.

A suitable curve for the top end rails can be marked by drawing small curves with the compass set to the thickness of a leg and linking these with a curve drawn with its center at floor level (FIG. 8-5B). Plow grooves for the plywood panel in the top and bottom rails and the legs and round their edges (FIG. 8-5C). The leg grooves need not go further than the length of the panel. They could be cut to this distance with a table saw, but if they must be worked by hand it is simpler to go the full length. No one is likely to notice the grooves down the insides of the projecting legs. For the best results, fill unwanted parts of grooves with strips of wood.

Join the rails to the pegs with mortise and tenon joints. Leave the top of each leg slightly too long so it can be finally shaped after the ends have been assembled (FIG. 8-5D). Have the plywood panel cut to size so it will have a little clearance at the bottom of the grooves.

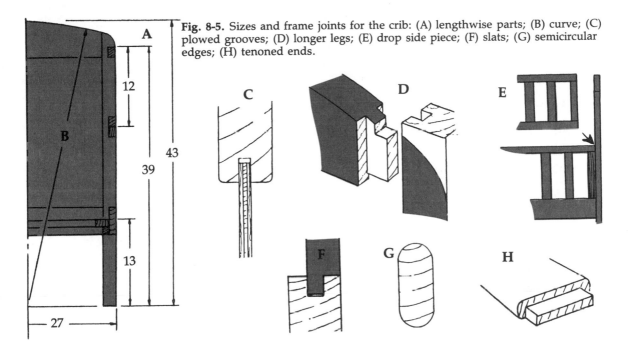

Fig. 8-5. Sizes and frame joints for the crib: (A) lengthwise parts; (B) curve; (C) plowed grooves; (D) longer legs; (E) drop side piece; (F) slats; (G) semicircular edges; (H) tenoned ends.

Join the upper and lower rails to one leg, slide in the plywood, then add the other leg. Full gluing all around the panel might not be necessary, but putting glue in the groove at intervals helps to make the whole assembly rigid. Sight across each end to see that it is not twisted and check one over the other for accuracy of shapes.

Although mortise and tenon joints are best for assembling the ends and they could be used for joining the lengthwise parts to them, it will be satisfactory to use dowels in most places. Use two ⅜-inch dowels in the narrow parts and four in the wide pieces.

The drop side must be made as a frame, but its lengthwise parts are similar in size to the fixed rails. Mark all these rails to length and prepare the ends of the fixed ones for dowel joints. Mark on the rails the positions of all the slats. Also key mark one end of each so that in the final assembly the risk of turning one end for end is reduced, as there will almost certainly be slight discrepancies somewhere along the length.

In the final assembly use two or three hinges to attach the drop front to the rail below it. To keep it up use sliding bolts at each end. These should be the type that require the knob to be moved sideways to unlock before withdrawing, as a child is unlikely to be able to open the side.

Next place a wide slat at the center of each side and narrower ones spaced equally on each side of them. To match the drop side allow for a piece of the same width as the end of the frame to be put between top and bottom rails alongside the legs (FIG. 8-5E). For the sake of a symmetrical appearance, do this at the back as well. Keep spaces between slats less than 4 inches. With a 6-inch central slat and the others 1½ inches, the spaces in the crib length shown are not much more than 3 inches.

The slats are about ⅜ inch thick and joined to the rails with short barefaced tenons, presenting a level surface on the inside (FIG. 8-5F). The slats are made with fully semicircular edges (FIG. 8-5G), so tenoned ends should be cut back to avoid the curves (FIG. 8-5H). Slat material is best if prepared in long pieces, whether the edge rounding is done by hand or machine.

The drop side frame can be made with mortise and tenon or dowel joints. It will be hinged on the rail below it so it will swing down (FIG. 8-6A). You can make it the same length as the fixed rails with a few shavings plained off after assembly. That way it will swing between the ends without excessive clearance.

The setting out on one of the ends will give the distances between rails. Use this as a guide to cutting the slats to length. The important distances are those between the shoulders. Mark across as many as possible at one time to get all of these the same.

Assemble the back with its slats into the rails. Use this as a guide when assembling the front parts, so the lower fixed part and the drop front match it in total depth and in squareness (FIG. 8-6B). Complete the dowel joints at the ends to join the sides into the legs. Check overall squareness and leave the assembly for the glue to set.

The supports for the bottom are 1-inch-square strips glued and screwed inside the bottom rails (FIG. 8-6C). There would probably be sufficient support if you only put them along the sides, but it is simple to continue them across the ends as

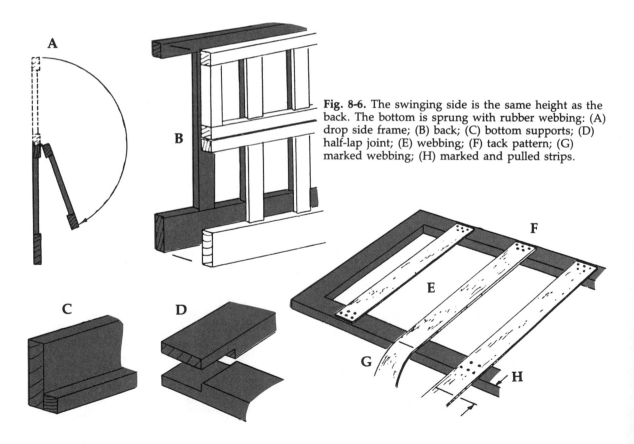

Fig. 8-6. The swinging side is the same height as the back. The bottom is sprung with rubber webbing: (A) drop side frame; (B) back; (C) bottom supports; (D) half-lap joint; (E) webbing; (F) tack pattern; (G) marked webbing; (H) marked and pulled strips.

well. Brackets are shown inside the legs (FIG. 8-4B). Glue and screw in position for appearance and to stiffen the legs.

There are several possible joints for the corners of the mattress support, but in this case a half lap would be satisfactory (FIG. 8-6D). Use screws as well as glue. Make this frame an easy fit inside the crib when it is dropped on its supports.

The bottom can be covered in any of the ways described for the previous crib and a thick mattress used. If the mattress is thinner, be sure there is some springing in the support. The easiest way to provide this is to use rubber webbing. You should have no difficulty fitting this. The only problem is getting even tension as it would be unsatisfactory to have some parts tighter than others.

Using the usual 2-inch-wide webbing, arrange across or in both directions leaving about 4-inch gaps (FIG. 8-6E). Tack to the frame. A pattern of five tacks should be enough (FIG. 8-6F).

Experiment with one piece to obtain a satisfactory stretch to give what seems to be a reasonable tension. Mark the webbing where it comes on the edge of the wood before it is stretched (FIG. 8-6G) and measure how far this mark is over the edge when you have the tension required. Mark and pull every other strip the same amount before tacking it and cutting off (FIG. 8-6H).

With a narrow mattress it might be unnecessary to include any lengthwise webbing. Fit the crosswise pieces first and try the mattress in place. If more support seems necessary, add two lengthwise strips interwoven with the crosswise webbing.

TRADITIONAL ROCKING CRADLE

For the first 6 months of his life, a child does not need much space in which to sleep and there is no need for a crib of the sizes just described. There is also the need for the child to be near the mother much of the time.

In colonial days small, box-like cradles or cots were commonly used. The majority of these could be rocked by a foot, leaving the mother free to knit or otherwise use her hands. Designs varied according to where the makers had come from. Some were elaborately carved and decorated, which might have been justified if the cot would have to last a long time, serving frequently arriving new babies. Some of the cots had hoods as a protection against drafts, but these are unlikely to be a problem in a modern home and any reproduction can be made without a hood, unless the maker was attracted by the novelty of it.

This rocking cradle follows the general lines of many early cradles (FIG. 8-7). The raised head end provides some protection there. The heart cutouts were not used just for sentimental reasons. They are a convenient shape for two fingers to be put in at each end to lift the cot. The rockers have projections at each end of the main curve. They limit movement and prevent anyone from rocking with their foot without looking at it and tilting the cradle too far.

See TABLE 8-3 for the materials list for this project. The main parts of the cradle are made from wood ½ inch thick. In a modern reproduction you can use plywood. If you use solid wood, you might have to join the pieces to make up widths and increase thickness slightly.

The grain in the ends should be horizontal. The rockers should be solid wood, although you can use thick plywood two ½-inch thicknesses together.

Set out the head end first (FIG. 8-8A). The sides should taper from the 14-inch bottom to 18 inches at a 12-inch height. Then draw a curve of about a 19-inch

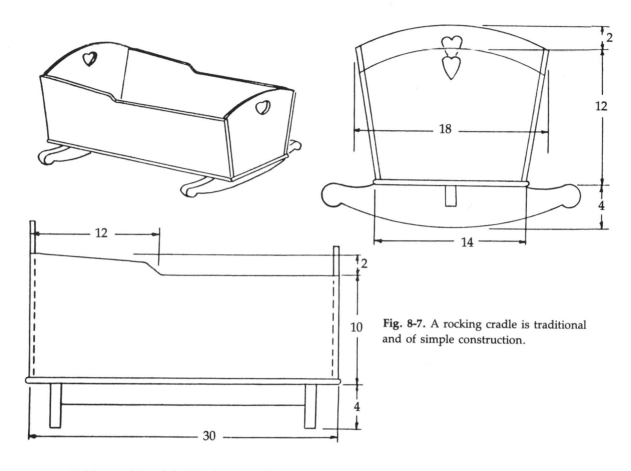

Fig. 8-7. A rocking cradle is traditional and of simple construction.

Table 8-3. Materials List for a Traditional Rocking Cradle.

19 × 20 × ½ plywood	2 ends
19 × 24 × ½ plywood	or
1 × 29 × 1	4 rails
½ × 12 × dowel rod	18 rungs
1½ × 29 × ½	2 bottom supports
14 × 29 × ¼ plywood	1 bottom

radius. The foot end should be 2 inches lower, but you can mark it out at the same time (FIG. 8-8B).

To get a uniform appearance, make a template of half a heart cutout with thin plywood or hardboard (FIG. 8-8C). Turn this over on the centerlines to draw the shape. Cut this out with a jig saw, using a fine narrow blade and thoroughly round the edges with a file and sandpaper.

Reduce the sides in depth about 12 inches from the head end and taper to this point (FIG. 8-8D). Many of the original cradles had dovetail joints at the corners, with the tails in the ends. They could be made this way in solid wood,

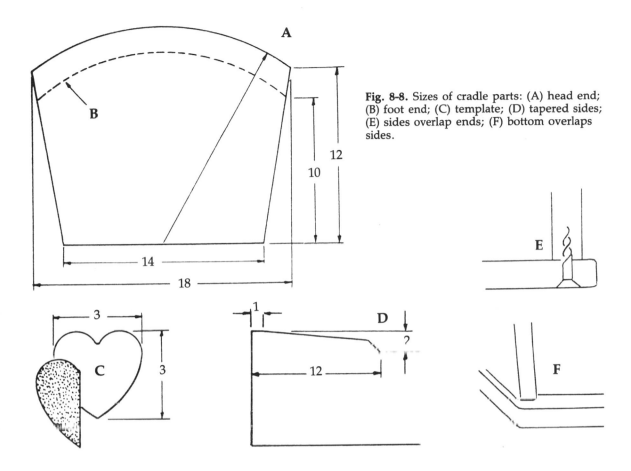

Fig. 8-8. Sizes of cradle parts: (A) head end; (B) foot end; (C) template; (D) tapered sides; (E) sides overlap ends; (F) bottom overlaps sides.

but for plywood it is satisfactory to use glue and screws, with the sides overlapping the ends slightly (FIG. 8-8E). Plane the bottom edges of the sides to the angles of the ends before assembly.

The bottom should also overlap the sides and ends. Be sure to round the edges (FIG. 8-8F). If a small foam mattress is to be put in the bottom of the cradle, drill a few holes in the bottom for air to pass in and out. Keep these clear of where the underframing will come.

The rockers are made from 4-×-1-inch wood. It is important for each to be symmetrical and match the other, so one could be made, drawn around, and turned over to see if it is the same both ways before using to mark the other rocker. Or you might set out a half template and use that to mark the rockers.

The main curve will be satisfactory with a radius of 26 inches. Small curves make the end projections (FIG. 8-9A). Curve the top edge into a flat surface a little narrower than the cradle bottom. Leave the part that will meet the bottom flat, but round all other edges so they will not mark carpets.

A good idea is to place a strut between the rockers (FIG. 8-9B). It could be screwed in place or joined to the rockers with dowels, but the traditional way would be with tenons (FIG. 8-9C). Fix with screws driven downward through the bottom (FIG. 8-9D).

Traditional Rocking Cradle   165

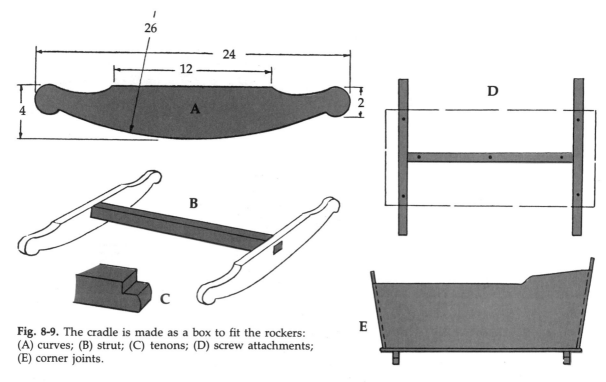

Fig. 8-9. The cradle is made as a box to fit the rockers: (A) curves; (B) strut; (C) tenons; (D) screw attachments; (E) corner joints.

Surviving old cradles of this sort were mostly left as untreated wood, possibly because all of the paints of those days might have been harmful if sucked by a child. A modern cradle, particularly if made of plywood, would look best if painted brightly, possibly with one color inside contrasting with another outside.

Also, many early cradles had the ends sloping as well as the sides. This looks more attractive, but it involves compound angles at the corners. If the slope at the ends is no more than at the sides, it is not difficult to cut the corner joints (FIG. 8-9E). Make the ends in the same way as for upright ones, but bevel the bottom edges. Then make the sides with the ends angled instead of square. The edges of the ends will be very slightly angled, but if you bring the parts together temporarily, you will see the amount of angle needed for a close fit. Final construction is the same as with upright ends.

TAKE-DOWN CRADLE

Because a small cradle is often not needed for a very long time, any simple assembly that can be reduced to a few flat pieces when not required has attractions. When it will no longer be needed, it can be taken completely apart to yield wood for other uses.

This cradle has about the same dimensions as the traditional cradle, but it is purely functional and does not follow earlier models (FIG. 8-10). However, it can be finished to look quite attractive.

There are two plywood ends, two ladder-like sides and a lift-out bottom piece of plywood. Assembly is with eight screws. When in use the cradle is rigid and cannot fold or collapse.

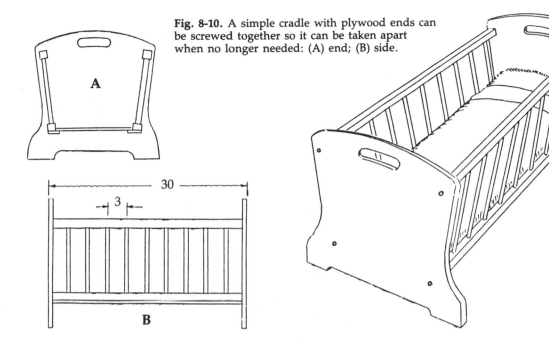

Fig. 8-10. A simple cradle with plywood ends can be screwed together so it can be taken apart when no longer needed: (A) end; (B) side.

A

30

3

B

Table 8-4. Materials List for a Take-Down Cradle.

1 head	14 × 18 × ½
1 foot	12 × 18 × ½
2 sides	13 × 31 × ½
1 bottom	15 × 31 × ½
2 rockers	4 × 24 × 1
1 strut	2 × 27 × 1

In the illustration two are shown. The ends can be made so the cradle can be rocked, or their bottoms can be arranged so that it will stand level. Except for the variations in the bottoms, the cradles are made the same way. TABLE 8-4 offers the detailed materials list.

Draw the end full size (FIGS. 8-11A or 8-11B). The rocking version is wider than the other, which is cut away to let the cradle stand on four feet. Hand holes can be provided for lifting. They can be hearts or the more usual cutout shape of about 5 × 1½ inches curved to match the shaped top (FIG. 8-10A). Round all external edges and inside the hand holes.

The two sides are made from square lengthwise strips. Mark these pieces together for rungs at 3-inch intervals (FIG. 8-10B). Make sure the lengths are exactly the same and the rung holes are of uniform depth. Cut all the pieces of dowel rod to length. If you are marking by hand, a simple jig or stop will suffice to set the length cut.

Except for rounding the edges, the top strips should be left square. The bottom strips have to be bevelled (FIG. 8-11C). The angle can be found from the shape of

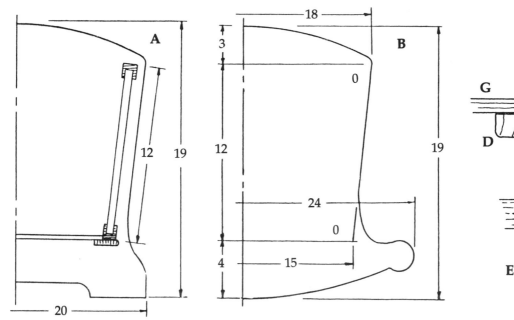

Fig. 8-11. Sizes and sections of two ways to make a cradle: (A) end; (B) end; (C) bottom strips; (D) supporting strips; (E) dowel rod; (F) cup washers; (G) bottom.

an end, but if it is planed on a jointer, the angle is 7°. Attach strips to support the bottom (FIG. 8-11D). They can finish level with the rail or have a rounded projection.

Assemble the sides. See that the rungs finish square to the rails. Place temporary stops between the ends to keep the rail spacing correct (FIG. 8-3B).

If you do not expect that the cradle will have to be disassembled, the side can be dowelled or screwed permanently to the ends. For disassembly it should be possible to screw and unscrew several times without the screw thread becoming worn.

There are special nut and bolt assemblies where one part is let into the wood to engage with the bolt, but in this case it should be possible to use wood screws. As they have to go into end grain, additional bite should be provided to prevent the screws from pulling out after several assemblies. This is done by putting pieces of dowel rod through the ends (FIG. 8-11E) so the screw engages across its grain.

Position the two sides on one end and pencil around the rails. Locate the screw holes through both ends centrally in each of these places. So the screws do not deface the wood when being driven and withdrawn several times, use screws with round heads over washers. Another way is to support flat head screws with cup washers (FIG. 8-11F).

The bottom is a piece of thin plywood or hardboard cut to rest in the assembled cradle (FIG. 8-11G). Drill a pattern of holes in it. There is no need to fasten it down.

SWING CRADLE

A small cradle on the floor certainly keeps the baby at a safe level and that type of cradle is easy to pick up so a parent can move the sleeping baby anywhere in the home. However, it does mean bending and kneeling frequently. The larger crib that might be needed later on is at a height that is more comfortable to deal with. This also brings the child to a safer height if there are pets in the home.

Several Europeans who emigrated to American had a tradition of higher cradles, but the Dutch in particular favored a high swinging type. This example is a modernized version of a Dutch style. The one shown has a small covered head (FIG. 8-12), but you can leave this off and make the head end slightly higher than the foot.

The cradle swings on a stand, so the baby can be rocked by hand, instead of by foot, as in the lower cradles. The amount of swing is limited so there is no fear of the cradle being turned over. If you don't want the swinging action, you can make the stand closer to the ends of the cradle and screw it to make a rigid assembly.

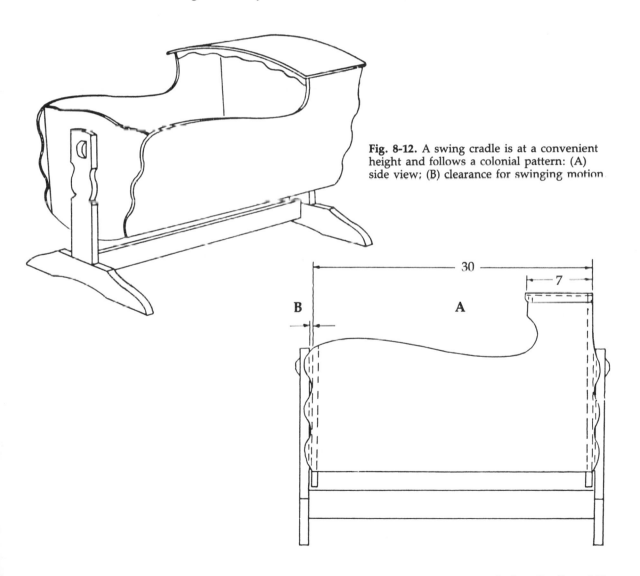

Fig. 8-12. A swing cradle is at a convenient height and follows a colonial pattern: (A) side view; (B) clearance for swinging motion

This design is particularly suited to anyone with a power saw for cutting curves, such as a bandsaw or saber saw. Hand sawing of most of the curves would not be laborious as most of the wood is thin, but if you want a simplified outline, some of the wavy edges can be modified to straight lines or broader sweeping curves. If alterations are made, be sure the ends of the sides project far enough to act as stops to prevent the cradle from being swung too far. TABLE 8-5 offers the material list.

Table 8-5. Materials List for a Swing Cradle.

2 sides	17 × 32 × ½	plywood
1 foot end	14 × 18 × ½	plywood
1 head end	18 × 19 × ½	plywood
1 bottom	14 × 30 × ¼	plywood
2 bottom bearers	½ × 30 × ½	
2 bottom bearers	½ × 14 × ½	
1 top	7 × 22 × ¼	plywood
1 arch	3 × 22 × ½	plywood
2 feet	5 × 20 × 1	
2 uprights	3 × 17 × 1	
1 rail	3 × 36 × 1	

In side view the ends are upright so the cradle will swing between its supports (FIG. 8-12A), but there should be a flair in the sides and a half drawing of the end should be drawn full size (FIG. 8-13A) so that you get the sizes of several parts.

Draw a line long enough to be the centerline and start marking out by drawing the shape of the foot end before its top curves (FIG. 8-13B). This will be the slope of the sides, which you can continue upward to get the outline of the head end. A convenient curve for the top is a 27-inch radius, with the center at floor level (FIG. 8-13C). Mark the pivot point and use this as a center for drawing the curve of the bottoms of the ends (FIG. 8-13D). Draw the straight outlines of the supports.

The top over the head is thin plywood sprung over the end of the cradle and an arched piece 1 inch deep (FIG. 8-13E). Draw this curve, then draw the wavy outline, but do not cut away the edge too much or the piece will be weakened. The curves can be drawn freehand, but suggested shapes are shown in FIG. 8-13F. Also shape the foot end (FIG. 8-13G), but in both cases, check overall sizes as there may be variations in individual cradles.

The shape of a side can be marked directly onto one piece of plywood (FIG. 8-14A). With the overall dimensions marked out with straight lines, show the top edge with a sweeping curve and mark the wavy edges at the ends (FIG. 8-13H) in a shape matching to the top. Cut both sides together or mark the second from the first. Also mark out the ends from the full-size drawing and cut them. Test these four parts together.

The ends fit between the sides. Bevel the bottom edges of the sides to match the ends. Round all upper edges. Put supports for the bottom on all four pieces (FIG. 8-14B). The bottom can be perforated hardboard or drilled plywood. It's a good idea to strengthen the corners of the cradle with square strips attached to the ends before the sides are added (FIG. 8-14C).

Assemble the sides and ends and fit the bottom, which could be left loose for lifting out. At the head end, fit the beam between the sides with glue and

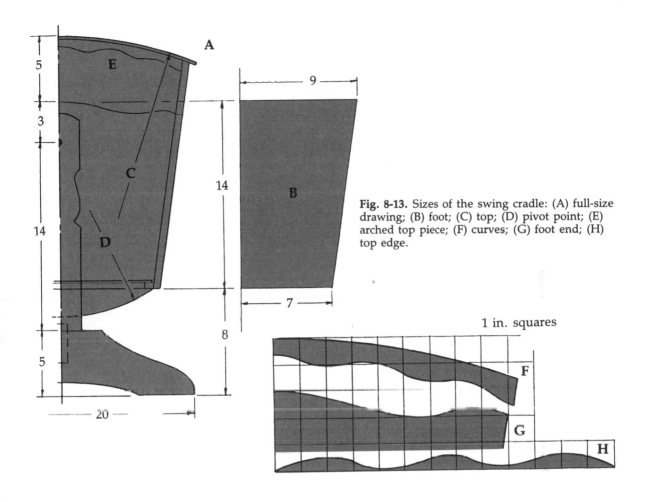

Fig. 8-13. Sizes of the swing cradle: (A) full-size drawing; (B) foot; (C) top; (D) pivot point; (E) arched top piece; (F) curves; (G) foot end; (H) top edge.

1 in. squares

screws from outside. Bend the plywood for the top to shape and mark the outline of the parts it touches. Leave it a little oversized, but round and sand the front edge before fitting. Bend it into place and fasten it down with glue and small nails, although a screw at each corner would help to hold the curve. Plane the rear edge level, but parallel to the sides. Then round them (FIG. 8-14D).

The supports are a simple assembly except for the rail having to fit into the joint between the upright and the foot. Shape the feet (FIG. 8-15A) and upright parts (FIG. 8-15B). Join these parts with ½-inch dowels, but keep the dowels clear of where the rail will come (FIG. 8-15C). Let this glue set so the joined parts can be treated as one piece when adding the rail. Make the rail long enough to allow sufficient clearance for the cradle to swing without rubbing the uprights (FIG. 8-12B). A gap of ⅛ inch should be enough.

The rail can be cut to the length specified and the joints made with dowels (FIG. 8-15D). The traditional joint is a mortise and tenon with the tenon taken through and its end rounded (FIG. 8-15E). In both cases it is the accuracy of the ends of the rail that keep the support in shape. Check squareness and make sure the ends stand upright when assembling.

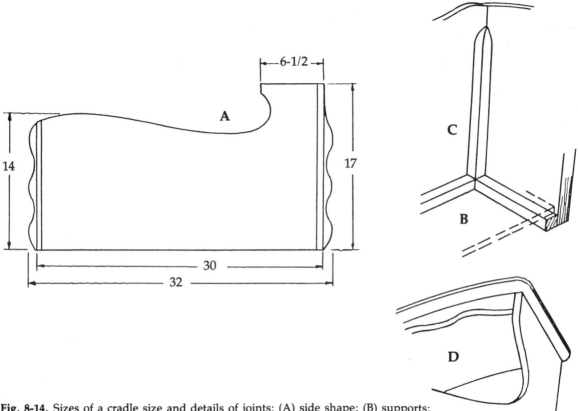

Fig. 8-14. Sizes of a cradle size and details of joints: (A) side shape; (B) supports; (C) corners; (D) round edges.

The pivots are ⅜-inch bolts with their shallow rounded heads inside the cradle and their square necks pulled into the wood. There should be a washer in each joint and another under the nut outside. Saw off the bolt end level with the nut (FIG. 8-15F). Cover the nut with a shaped block of wood. Drill out enough to fit over the nut and taper the outside (FIG. 8-15G). If you screw these blocks in place without glue, they can be removed if the cradle has to be taken out of the stand for transport or storage. If you would like the cradle to stand on the floor away from the stand, cut the bottom edges of the ends straight across, although the curve shown matches the general curve of the edges elsewhere.

Although these traditional cradles made of solid wood were often left the natural color, a plywood cradle is better painted. Light colors inside the top alleviate the confined look otherwise possible and the outside can be decorated like other similar furniture with painted patterns or decals.

UNIT BED

At one time it was common for beds to have built-in springing to support a mattress. The total amount of springing needed to sleep in comfort was then divided between the lift-off mattress and its more permanent lower part. With the coming of deep interior-sprung and rubber foam mattresses it became possible

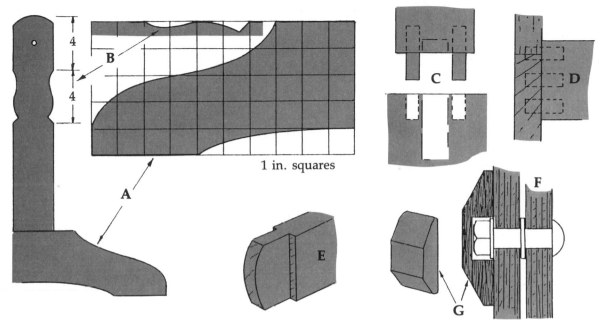

Fig. 8-15. Details of the cradle stand and pivot: (A) feet; (B) upright parts; (C) dowels; (D) rail with doweled joints; (E) traditional joint; (F) level with nut; (G) cover for nut.

to get all of the necessary springing in the top part and so simplify the construction of the bed. Instead of a frame to support a system of coil springs, the mattress support could be flat.

In some children's beds there might be springing provided by rubber webbing, but in most cases a child can sleep comfortably on 4 inches or more of foam over any unyielding base. The bed described here and most of those that follow are made that way.

The size of a bed is determined by the size of an available mattress. Although there are small mattresses available, one of a standard length of about 78 inches is a good choice so the same bed is used until the child is fully grown. If space is restricted, it is possible to sleep in reasonable comfort on a bed only 24 inches wide, but it is better for a single bed to be 36 inches wide. This and other beds are designed for mattresses 78 × 36 inches. This can be modified if you choose another mattress (FIG. 8-16). Obviously, a mattress should be selected before starting on any work.

This basic bed can also be made without additions as a divan that can be completely covered during the day. Head and foot boards can be added as well as a guard rail for a child who might roll out of bed.

For a complete materials list, refer to TABLE 8-6. The main frame is made like a simple open box (FIG. 8-17A). Corners can be screwed, although a comb joint is an alternative (FIG. 8-17B). Choose straight-grained wood, free of large knots, as it would be troublesome if the long pieces warped after the bed has been put into use.

Much of the main frame is not normally in view so it need not be made of a good quality wood, but the legs will show and they are better if made of

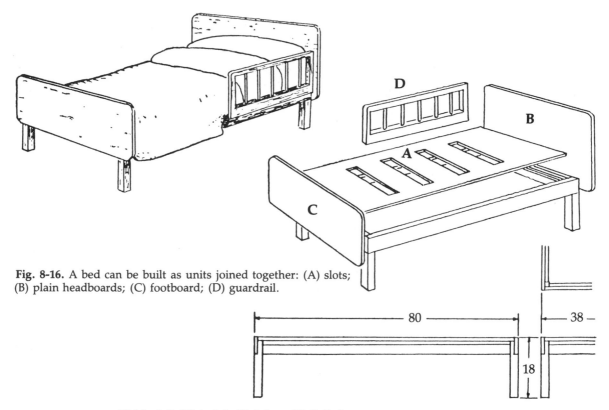

Fig. 8-16. A bed can be built as units joined together: (A) slots; (B) plain headboards; (C) footboard; (D) guardrail.

Table 8-6. Materials List for a Unit Bed.

4 legs	2 × 18 × 2
2 sides	5 × 80 × ⅞
2 ends	5 × 38 × ⅞
2 mattress bearers	1 × 78 × 1
2 mattress bearers	1 × 36 × 1
1 mattress support	36 × 78 × ½ plywood
or 13	4 × 36 × ½
1 headboard	4 × 46 × ½ plywood
1 footboard	18 × 46 × ½ plywood
1 guardrail	1¼ × 36 × 1¼
2 guardrail	1¼ × 15 × 1¼
5 rungs	½ × 15 × dowel rods
1 guardrail	2½ × 36 × 1¼

hardwood, with a good furniture finish. They should be square, but cut away to fit inside the main frame (FIG. 8-17C). Their tops come at the same level as pieces inside that form bearers for the mattress support (FIG. 8-17D).

It would be satisfactory to leave the legs square in section, but the appearance can be lightened, without actually tapering the inner surfaces, if you gave the inner corner a tapered beveled cut (FIG. 8-17E). You could put glides on the bottoms of the legs, but casters are better if the bed has to be moved frequently.

Most casters raise the bed about 2 inches so this should be allowed for in the lengths of the legs. Suitable casters are the type that fit into a drilled hole in the leg and do not require a large area for an attachment plate.

Glue and nail or screw the bearers for the mattress support to the frame. Round the top edges of the frame before assembly and check squareness. See that the legs are upright and sight across opposite sides and ends of the assembly to confirm there is no twist.

Several types of mattress support are possible. A solid piece of ½-inch plywood would do, except that it ought to be perforated with a pattern of holes for ventilation (FIG. 8-17F). Perforated hardboard would not be stiff enough in itself, but it could be used on a frame, with cross members at intervals (FIG. 8-17G). If you use ½-inch plywood, you could also make slots across it (FIG. 8-16A). If you use solid wood, you could put it across with ventilating gaps between (FIG. 8-17H).

This basic bed can be used alone as a divan or joined to any of the headboards described later, but here it is shown with a plain headboard (FIG. 8-16B), made from a piece of ½-inch plywood preferably with veneer on one or both sides to match other furniture. If you want a painted finish, it could be plain plywood.

The headboard extends on each side of the bed (FIG. 8-18A), but if the bed is to go into the corner of a room, that side should be level with the bed frame. It is attached by screwing into the frame (FIG. 8-18B).

The footboard is similar, but lower (FIG. 8-16C), although screws through it into the frame would spoil its appearance. There is not much grip for screws driven the other way and the joint would not be strong enough if there is no further fastening. Screws can be driven through the plywood with counterbores and plugs over their heads. If you carefully mark it out and give it a neat pattern, this should be acceptable.

Another treatment is to cover screw heads with molding. You could use half round or other molding on the surface, with the lower piece covering the screw heads. (FIG. 8-18C).

If you want to include a guardrail, it should be sufficient to make it less then half the length of the bed, say 36 inches long (FIG. 8-16D). For a bed in the corner of a room, you need a rail on one side. Otherwise make two. Square-sectioned top and end rails are shown, with a deeper bottom piece to screw to the side frame (FIG. 8-18D). Corners can be doweled, tenoned, dovetailed, or made as open bridle joints (FIG. 8-18E). Pieces of dowel rod fit into holes. For an attached frame, prepare for screws into the side frame and through the backboard. The guard rail assembly will then brace the bed. Round the free corner and all exposed edges.

You might want the guardrails to be removable. This eases the work of bedmaking and allows the rails to be taken away when the older child has no further need for them. Then they will be available if needed again for a younger child.

In this case the lower rail can be the same section as the other rails so it rests on a similar rail attached to the bed frame side (FIG. 8-18F). Take three of the dowel rods through the bottom guardrail so they can be plugged into holes in the attached piece (FIG. 8-18G). Sand and round the extending dowel rods so they are push fits into the holes. At the top fit a small sliding bolt to the end of the rail so it will go into a hole in the backboard (FIG. 8-18H).

This type of bed is usually best if left fairly plain, but the head and foot boards can be decorated, either by painting or by varying the outlines. The top and outer edges could be given decorative curves, either board sweeps or wavy outlines

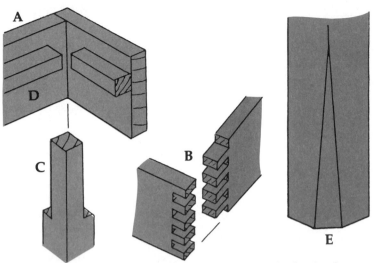

Fig. 8-17. The bed can be framed in several ways, the leg can have an inner corner beveled and the mattress support may be plywood or slats: (A) main frame; (B) corners; (C) legs; (D) tops of legs; (E) tapered beveled cut; (F) pattern of holes; (G) perforated hardboard; (H) solid wood.

Fig. 8-18. The bed ends are plywood. The guardrail pegs into a strip on the bed side and is bolted to the headboard: (A) headboard; (B) headboard attachment; (C) molding; (D) bottom piece; (E) corners; (F) lower rail; (G) attached piece; (H) backboard hole.

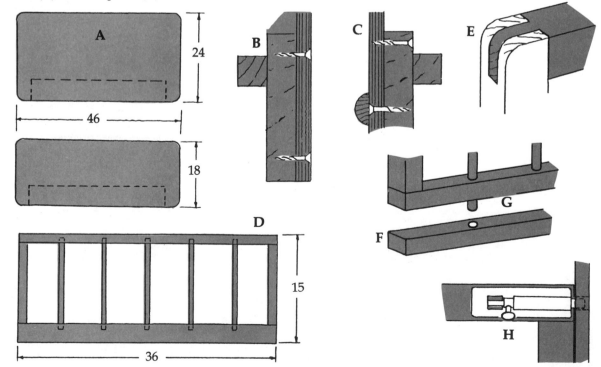

on generally straight lines. Another possibility is to cut the whole outline in the form of an animal or bird, then leaving it as a silhouette or painting details on the surface. If this is done you have to remember that the bed might be in service for many years and an older child will not appreciate having to sleep in something designed for his more babyish days.

HEADBOARD

Although much can be done with bedside tables and racks it is often better to include various items in a combined assembly forming the head of the bed (FIG. 8-19). If all a child should need is within reach, he has less reasons for getting out of bed, and if these things are on fixed furniture there is no risk of them being pushed about or knocked over.

In a small room a headboard unit can take the place of several items of furniture and economize on space. A headboard can also make an attractive feature along a wall.

The headboard can be attached to the bed itself, it can be attached to the wall so the bed can be moved away from it, or it can be attached to both bed and wall, usually in a temporary manner so the parts can be moved for cleaning. Only the lighter structures are suitable for attaching to the bed. If the unit has depth, possibly enough to contain a bookrack, it might not be steady enough to stand

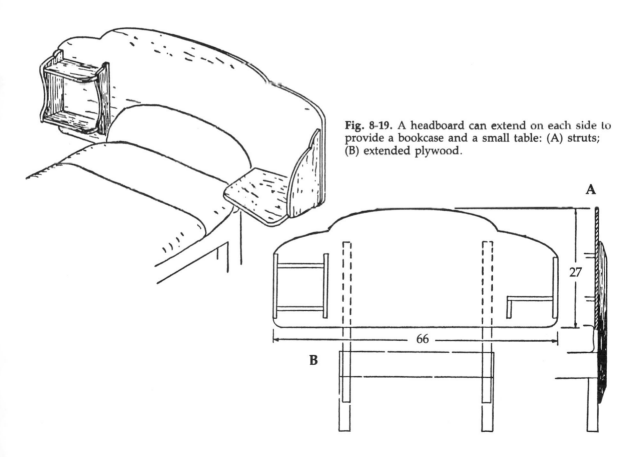

Fig. 8-19. A headboard can extend on each side to provide a bookcase and a small table: (A) struts; (B) extended plywood.

unaided, so it must be attached to the wall. Built-in side tables or cabinets can also give the wider base needed by a deeper unit for steadiness without fastenings.

The simplest headboard is made like the headboard on the bed just described, but extended at the side enough to take shelves. That arrangement should not be made too big or the load on the screws into the bed frame will be too much. Instead, provide struts behind the board and let them extend down the legs (FIG. 8-19A). In the example the board is a piece of plywood extended on both sides, so there can be a shelf to serve as a table on one side and racks for books at the other side (FIG. 8-19B). The sizes suit a 36-inch bed. The height might have to be adjusted according to the thickness of the mattress and bedding. A complete materials list is supplied on TABLE 8-7.

Table 8-7. Materials List for a Headboard.

1 back	27 × 66 × ½ plywood
2 struts	1½ × 36 × 1½
1 table	15 × 15 × ½ plywood
1 table bracket	5 × 12 × ½ plywood
1 table bracket	12 × 13 × ½ plywood
2 book shelves	5 × 15 × ½ plywood
1 book shelf	5 × 15 × ½ plywood
1 book shelf upright	3 × 13 × ½ plywood

The backboard is a piece of ½-inch plywood supported by two struts that extend down the bed legs (FIG. 8-20A). Taper the ends of the struts and round their exposed edges as they might be pushed against or be rubbed along the wall when you are moving the bed. You might want to glue strips of foam rubber or plastic along them to avoid marking wall coverings.

Shape the top of the back with stepped curves that are carried into the brackets as well. A suggested curve for the top edges is shown in FIG. 8-21A. You can make a half paper template. Turn it over to get the back symmetrical. Round the bottom corners. For most beds it will be sufficient to cut the bottom edge straight across, but in some cases, it will be necessary to cut away the center of the bottom edge so the two wings hang lower.

The parts attached to the back as shown are plywood, but they could be particleboard with a plastic facing. If possible, make the joints to supports with dado joints. If the material you choose is unsuitable for cutting in this way, put strips under the shelves, screwed both ways. The sizes for bookcase and table will give reasonable proportions, but they can be adapted to suit a particular situation.

If the bed is in a corner and the extension can only be at one side, bookshelves could be arranged above the table. Too great an extension of the table should be avoided because of the method of supporting it. A larger table would need supports to the floor.

The tabletop should taper toward the bed (FIG. 8-20B). Put a strut underneath the edge toward the bed (FIG. 8-20C and 8-21B). At the outer edge the bracket should extend above and below the table (FIGS. 8-20D and 8-20E) with a matching outline (FIG. 8-21C). If the table is notched around it, cut a dado groove right across. If

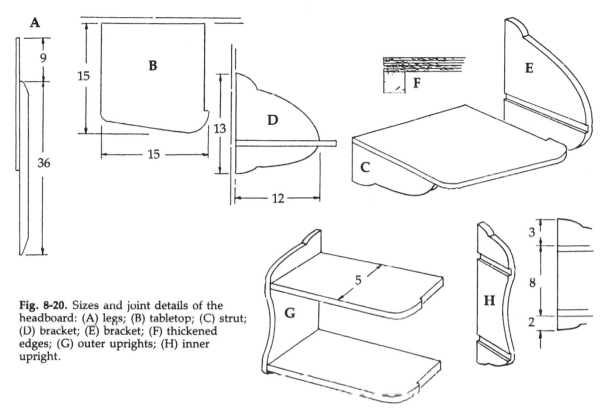

Fig. 8-20. Sizes and joint details of the headboard: (A) legs; (B) tabletop; (C) strut; (D) bracket; (E) bracket; (F) thickened edges; (G) outer uprights; (H) inner upright.

you use ½ inch plywood, this might not give a very secure hold for screws driven through the back, so thicken edges with strips where they will not show (FIG. 8-20F).

The bookrack has shelves of the same width, but the supports are a different width to give a tapered effect toward the bed so books are easily removed. Cut the outer upright (FIG. 8-20G) with stopped dado joints for the shelves since they are the same width. You should also give the outer a shaped outline (FIG. 8-21D). Cut the dados through the inner upright (FIG. 8-20H) and notch the shelves upright around in a way similar to the table bracket. Cut it to a matching outline (FIG. 8-21E).

Thicken under the shelves so that screws can be taken through the back (FIG. 8-20F). You will have to drive screws directly into plywood in some parts of both fitments, but the main load will rest on the reinforced parts.

WALL HEADBOARD

This is a piece of furniture that is not attached to the bed, but is screwed to the wall (FIG. 8-22). As shown, it is intended to go into a corner, but with the side fitment repeated at the other side for use in an open position. A piece of plywood is shown at the corner that extends upward so that it provides the child with somewhere to mount picture cutouts and the like, rather than sticking them to the wall. When the bed is moved away and the headboard is closed, there are no projections into the room.

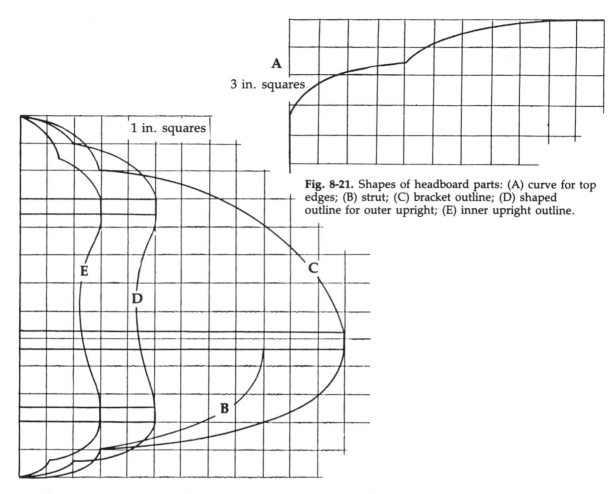

A

3 in. squares

1 in. squares

E

D

C

B

Fig. 8-21. Shapes of headboard parts: (A) curve for top edges; (B) strut; (C) bracket outline; (D) shaped outline for outer upright; (E) inner upright outline.

The part where the bed will come is shown closed. It could be made open so the bed can be pushed under the shelf, but this would mean about a 6-inch projection over the pillow. If the child is much shorter than the bed, this would not matter as the pillow could be drawn down, but for a taller person, the overhanging shelf would then be a nuisance. The side table is made with a flap that swings down and is then supported by a partly open door below, which covers some storage space. With the flap up and the door closed, there is a level front to the headboard.

Construction involves solid wood for the main framing and plywood for the back, door, and flap. For a quality finish the exposed edges of the flap should be lipped, but for a painted finish it would not matter if the plywood edges showed. A materials list is found in TABLE 8-8.

The main frame is made like a box. Any of the usual corner joints can be used (FIG. 8-23A). Top and bottom can overlap the upright for dado joints (FIG. 8-23B). At the room corner, the top and bottom can be notched so the upright can be screwed into it (FIG. 8-23C). The bottom should be cut back for the door to overlap, so when it opens it can rest on the floor to take the thrust from the flap (FIG. 8-23D).

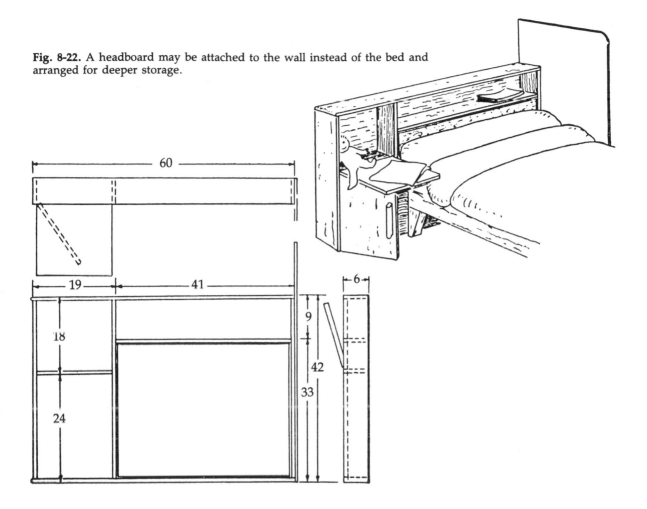

Fig. 8-22. A headboard may be attached to the wall instead of the bed and arranged for deeper storage.

The intermediate upright and the shelves can have dado joints (FIG. 8-23E) or the bottom of the upright can be tenoned. The simplest way to make the closed panel is to fit plywood on the surface (FIG. 8-23F), but it would look better if you fit the plywood inside against strips and then fill the angle with quarter-round molding (FIG. 8-23G). The back could be a piece of plywood all over the frame, but if there is to be a closed panel behind the bed, you could cut the panel carefully from the back with the remainder fitted behind the parts that show.

The flap fits into its opening and is hinged at the front edge. A strip at the top acts as a stop (FIG. 8-24A) and can carry a catch to hold the flap closed. The door is hinged on the outer upright. It is cut to clear the shelf, but with no more clearance at the bottom than is needed to swing over the floor. The piece at the end that will support the flap could be cut in one piece with the door, but it will be simpler to attach a separate piece (FIG. 8-24B). This goes into a notch in the shelf when the door is closed and should come level with its top surface. It will act as a door stop, but there should be a catch lower down. A piece of thick cloth glued to the top of the support will reduce the risk of marking the flap.

Wall Headboard 181

If the flap is merely resting on the door, it will have a slight downward slope. It should be level or slope very slightly the other way. To achieve this, allow the door to open against a wedged stop that lifts the flap. The stop forms part of the flap handle.

To get the position and shape of the handle stop, first draw the flap with an arc showing the swing of the door (FIG. 8-24C). Draw on the outline of the handle. Make the stop with a taper to a flat surface and notch so the door is

Table 8-8. Materials List for a Wall Headboard.

2 ends	6 × 42 × ¾
1 top	6 × 60 × ¾
1 upright	6 × 42 × ¾
1 shelf	6 × 41 × ¾
1 shelf	6 × 19 × ¾
1 flap	18 × 18 × ¾ plywood
1 door	18 × 24 × ¾ plywood
2 handles	1¼ × 8 × 1
1 back	42 × 60 × ¼ plywood
1 panel (cut from back)	33 × 41 × ¼ plywood
1 bulletin board	30 × 54 × ½ plywood
2 panel frames	½ × 41 × ½
2 panel frames	½ × 33 × ½
2 panel moldings	½ × 41 × quarter-round
2 panel moldings	½ × 33 × quarter-round

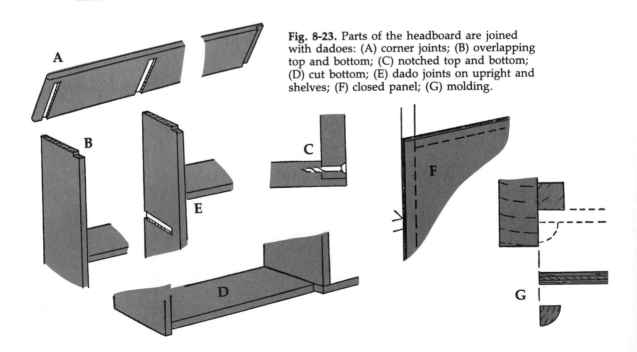

Fig. 8-23. Parts of the headboard are joined with dadoes: (A) corner joints; (B) overlapping top and bottom; (C) notched top and bottom; (D) cut bottom; (E) dado joints on upright and shelves; (F) closed panel; (G) molding.

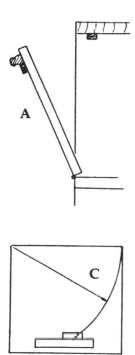

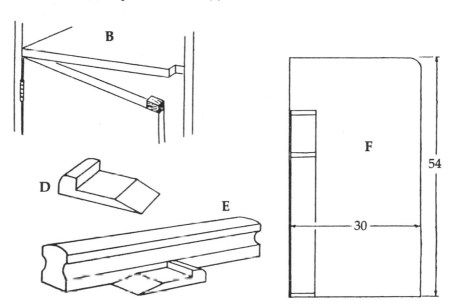

Fig. 8-24. The side table is made by swinging down the top flap to rest on the door below: (A) flap; (B) supporting piece; (C) arc of door swing; (D) flat part thickness; (E) strip wood handle; (F) bulletin board.

stopped from going further. The thickness of the flat part is the amount needed to bring the flap level. With the usual hinges and the clearance that must be allowed, this is unlikely to be more than ¼ inch (FIG. 8-24D). Position this piece on the flap and make a strip wood handle to fit against it (FIG. 8-24E). A similar handle can be used on the door.

If you want to add a corner plywood bulletin board, it should be higher than the headboard to allow the child to use it when sitting on the bed. The bulletin board needn't extend to the floor, instead, it can be cut off at the bed level, although making it full depth provides added wall protection when the bed is moved about.

INDEPENDENT HEADBOARD

If there is space in a room for a headboard unit that stands out from the wall and so causes the bed to project further, it is possible to make a unit into a piece of furniture in its own right that can stand unaided when the bed is removed. This allows the headboard plenty of storage capacity. One way of doing this is shown in FIG. 8-25. You could make it with an extension at one side only for a corner situation, or make one side a different size from the other. A further possibility is to make one side entirely a bookcase or other sort of storage unit. TABLE 8-9 offers a complete materials list.

The unit is in one piece, but you could make it in three pieces if this would be better for transport or possible rearrangement at a future date. There would then be a central part slightly wider than the bed and side pieces with their own sides fitting against the sides of the central part.

In the arrangement shown, the central part that projects above the bed level slopes back, so it could be used as a pillow support when sitting in bed. This

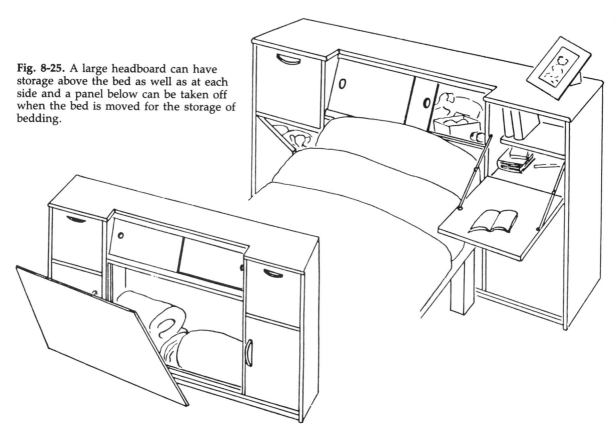

Fig. 8-25. A large headboard can have storage above the bed as well as at each side and a panel below can be taken off when the bed is moved for the storage of bedding.

Table 8-9. Materials List for an Independent Headboard.

2 ends	12 × 42 × ¾
2 uprights	12 × 40 × ¾
1 bottom	12 × 76 × ¾
1 top	12 × 78 × ¾
1 divider	12 × 41 × ¾
2 dividers	12 × 18 × ¾
4 shelves	9 × 18 × ¼ plywood
4 shelves	1 × 18 × 1
1 plinth	2 × 76 × ¾
2 flaps	18 × 18 × ¾ plywood
2 doors	18 × 22 × ¾ plywood
2 doors	15 × 22 × ¼ plywood
1 panel	25 × 40 × ¼ plywood
2 panel frames	1½ × 25 × ½
2 panel frames	1½ × 40 × ½
2 panel stops	½ × 25 × ½
2 panel stops	½ × 40 × ½
1 back	42 × 76 × ¼ plywood

features sliding doors for access while in bed to a large storage space behind. Below that the front is arranged as a removeable panel. It would not be accessible when the bed is in position, but when the bed is pulled away the front can be lifted out for getting at a blanket store.

The side parts have doors to the bottom sections and flaps to the top sections. The doors can be arranged to support the flaps in the same way as in the previous example, but the design shows them with folding stays. The insides of both parts can be arranged with one or more shelves.

Sizes are dependent on the bed. The center section should be a few inches wider than the bed and the bottom of the top compartment should be above the mattress level and preferably nearly as high as the pillow. Other dimensions will have to be adjusted around these measurements.

To make the headboard use solid wood, thick plywood, or faced particleboard. Plywood panels should be lipped on their exposed edges for a clear finish. Particleboard should have suitable edging added where it is not already on manufactured edges.

The four uprights are almost the same. Mark one outer upright (FIG. 8-26A and 8-27A) with the positions of parts that will be attached to it and the location of center section parts, so that it can be used as a pattern for marking the other uprights. The outer uprights go to the floor to act as feet, but the intermediate ones stop at the bottom board.

The bottom goes right through and can fit into dados or rest on battens that fit behind the front plinth (FIG. 8-27B). Rabbet the backs of the outer uprights to take the thin plywood back and make the intermediate uprights narrow enough for the plywood to pass over them.

The top goes right through, but is cut back over the center section (FIGS. 8-26B and 8-27C). The simplest satisfactory joints are made be letting the top overhang for stopped dado joints to be used (FIG. 8-27D). The alternatives are any of the corner joints, such as dovetail or notched.

The central divider and those for the side parts can be joined with dado joints, but for the sake of rigidity there should be battens below (FIG. 8-27E). They should be kept back at the front to clear the flaps and doors.

The shelves can also be fitted into dados, although it might be better to rest them on battens so they can be removed to allow storage space for large items. One way of making the battens unobtrusive is to put a solid front on a thin plywood shelf (FIG. 8-27F).

The doors and flaps do not involve cutting into the main parts before they are assembled, so it is best to finish and sand the parts described so far and assemble them. Make the back out of one piece of plywood is possible, but if this is an opportunity to use up smaller pieces where joints will not show, you can butt edges over the solid framing. If there is any doubt about whether the floor is level or the wall upright, the bottoms of the sides can be cut away to form feet or their angles adjusted to suit.

It is better for the headboard to tilt slightly towards the wall than away from it, if you cannot make it stand vertically. Check squareness, but if the back plywood is carefully shaped, this should keep the assembly accurate.

The flaps can be made in one piece or you can let plywood flush into rabbets in a frame to give a paneled effect when closed and a flat surface when lowered (FIG. 8-28A). The doors can be made in the same manner.

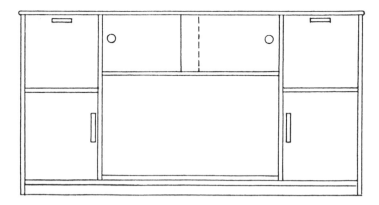

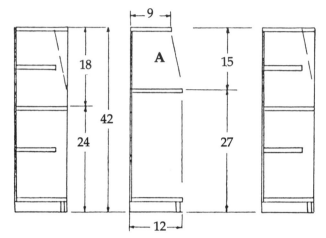

Fig. 8-26. Sizes of the large headboard: (A) uprights; (B) top.

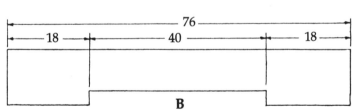

Another way to provide a thicker door without excess weight would be to use plywood on each side of a frame, mitered on the top corners, but allowed to overlap where it would not show at the bottom (FIG. 8-28B). Provide matching handles on the flaps and doors.

Hinge the doors on the outer uprights and put stops and catches at their other edges. The flaps swing down on hinges and are arranged with two folding stays each, so there is less risk of distortion with uneven pressures. It might be necessary to try the action of the stays before fitting shelves to allow for their movement as they fold.

The sliding doors on the sloping center section are pieces of plywood. Projecting handles would interfere with their movement. Finger holes are all that

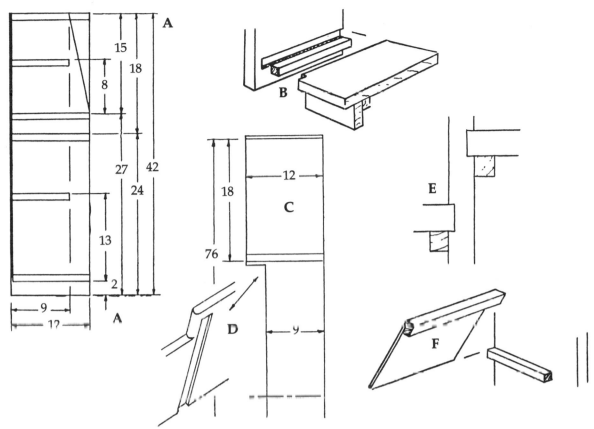

Fig. 8-27. Sizes of headboard parts and some of the joints: (A) uprights; (B) bottom; (C) top; (D) stopped dado joints; (E) battens; (F) solid front.

are needed, although these could be lined with a type of flush handle intended for the purpose.

The doors slide in plowed grooves. They rest against the bottoms of the lower grooves (FIG. 8-28C), but at the top the grooves should be deep enough to allow the doors to be lifted clear of the bottoms for removal or insertion (FIG. 8-28D). The clearance in the top grooves should be only just enough to release the doors, otherwise there is a risk of unintentionally lifting a door free when sliding it.

The best way to make both door guides is to plow the grooves on a rectangular piece and bevel it afterwards (FIG. 8-28E). Sand the insides of the grooves with abrasive paper wrapped around a thin piece of wood or a door edge. The sliding action should be easy, so allow for the slight thickening of a coat of paint or varnish. Fit one of the guides in place and make a trial assembly of the other guide and the doors, to check that the action is correct and one guide is not twisted in relation to the other.

The lower removable panel is a piece of plywood that rests against stops in the opening, which should be taken all around the sides and top. Put strips of wood inside the panel edges and across the bottom, with the upright pieces long enough to fit inside a strip across the headboard bottom (FIG. 8-28F). There can

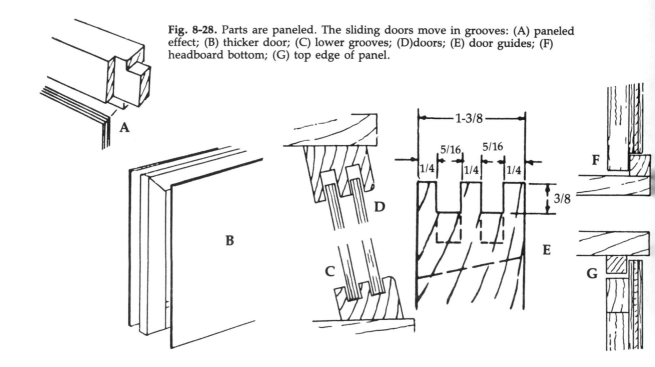

Fig. 8-28. Parts are paneled. The sliding doors move in grooves: (A) paneled effect; (B) thicker door; (C) lower grooves; (D)doors; (E) door guides; (F) headboard bottom; (G) top edge of panel.

be a strip across the top edge of the panel to fit easily inside the stop (FIG. 8-28G), then there can be two catches arranged to hold the panel in place. To remove it, tilt outwards and lift.

No shelves are shown in the example inside the lower compartment, but if folded blankets and similar things are to be stored there, the space might be better left unimpeded.

SPRUNG BED

This is a bed of simple design that is intended to be comfortable, yet strong enough to stand up to the activity and energy of a child as he grows to adult size (FIG. 8-29). The sizes suit a mattress of standard length (FIG. 8-29A) and a 30-inch width, but it is easy to adapt to other sizes in the first planning. The base is sprung with rubber webbing, but it could be made with plywood or other supports (FIG. 8-17). Having rubber webbing allows a thinner mattress to be used, or with a deep mattress it increases comfort. TABLE 8-10 lists the necessary materials for this project.

The head and foot are made in the same way, but the head is 9 inches deeper (FIG. 8-29B). As shown, these stand well above the bedding level. The head is high enough to lean against when sitting and the foot allows clothes to be hung over it. Both parts could be lowered by about 6 inches if less projection is preferred.

Mark out the legs together (FIG. 8-30A) to get matching positions level. Leave some excess wood at the tops until after the joints have been made. The rails are simple and all the same length (FIG. 8-30B). Cut grooves for the plywood panels in all of these parts. The grooves in the legs are only needed as far as the bottom rail, but if they have to be cut right through, the lower parts can be filled with glued strips.

It is possible to dowel the corners of the two end frames, but it is better to use mortise and tenon joints. Make the tenons about one-third the width of the wood, not just the thickness of the plywood. At the top cut a stub on the tenon to go to the depth of the groove, then take the main tenon at least 1 inch deep (FIG. 8-30C). For the wider lower rails use double tenons (FIG. 8-30D). After assembly, trim the tops of the legs and round their corners. Bevel the bottoms of the legs and add glides. Take off sharpness all around.

Table 8-10. Materials List for a Sprung Bed.

2 legs	$1\frac{3}{4} \times 42 \times 1\frac{3}{4}$
2 legs	$1\frac{3}{4} \times 33 \times 1\frac{3}{4}$
2 rails	$1\frac{3}{4} \times 30 \times 1\frac{3}{4}$
2 rails	$4 \times 30 \times 1\frac{3}{4}$
1 panel	$24 \times 30 \times \frac{1}{4}$ plywood
1 panel	$15 \times 30 \times \frac{1}{4}$ plywood
2 sides	$4 \times 75 \times 1$
2 ends	$4 \times 30 \times 1$
2 cross members	$4 \times 30 \times \frac{3}{4}$

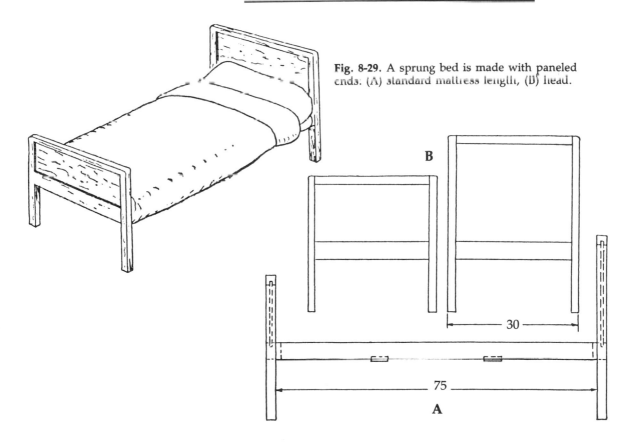

Fig. 8-29. A sprung bed is made with paneled ends. (A) standard mattress length, (B) head.

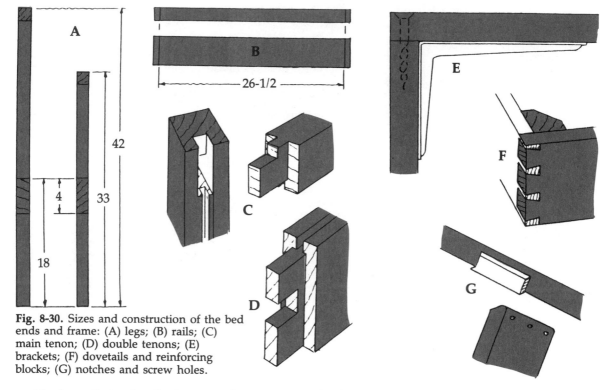

Fig. 8-30. Sizes and construction of the bed ends and frame: (A) legs; (B) rails; (C) main tenon; (D) double tenons; (E) brackets; (F) dovetails and reinforcing blocks; (G) notches and screw holes.

The frame that makes the base must be strong enough to resist strain, direct loads, rocking action, and twisting. This means that the corner joints should be good ones and some bracing underneath is advisable. A simple way of joining the corners is to let the sides overlap the ends, attached with long screws, then put shelf brackets inside (FIG. 8-30E), either one or two at each corner.

A better joint involves dovetails and reinforcing blocks glued in the angles (FIG. 8-30F). In both cases, further strengthening of the sides comes from two cross members below the frame. Divide the length into three. Screw these pieces into shallow notches from below (FIG. 8-30G). Keep the notches shallow to avoid weakening the sides and round the exposed parts so they will not be visible in normal use. Mark out and prepare these joints, but deal with the edges to suit the method of mattress support before assembly.

It should be satisfactory to interlace 2-inch-wide rubber webbing with gaps of about 4 inches. The simplest way to attach it is to tack directly on the surface, but this might show and it is better to leave the outer edge plain. There are several ways of doing this.

You can cut a rabbet wide enough to take the tacked webbing, but with a narrow edge to hide it (FIG. 8-31A). The depth needs to be little more than the webbing thickness. Also, there are metal clips obtainable for attaching to the ends of webbing. One type goes over the webbing and is squeezed tight in a vise, so its points pierce the fabric (FIG. 8-31B). One way of attaching this to the wood is to press it into a plowed groove about ⅛ inch wide and ½ inch deep (FIG. 8-31C), but check the actual clips used. A perpendicular groove should be safe, but it is better to angle the cut slightly. The groove could be cut on the surface or

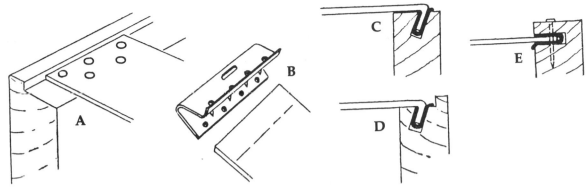

Fig. 8-31. Rubber webbing can be tacked in a rabbet or used with metal clips in a groove: (A) rabbet; (B) pierced fabric; (C) plowed groove; (D) groove; (E) driven nail or screw.

combined with a rabbet (FIG. 8-31D). If the clip has a slot hole in it, this allows another method of attaching, using a groove plowed on the inside of the wood and a stout nail or screw driven downward (FIG. 8-31E).

Attach the bed frame to the head and foot by screwing from inside. Alternatively there could be a set of the metal bed fittings that allow easier disassembly. Wood screws are satisfactory if you only plan to take the unit apart a few times.

The bed as described is functional and quite satisfactory, but there are ways of decorating it besides painting. The appearance of the wide lower rail at the foot can be lightened by chamfering its lower edge. This can be a sweep (FIG. 8-32A) or a stopped chamfer with a rounded end if made with a spindle molder (FIG. 8-32B). Or it can be an angular cut if made by hand (FIG. 8-32C).

There could be matching chamfers around the panels on the fronts of head and foot (FIG. 8-32D) and along the lower edges of the sides, but they would usually be hidden. Round the inner edges of the sides in any case for a comfortable grip if fingers are curled under to move the bed.

You can also add molding to break up the plainness of the panels. Avoid complicated sections, but use half round molding to make a border or diamond pattern (FIG. 8-32E).

As an alternative to plywood panels, the ends can be made with slats. They could be all the same width and either vertical or horizontal. Graduating the widths, with the widest in the middle gives a pleasing appearance (FIG. 8-32F). There could be a fretted cutout or an applied carving or other decoration on the center slat. The best way to fit the slats is with barefaced tenons that need not go very deeply into the rails (FIG. 8-32G). Round the edges before assembly.

BUNK BEDS

If two children are to sleep in the same room it is convenient to have two identical beds that can be used independently or stacked one over the other to give double-decker sleeping accommodations (FIGS. 8-33 and 8-34). It is then possible to use both beds on the floor where there is plenty of space or have them in different rooms. But for more crowded conditions, one can fit over the other.

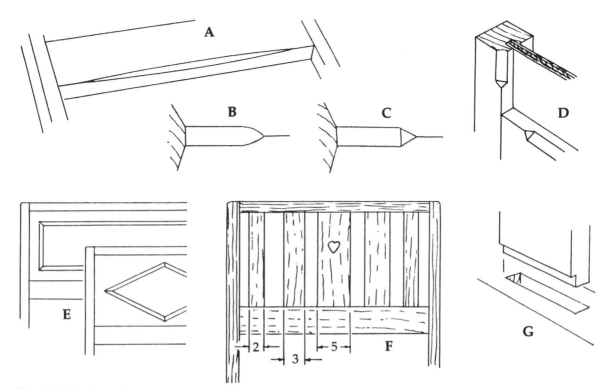

Fig. 8-32. End panels can be decorated with chamfered edges, molded panels, or by using slats instead of plywood: (A) sweep; (B) stopped chamfer; (C) angular cut; (D) matching chamfers; (E) molding; (F) graduating widths; (G) tenons.

For convenience in getting into the upper bed there is a ladder. A safety guard can be fitted at the head end of it, assuming the other side of the stacked beds are against a wall. If not, there should be guardrails on both sides.

One bed fits on to the other with pegs or dowels projecting upward to engage with holes. Obviously the two beds must match or they cannot be joined. If the safety guard is made to fit only one bed, that should be the upper one and it need not have pegs at the top of its legs.

To make sure the beds will match, mark all similar parts for both beds at the same time and assemble the two beds in matching stages, rather than completing one before the other. A detailed materials list is found in TABLE 8-11.

Sizes are intended for mattresses of standard length and 36-inch widths (FIG. 8-34), but the two mattresses should be obtained first and measured before marking out wood. There should be enough clearance for bedmaking, but make sure the mattresses are not too loose or there will be a risk of a restless sleeper twisting the mattress in relation to the bed.

All four end frames are made in the same manner. Join the legs by rails and put plywood panels on the surface. Make all eight legs first (FIG. 8-35A). Note that the tops of the legs or posts stand above the top rails and the lower rails are below the level of the bed sides. The rails could be joined to the legs with single ¾-inch dowels, but tenons would be stronger (FIG. 8-35B).

Fig. 8-33. Two matching beds can be stacked to form bunks.

Drill the tops and bottoms of the legs for hardwood dowels—¾-inch diameter should be satisfactory. For the sake of appearance, you can taper the squares to round. Draw a circle, then chisel and sand the shapes (FIG. 8-35C). The dowels should go about 1½ inches into each leg and the projecting top should be rounded to ease assembly (FIG. 8-35D). If a lathe is available you can give the end a slight taper as well (FIG. 8-35E).

The bed sides should have their inner surfaces level with the inner edges of the legs. You can dowel or tenon into the legs, and then place plywood gussets on the inner surfaces to provide extra bracing (FIG. 8-35F). Glue and screw the gussets after attaching the bed sides to the legs.

It would be possible to use rubber webbing, but to keep the beds light for lifting, you can drill the plywood mattress supports with a pattern of holes and support them on strips inside the sides and ends (FIG. 8-35G). The plywood need not be fastened down.

Attach the end plywood panels to the bed ends with glue and nails, the nails punching below the surface and then covering them with stopping. Round all exposed edges. When the two beds are stacked, they should hold together safely without further fastening, but if you want additional security, you could add fasteners of the hook-and-screw-eye-type joining one leg to the other at each corner.

Table 8-11. Materials List for Bunk Beds.

8 legs	1¾ × 34 × 1¾
8 rails	1¾ × 37 × 1¾
4 panels	22 × 38 × ¼ plywood
4 sides	5 × 75 × 1
4 mattress supports	1 × 75 × 1
4 mattress supports	1 × 36 × 1
2 mattress supports	36 × 75 × ½ plywood
2 ladder sides	1½ × 60 × 1
5 ladder sides	1½ × 12 × dowel rods
8 pegs	¾ × 3 × dowel rods
1 ladder top	1 × 14 × ½
2 safety guards	1½ × 36 × 1½
2 safety guards	1½ × 13 × 1½
5 safety guards	½ × 12 × dowel rods

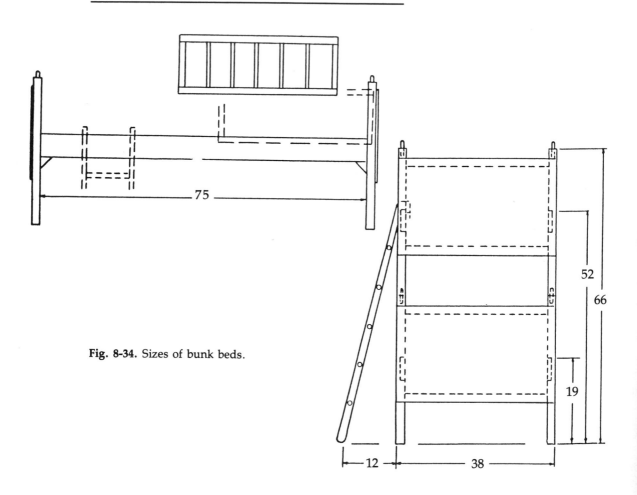

Fig. 8-34. Sizes of bunk beds.

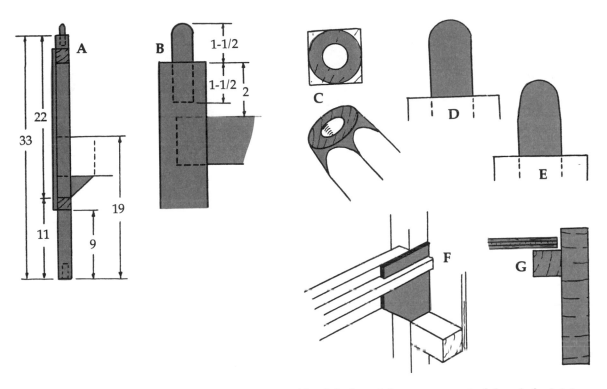

Fig. 8-35. Construction of bunk beds and the arrangement of dowels for joining them: (A) legs; (B) tenons; (C) sand shapes; (D) rounded projecting top; (E) tapered end; (F) plywood gussets; (G) inside strips.

The ladder is intended to slope (FIG. 8-34) and hook over the side of the upper bed. Its length is best determined by putting the wood for one side against the stacked beds and marking the top edge when the slope is satisfactory.

The hook over the top is made with plywood cheeks and a crossbar inside (FIG. 8-36A). This does not have to make a tight fit over the bed side. It can be loose enough to be lined with cloth. The bottoms of the ladder sides should be rounded.

Divide the distance from the bed edge to the ground equally. The child should step the same distance at the top and bottom as he does between the rungs. Spaces of about 9 inches should be satisfactory (FIG. 8-36B). The rungs can be ¾-inch dowel rods taken right through the sides. For the strongest construction make saw cuts across the ends before assembly and drive in glued wedges across the grain (FIG. 8-36C).

The safety guard is made in a similar way to that described earlier, with its corners doweled or tenoned and dowel rods set into holes (FIG. 8-36D). The simplest way to attach the safety rod securely is to use bolts and butterfly nuts, two through the bed side and one through the post (FIG. 8-36E).

When the two beds are to be used independently, it is possible to arrange storage for the ladder and guard under the mattress support of the lower bed. Storage under the upper bed would limit headroom in the lower bed when the two are fitted together.

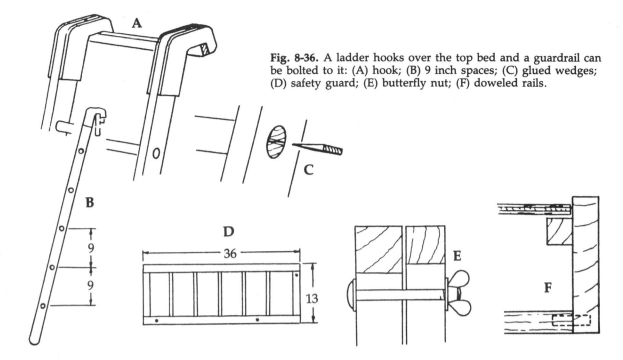

Fig. 8-36. A ladder hooks over the top bed and a guardrail can be bolted to it: (A) hook; (B) 9 inch spaces; (C) glued wedges; (D) safety guard; (E) butterfly nut; (F) doweled rails.

For this storage space the mattress support must be left loose so it can be lifted out. Three rails are equally spaced in the length of the bed and fitted across between the sides. They can be doweled or tenoned when the bed is assembled (FIG. 8-36F). There will then be space for both items to be put away out of sight.

BED TRAY

If the child is ill and has to eat in bed and you want to avoid spilled food and drink, there has to be something rigid on which to put things. This tray or table stands on legs far enough apart to straddle the legs of anyone in bed and rest on the comparatively steady mattress (FIG. 8-37). The size is sufficient to allow leg movement without tipping the table and the same item could be used by an adult. This materials list can be found in TABLE 8-12.

The legs of the table fold inward so the folded thickness is less than 3 inches for storage. The tray can be carried with the legs folded and opened when it is put in position on the bed. If the sizes are altered they must be arranged so there is space for both sets of legs to fold inward without interfering with each other. The distance between the legs must be slightly more than double the leg length.

It will help visualize sizes if you draw one corner full-size (FIG. 8-38A). The legs should be set in 1 inch from the ends and sides of the top. The lips around the tray should come midway between the leg tops and the edge of the tray.

Join the legs at each end with a crossbar (FIG. 8-38B). The only joints to make are between these parts. You could use two dowels in each joint, but cut mortise and tenon joints would be better (FIG. 8-38C). Mark out the legs together and taper them to 1 inch square at their bottoms. Leave some waste wood at the top until the joints have been made.

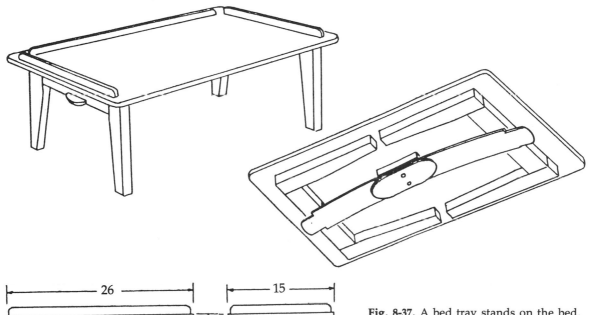

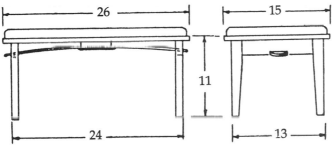

Fig. 8-37. A bed tray stands on the bed, but its legs can be folded. They are held in both positions with a springy piece of wood.

Table 8-12. Materials List for a Bed Tray.

1 top	15 × 26 × ½ plywood
4 legs	1½ × 11 × ¾
2 crossbars	2 × 12 × ¾
2 lips	1 × 25 × ½
2 lips	1 × 14 × ½
1 spring	3 × 26 × ¼
1 packing	3 × 6 × ½
1 stiffener	3 × 6 × ¼

Carefully square the joints during assembly and check that the tops of the assemblies are both straight and with right angles between the faces, as the accuracy of the top edge controls the leg attitude when open.

The top is a piece of ½-inch plywood. Round its corners and angles. There could be a frame all around the top with mitered corners. It could have a long side open toward the user. In the arrangement shown, the frame is made of three lips on top. They do not meet at the corners. This allows easier cleaning (FIG. 8-38D). The long side without a lip will probably be stiff enough as it is, but there

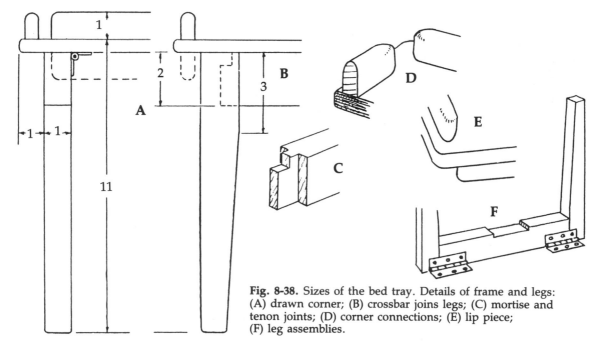

Fig. 8-38. Sizes of the bed tray. Details of frame and legs: (A) drawn corner; (B) crossbar joins legs; (C) mortise and tenon joints; (D) corner connections; (E) lip piece; (F) leg assemblies.

could be another lip piece put underneath (FIG. 8-38E). All of the lips should be well rounded. Fix them with glue and screws through the plywood.

The leg assemblies have hinges on the inside (FIG. 8-38F). They could be piano hinges taken across the full width, or a pair of shorter hinges at each end. Do not let them in. The legs will swing clear as they are folded. Arrange the hinges so the tops of the legs bear against the tray when they are upright.

Locking the legs in position is done with a springy piece of wood. The amount of spring needed is not excessive and there are several hardwoods that could be used, but something with known springy characteristics, like ash, would be best. The thickness might have to be adjusted by trial thinning of the wood to give an easier action, but ¼ inch should be satisfactory.

The spring piece is fitted under the tray on a packing (FIG. 8-39A). There are two screws across its center, but to spread the load on them and prevent cracking there, put a stiffener under the screw heads. This is elliptical and thinned toward the ends (FIG. 8-39B). It should be satisfactory if the same length as the packing, but if the spring is not stiff enough, a longer stiffener can be used. Have the spring too long at first.

Cut notches in the centers of the crossbar, ½ inch narrower than the spring and ¼ inch deep at first (FIG. 8-39C). Temporarily assemble the table. One screw in each hinge will do. Flex the spring in position and mark where it will have to be shouldered to drop into the notches. Cut these shoulders (FIG. 8-39D). Trim and round the projecting ends (FIG. 8-39E). Note how much the notches in the crossbars should be trimmed for the spring to drop in neatly. Taper the bottoms of the notches to suit (FIG. 8-39F).

Take the sharpness off any projecting edges or angles. The spring has to be lifted from each notch to allow the legs to fold, but it should then close on to them and prevent them from swinging away from the tray.

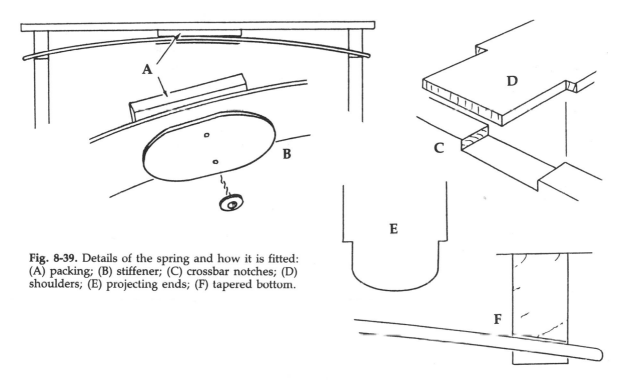

Fig. 8-39. Details of the spring and how it is fitted: (A) packing; (B) stiffener; (C) crossbar notches; (D) shoulders; (E) projecting ends; (F) tapered bottom.

A painted finish is probably best, although the spring could be given a clear varnish treatment. There could be a picture on the surface of the tray for a young child, but it would probably be better to allow for the use of a cloth or place mat. An alternative to paint is to use plywood veneered on the surface and hardwood for the lips. A clear finish would make a more attractive piece of furniture for an older child.

DRESSING CHEST

This is a three-part dressing chest, dressing table, or dresser, consisting of a two-drawer chest that fits onto a stand and a mirror that can be separate or attached to the chest (FIG. 8-40). The stand is made of wood like the under part of a low table. The chest could be made of solid wood or plywood, but it is described as made from veneered or plastic-faced particleboard. The mirror assembly is made of wood.

You can choose the solid wood parts to match the veneer on the particleboard, but the appearance would also be attractive if the stand and mirror parts were of a color to contrast with the chest. A complete materials list can be found in TABLE 8-13.

The chest could be arranged to use some of the standard drawer assemblies with their runners. You would then have to adapt its sizes to suit. It would also be helpful to use stock widths of faced particleboard and that shown in FIG. 8-40 is one of them. Variations in the back-to-front measurements by a few inches would not matter, however.

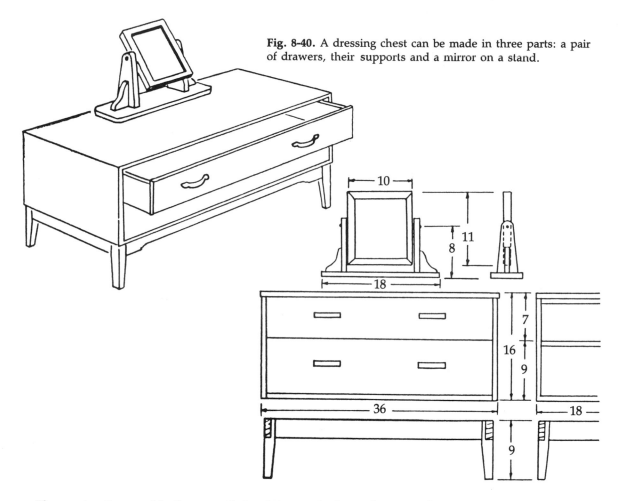

Fig. 8-40. A dressing chest can be made in three parts: a pair of drawers, their supports and a mirror on a stand.

The construction used in the example involves standard wood construction for the drawers, except the fronts, which are matching particleboard. The wooden parts are adaptable to match the chest, so its sizes and assembly should be dealt with first.

The chest ends (FIG. 8-41A) have strips of wood across the top to make the joint and act as drawer kickers. Similar strips also act as runners and kickers between the drawers. All are cut back to clear the drawer fronts. More strips at the back take the plywood or hardboard back and act as drawer stops. You could put strips across the bottom also, but they would reduce the depth of the bottom drawer and it would be better to use counterbored screws covered with plastic plugs (FIG. 8-41B).

The chest bottom fits between the ends and is plain except for a strip across it to take the back (FIG. 8-41C). The top is similar except it overlaps the ends (FIG. 8-41D) and its extending parts should be covered with matching strips of veneer. These parts can be assembled and the back glued, nailed, or screwed in to hold the carcass true while drawers are made and fitted.

The drawer sides should fit between the strips and the particleboard fronts should come inside the chest, level with the front edges. Make sure there is

Table 8-13. Materials List for a Dressing Chest.

2 chest ends	16 × 18 × ¾
1 chest bottom	18 × 35 × ¾
1 chest top	18 × 37 × ¾
1 chest back	16 × 36 × ¼ plywood
6 chest joints	⅝ × 17 × ⅝
1 drawer front	7 × 35 × ¾
1 drawer front	9 × 35 × ¾
1 inner drawer front	6 × 35 × ⅝
1 inner drawer front	8 × 35 × ⅝
2 drawer sides	6 × 17 × ⅝
2 drawer sides	8 × 17 × ⅝
1 drawer back	5½ × 35 × ⅝
1 drawer back	7½ × 35 × ⅝
2 drawer bottoms	17 × 35 × ¼ plywood
4 legs	1½ × 9 × 1½
2 rails	3 × 35 × 1
2 rails	3 × 17 × 1
2 mirror frames	1 × 11 × 1
2 mirror frames	1 × 10 × 1
2 mirror supports	3 × 10 × ¾
1 mirror base	5 × 18 × ¾
2 mirror brackets	3 × 5 × ¾

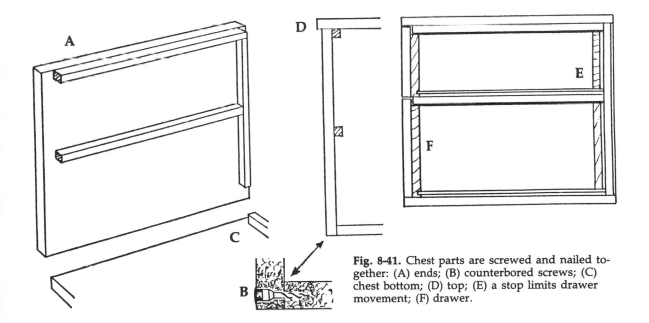

Fig. 8-41. Chest parts are screwed and nailed together: (A) ends; (B) counterbored screws; (C) chest bottom; (D) top; (E) a stop limits drawer movement; (F) drawer.

clearance behind these fronts and the strips across the chest ends so it is the back of each drawer against its stop that limits the drawer movement (FIG. 8-41E). This should prevent the front from becoming strained.

The drawers are made in any of the usual ways, with the inner front set back enough for the particleboard front to be attached by screwing from inside (FIG. 8-41F). The two fronts should have only enough space between them for clearance and the top edge of each should be veneered.

Handles can be any type that match the veneered particleboard, but if a child is to use them, do not space them too far apart and choose a type that allows small fingers to get a good grip as a packed drawer may be quite heavy.

The stand is made like table framing with doweled or mortised and tenoned corner joints (FIG. 8-42A). The inner surfaces of the legs can taper. Leg bottoms should be rounded and can be fitted with glides. You could also add some shaping to the lower edge of the front rail (FIG. 8-42B).

The outside of the stand rails should be level with the outsides of the legs and the overall size should be arranged so the stand ends are ½ inch in from the chest ends and the front is set back a similar amount. If there is a baseboard around the room and you want the chest close to the wall, you can bring the back of the stand forward enough to clear this, but otherwise the rear legs should be level with the back of the chest.

To locate the chest on its stand, put strips around the bottom to fit inside the rails (FIG. 8-42C). They do not have to be the full lengths of the stand rails, nor in single pieces.

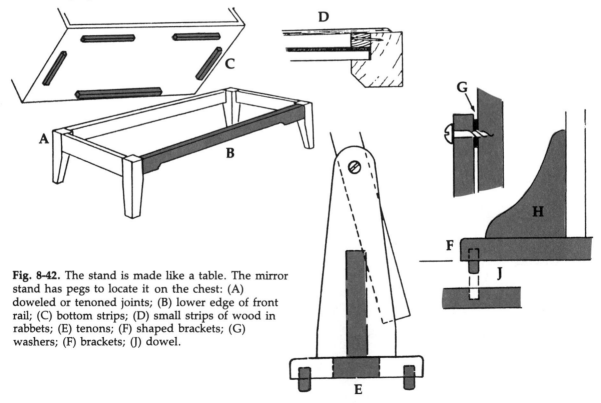

Fig. 8-42. The stand is made like a table. The mirror stand has pegs to locate it on the chest: (A) doweled or tenoned joints; (B) lower edge of front rail; (C) bottom strips; (D) small strips of wood in rabbets; (E) tenons; (F) shaped brackets; (G) washers; (F) brackets; (J) dowel.

The swivel mirror shown has the glass framed. The suggested sizes can be modified to suit any size mirror. A similar construction could be used for quite a long mirror which would be appreciated by an older girl.

Rabbit and miter the mirror frame like a picture frame. The mirror can be held with a piece of card to protect its back and small strips of wood in the rabbets (FIG. 8-42D). You can screw a piece of thin plywood on the back as further protection. This will also strengthen the corner miters.

The pivot points should come above the halfway point on the sides. Arrange the height of the supports to suit this and allow some clearance for the bottom edge to swing over the base. Tenons into the base are the best joints (FIG. 8-42E), but you could use dowels or the supports could be screwed from below.

The mirror baseboard is a piece of wood long enough to allow shaped brackets to be fitted (FIG. 8-42F). Space the supports so they will stand upright with enough clearance on each side of the mirror for washers at the pivots. The pivots are two wood screws, but to provide friction in the joints to hold the mirror at any angle, include rubber or fiber washers between the wood surfaces (FIG. 8-42G).

Smooth and round the shaped outlines of the brackets (FIG. 8-42H). Then attach them with glue and screws through the baseboard. Round the corners of the baseboard and chamfer or round the upper edges.

The mirror stand can be treated as a separate item, so it can be moved about. In that case cover its bottom with cloth or rubber to avoid damage to a surface or accidental sliding. If you want it in a fixed position on a chest, you could either screw it in place or use dowels.

Locate four dowels near the corners of the baseboard (FIG. 8-42J). Glue them in place with rounded ends projecting about ⅜ inch. Drill holes in the chest top so the dowels can be pressed in. This should give enough security against unintentional movement, but the mirror stand can still be lifted out and used elsewhere standing on the dowel ends.

KIDNEY-SHAPED DRESSING TABLE

A dresser with a kidney-shaped top and drapes below is appropriate in a girl's bedroom. It looks particularly attractive if you add an oval mirror (FIG. 8-43).

TABLE 8-14 lists the necessary materials. Construction is not as difficult as it might seem due to the shape, because only the top has the kidney shape and the support underneath is a four-legged table structure. In this case the drapes can be opened to show a light framework with a shelf directly below the top and a drawer below that.

The only complication in making the table is having to slope the front legs. This is done to give a wide enough spread on the floor for steadiness, yet also be narrow enough at the top to allow the drapes to slide on their rail without touching the legs.

The top can be made in several ways. You could use a piece of thick plywood or use thin plywood thickened with strips underneath the shaped edge. This would have to be done with several pieces butted against each other to follow the curves.

The best top, however, is a piece of veneered particleboard. The structural parts are nearly all of 1-×-2-inch section. For a clear finish they should be hardwood, but they are not normally visible and for a painted finish they could be softwood.

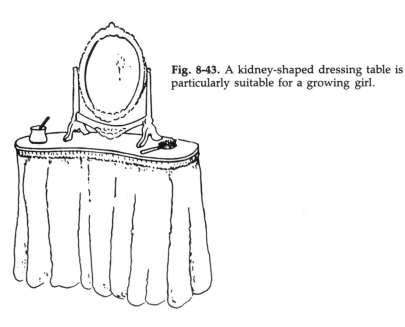

Fig. 8-43. A kidney-shaped dressing table is particularly suitable for a growing girl.

Table 8-14. Materials List for a Kidney-Shaped Dressing Table.

1 top	21 × 6 × ¾
4 legs	2 × 30 × 1
5 rails	2 × 24 × 1
1 stretcher	2 × 24 × 1
2 top rails	2 × 11 × 1
2 bottom rails	2 × 15 × 1
1 shelf	14 × 32 × ¼ plywood
2 top strips	1 × 15 × 1
1 false drawer front	5 × 22 × ¾
1 drawer front	4 × 22 × ⅝
2 drawer sides	4 × 15 × ⅝
1 drawer back	3½ × 22 × ¼ plywood
2 drawer guides	6 × 15 × ¼ plywood

Mark out the top first (FIG. 8-45A). A paper template of half the top will help get it symmetrical. Cut the shape carefully, preferably with a fine-toothed saw. This will leave little raggedness to clean off. Keep the section square and the edge flat. Strip self-adhesive veneer or plastic can then be ironed on. Arrange the joint in the edge veneer near the center of the back.

It might be just as well to prepare the curtain rail at this stage. A metal rail is easier to shape than a plastic one. Bend it to follow the outline about 1 inch in from the edge and allow for more brackets to hold it in place than you would need for the usual straight method of hanging drapes.

Let the ends come at the back. There is no need for the rail to make a complete circuit unless the table will be standing away from a wall and will be visible all

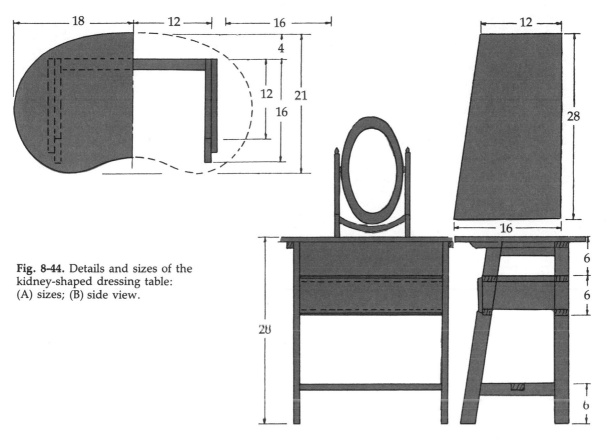

Fig. 8-44. Details and sizes of the kidney-shaped dressing table: (A) sizes; (B) side view.

around. For a wall position the rail ends can leave a gap of 12 inches or more at the back.

The supporting table frame must fit inside the rail and not interfere with the running of the drapes. Check that the sizes shown (FIG. 8-44A) will allow this with the chosen type of rail.

Draw a full-size side view of the table (FIG. 8-44B). The back leg is upright and the other members are at right angles to it, but you need the full-size drawing to obtain their lengths and angles at the other end.

The top and bottom rails can be tenoned or doweled into the legs (FIG. 8-45B). Check squareness of the rails to the back legs and see that both end assemblies match. The stretcher could be tenoned into the bottom rails; however, the assembly would be stronger if it was dovetailed (FIG. 8-45C). Cut this joint before assembling the ends.

There are also upper and lower drawer rails. At the upright leg they should be the same, but at the front leg the bottom rail should be narrower to allow the drawer front to be upright (FIG. 8-45D). It would be possible to make a sloping drawer front to match the angle of the legs, but it is simpler and more common to have it upright.

Tenon these rails into the legs. They need not go right through (FIG. 8-45E). There is no top rail across at the front, but the back rail can have a dovetail lap joint to the tops of the legs (FIG. 8-45F).

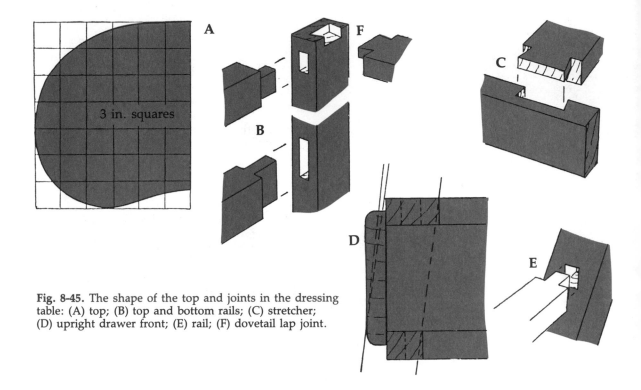

Fig. 8-45. The shape of the top and joints in the dressing table: (A) top; (B) top and bottom rails; (C) stretcher; (D) upright drawer front; (E) rail; (F) dovetail lap joint.

The shelf is a piece of plywood attached to the top drawer rails. It can be made the width of the frame, although it can also be extended between the legs to provide extra storage space outside of them, yet inside the drapes (FIG. 8-46A). Prepare this piece, but do not fit it finally until after the drawer and its runners have been made, although if the extensions are very long it will have to be put loosely in position when the framework is assembled.

Cut pieces of plywood to fit across the legs between the drawer rails. The drawer could be made to run on metal or plastic runners attached to the plywood sides. Another alternative is to groove the drawer sides so they will slide on strips of wood on the plywood (FIG. 8-46B). If there are no facilities for making a suitable groove, you can add a strip of wood on the side of the drawer and two slides for it to run between on each piece of plywood (FIG. 8-46C). The chosen method of running affects the width the body of the drawer has to be.

The drawer is made in any of the usual ways with a false front that hides the running arrangements and fits between the legs. Its top and bottom edges should be rounded and overlap the front rails (FIG. 8-46D). Attach the false front with glue and screws from inside. It can act as the drawer stop when it hits the rails. Or you can use a piece of plywood to close the space behind the back of the drawer. Adjust the drawer length to hit the piece.

The drawer handle should not project very far or it might show through the drapes. One of the type that swings down would be suitable. Another way of providing a pull without a handle would be to cut the false front so its center comes below the bottom rail. This would provide a hand hold (FIG. 8-46E).

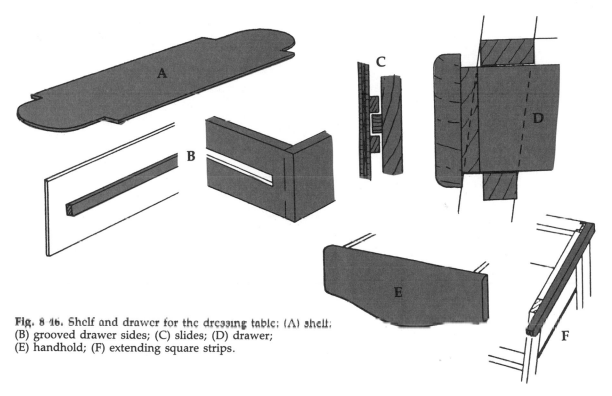

Fig. 8-46. Shelf and drawer for the dressing table: (A) shelf;
(B) grooved drawer sides; (C) slides; (D) drawer;
(E) handhold; (F) extending square strips.

Attach the top by screwing from below. You can drill screw holes in the rear rail and deeply counterbore holes in the top rails between back and front legs, but it would be simpler to screw on square strips outside the framework and drive screws upward through them into the top. They could extend a little at the front to give a broader contact (FIG. 8-46F). Invert the top and locate the framework squarely for screwing on.

Finally, make a trial assembly to the top, then remove the framework for finishing while the drapes are also being made. No mirror construction is suggested as this table looks best with a fairly ornate oval adjustable mirror.

WARDROBE

A full-size wardrobe is bigger than a child needs and much of it might be out of his reach. This is a smaller version with hanging space at a reasonable height and shelves for folded garments (FIGS. 8-47 AND 8-48). The overall size would be large enough for adult clothes, so it is possible to remove the internal parts and adapt the inside arrangements when the child gets older.

A materials list is found in TABLE 8-15. Construction is based on four corner posts, joined with framing and with plywood panels. The door is a sheet of plywood with stiffening inside to prevent warping. The whole piece of furniture is intended to be painted and the outside could be decorated with painted patterns or decals. Whatever color is used on the outside, a pastel shade inside will encourage cleanliness and help to make the contents visible.

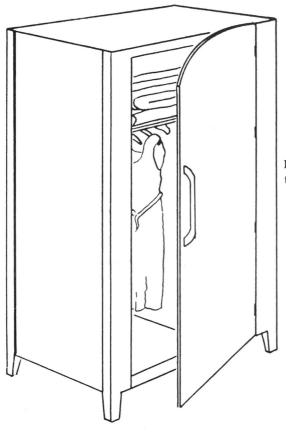

Fig. 8-47. A wardrobe scaled to size will hold a child's clothes.

Start by laying out one side (FIG. 8-49A). The bottom should be high enough for cleaning underneath. The main shelf settles the height of the rail for clothes hangers. This might be a little higher for a girl than a boy in order to accommodate long dresses. The side shelves could be equally spaced, but they look better if the spaces reduce in depth toward the top.

Next, groove the two rear posts both ways for plywood panels (FIG. 8-49B). Groove the front ones only at the sides, but increase at the front their width with glued on strips (FIG. 8-49C). Taper the feet below the bottom.

The rails at the sides should all come inside the plywood. The top rail should be low enough for the plywood top to come inside (FIG. 8-49D). At the bottom the rail supports the plywood base (FIG. 8-49E). Other lighter rails will support the main shelf and some on the right hand side support the other shelves. All of the rails should have their faces level with the edges of the groove and are tenoned to the posts.

The door can be hinged either way, but it is better if the internal divisions have the narrow shelves on the hinge side and hanging garments are on the side the door is opened.

At the top of the back place a similar rail inside the rear plywood at the level to take the top plywood (FIG. 8-49F). At the front dowel or tenon a deeper rail into the widened posts and rabbet it so the edge of the top plywood does not show

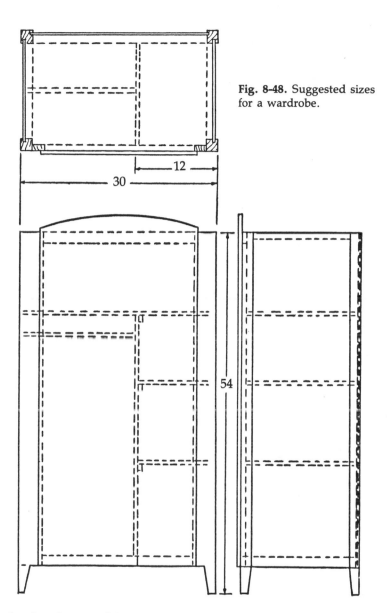

Fig. 8-48. Suggested sizes for a wardrobe.

when the door is opened (FIG. 8-49G). Also rabbet the rail at the bottom for the base plywood. At the back the base can go over the rail.

The inside parts can be made before assembly, but they will probably need some adjustments later. Mark the shelf support positions of the upright division from the wardrobe side. It could be a piece of ½-inch plywood, but lip its front edge (FIG. 8-49H) or put a grooved strip at the front with thinner plywood (FIG. 8-49J).

The shelves can be treated in a similar way, but with thin plywood there should be rabbets to bring the tops level (FIG. 8-49K). All of the internal parts

Table 8-15. Materials List for a Wardrobe.

4 posts	1¾ × 54 × 1¾
2 front strips	2¼ × 54 × ⅝
2 panels	16 × 50 × ¼ plywood
4 side rails	1¼ × 16 × 1¼
2 back rails	1¼ × 28 × 1¼
1 front top rail	2 × 28 × ⅝
1 front bottom rail	1½ × 28 × 1¼
1 back panel	28 × 50 × ¼ plywood
1 top	18 × 30 × ¼ plywood
1 bottom	18 × 30 × ¼ plywood
1 divider	17 × 38 × ½ plywood
1 main shelf	17 × 30 × ½ plywood
2 side shelves	12 × 17 × ½ plywood
7 shelf supports	1 × 17 × ¾
1 door	24 × 54 × ½ plywood
2 door frames	1½ × 50 × ⅝
2 door frames	1½ × 23 × ⅝

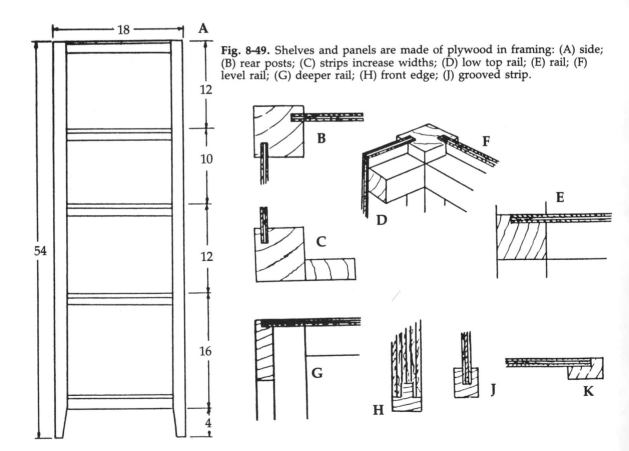

Fig. 8-49. Shelves and panels are made of plywood in framing: (A) side; (B) rear posts; (C) strips increase widths; (D) low top rail; (E) rail; (F) level rail; (G) deeper rail; (H) front edge; (J) grooved strip.

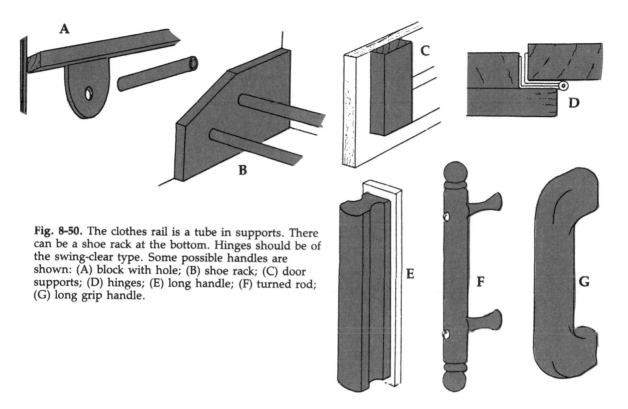

Fig. 8-50. The clothes rail is a tube in supports. There can be a shoe rack at the bottom. Hinges should be of the swing-clear type. Some possible handles are shown: (A) block with hole; (B) shoe rack; (C) door supports; (D) hinges; (E) long handle; (F) turned rod; (G) long grip handle.

should not come further forward than the insides of the widening pieces on the front posts. This gives clearance for the door framing.

With the parts prepared, start assembly with the sides. Although the plywood panels should be a good fit in the grooves, they need not go to the full depth. It is more important that the rail joints pull tight, which they would not do if the plywood reached the bottoms of the grooves first.

Cut the bottom of a plywood panel square and use this to true the assembly. At the top there can be some excess length to cut off later. Where plywood comes over intermediate rails, use glue and a few thin nails, punched and covered with stopping. See that the opposite sides match and be careful that they do not develop twists while the glue is setting. Put them under weights.

The top and the bottom have to be assembled next. The internal parts all rest on supports so they can be fitted in after the external parts are joined. Check the top and bottom rails for size and position. Mark joints that come together. Have the base plywood ready. The top plywood can be added after the other parts are assembled. Treat the back plywood like the side panels, using the squared bottom to get the assembly true and leaving some excess length at the top to trim after assembly.

Check that the wardrobe stands upright when placed on a flat surface. View it from all directions. When the glue has set, fit the top plywood. Try the inside parts in position. Before fitting them, make the clothes rail. This can be a piece of ¾-inch dowel rod, but it is probably better if made of a piece of aluminum tube. Support it with a block with a hole in each end (FIG. 8-50A). A shoe rack could be made in a similar way across the back of the base (FIG. 8-50B).

The door is a single piece of ½-inch plywood. It will probably hold its shape, but to reduce the risk of warping, it should be framed on the inside with strips that fit easily into the opening and are not more than ⅝ inch thick. This way they will not touch the edges of the shelves (FIG. 8-50C). The hinges will have to be of the cranked type. You will need three or four for a door of this height. So that stock sizes of hinges can be used, suitable ones should be obtained before laying out the framing (FIG. 8-50D).

It will probably be best to use spring catches. Although one might be sufficient, the door will close tighter if you use two, spaced about one-quarter of the depth from top and bottom.

The door top is shown rounded, but any other outline could be used. Slightly round the exposed edges all round. It is better for the bottom of the door to be a little way below the bottom rail than to have part of the rail showing.

A piece of furniture with a tall door looks best with a long handle. It could be a metal or plastic one or it could be of the hollowed wood type used on earlier furniture (FIG. 8-50E). A turned rod could be held out with spacer pieces (FIG. 8-50F) or a block of wood could be cut away to provide a long grip (FIG. 8-50G). The door could be finished a different color from the rest of the wardrobe and the handle made the body color or a third color.

9

Play Equipment

A CHILD'S IDEA OF TOYS is not always the same as an adult's, as many parents know after seeing a child reject an elaborate and expensive toy in favor of something simple. This is not a book on making toys, but there are many pieces of furniture that have play possibilities and there are some toys related to furniture that are worth including. A table with a cloth over it may be all the conversion needed to make a playhouse, but something looking at least a little more real might give longer pleasure and serve to keep young children occupied and within bounds. Other toys might actually be containers for smaller toys and their use encourage the child to clean up after a play session. The few ideas given in this chapter can be elaborated and adapted to other uses.

WALKER TRUCK

A child who is still hesitant about walking will appreciate something to hold on to that he can push around. If it is a box on wheels, he can load other toys into it or use it for their storage (FIG. 9-1).

As this is a toy that the child will outgrow, there is no need for an elaborate construction. The assembly is kept low and the handle comes within the wheel area, so there is little risk of the truck being pulled over. TABLE 9-1 lists the necessary materials.

The main body is a box with the sides extended. Nailed joints could be used, but dados are shown. Mark the sides together (FIG. 9-2A). The ends are plain pieces to fit between them (FIG. 9-2B). Although the bottom could be nailed on, it is better to put it inside on supporting strips (FIG. 9-2C). Round the corners of the extending sides and take the sharpness off all edges.

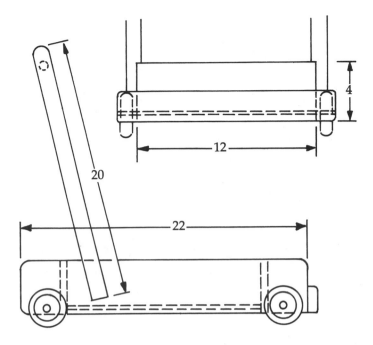

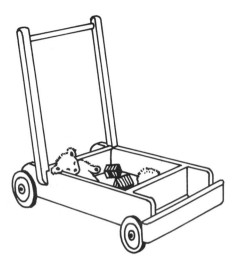

Fig. 9-1. A walker truck provides mobile storage for a young child who is just learning to walk.

Table 9-1. Materials List for a Walker Truck.

2 sides	4	×	22	× ½
2 ends	4	×	11¼	× ½
1 bottom	11	×	16	× ¼ plywood
2 handle sides	1	×	20	× 1
1 handle	⅝	×	13	× dowel rod

Slope the handle sides, but arrange their tops so the handle is above the rear-axle position. Notch the handles over the box sides, but do not cut out so much as to weaken them (FIG. 10-2D). Drill the tops for a piece of dowel rod, which can have a thin nail driven across to supplement glue (FIG. 9-2E).

How the wheels and axles are arranged depends on available equipment. In the arrangement shown there are 3-inch-diameter wheels with rubber tires on iron rod axles that suit the wheels, probably ¼ inch diameter. The axles go through the sides, then there are washers on each side of each wheel. The end of the rod is lightly riveted to prevent the wheel from coming off (FIG. 9-2F).

The front end of the truck could be hazardous to furniture that it is pushed against, so a strip of wood across the front, just wide enough to overlap the wheels to act as a fender would help (FIG. 9-2G). It might be sufficient to round its edges or add some rubber padding.

If the truck will be used outdoors, paint the axles and wheels as well as the woodwork. A few holes in the bottom will let rainwater run out, although they would not be appreciated if the young operator wanted to transport sand.

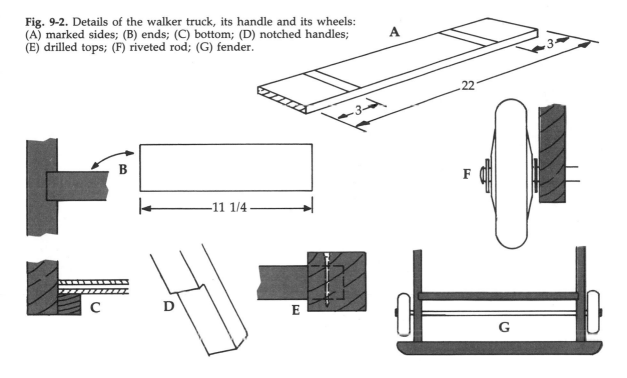

Fig. 9-2. Details of the walker truck, its handle and its wheels: (A) marked sides; (B) ends; (C) bottom; (D) notched handles; (E) drilled tops; (F) riveted rod; (G) fender.

ROCKING HORSE

Any sort of rocking seat appeals to a child and it is particularly attractive if it is in the form of an animal or bird. A traditional rocking horse, that is carved to be a fairly lifelike representation of the animal is an ambitious and difficult project, but a simplified version will be just as satisfying.

This is a symmetrical inverted V sectioned seat (FIG. 9-3) that only becomes a horse or any other animal with the addition of a head and tail. Construction can be nailed throughout, although fitted joints could be cut if you wish. How elaborately the horse is decorated and how much harness is added depends on you. For the basic materials, refer to TABLE 9-2.

As the legs slope in two directions, first draw the main lines that will give the angles to cut and bevel the wood. There is no need to draw the whole horse, but lines representing the outer edges of the legs will provide the information (FIG. 9-3A). The sizes suit a very young child. If tests with a particular child show a greater leg length, increase the overall height, but keep the length and width the same.

Cut the top part from a too-long piece of 2-×-3-inch section. Next, plane the bevels on each side (FIG. 9-4A). Put the boards that will form the sides against it, mark its width and mark where the legs will come. Bevel the top edges of these boards and shape the bottom edges (FIG. 9-4B). Some more rounding will be necessary after assembly, but this is the main outline. Cut pieces for the legs a little too long. Shape their tops to fit against the top part. Nail the legs to the sides and the sides to the top part.

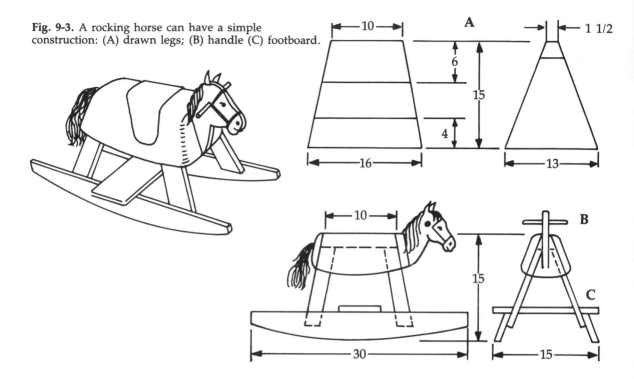

Fig. 9-3. A rocking horse can have a simple construction: (A) drawn legs; (B) handle (C) footboard.

Table 9-2. Materials List for a Rocking Horse.

1 back	3 × 12 × 2
2 sides	6 × 15 × 1
2 ends	6 × 8 × 1
4 legs	3 × 14 × ¾
2 rockers	4 × 30 × ¾
1 footboard	5 × 15 × ¾
1 head	8 × 10 × ¾ plywood
1 handle	⅝ × 8 × dowel rod

The compound angle at which the legs are spread means that the ends of the body do not assemble squarely. Plane the surfaces on which the end pieces will be nailed (FIG. 9-4C). Make the end pieces, do not nail them on yet.

The tail is made from a piece of rope. Drill a hole in the end to fit it fairly close. Glue the rope with part of it spread on the inside and then tack to resist pulling out. After the glue has set the hanging part should be completely unlaid so all of the fibers hang loosely like hairs (FIG. 9-5A).

The head could be made of fairly thick solid wood and carved to something like a lifelike section, but a simpler alternative is to keep it thinner and flat, then decorate it by painting. For strength it is best to use plywood ¾ inch or thicker and then gluing two pieces together. Cut the head to shape (FIG. 9-5B). It could be held to the end of the body with glue and screws, but as screws might not hold very well in the edge of plywood, it would be better to use dowels (FIG. 9-5C).

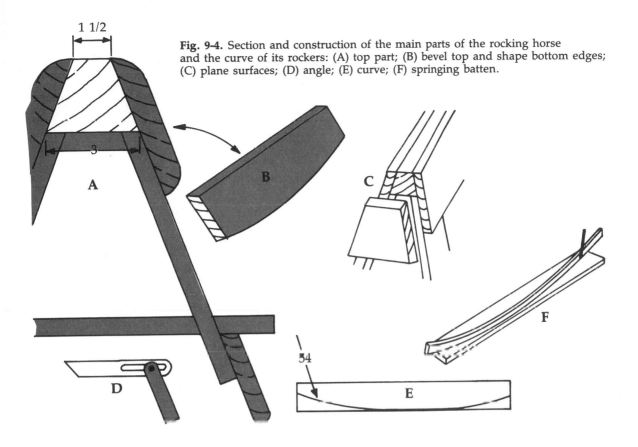

Fig. 9-4. Section and construction of the main parts of the rocking horse and the curve of its rockers: (A) top part; (B) bevel top and shape bottom edges; (C) plane surfaces; (D) angle; (E) curve; (F) springing batten.

1 1/2

3

54

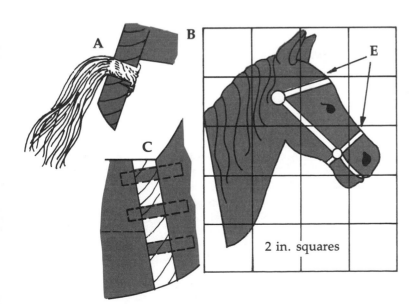

Fig. 9-5. Head and tail details:
(A) loosely hanging fibers;
(B) head shape;
(C) dowels; (D) reins;
(E) harness of plastic straps.

2 in. squares

Keep the edge that will be joined flat, but all other edges should be rounded. There could be a handle put through the head (FIG. 9-3B), made from a piece of dowel rod with rounded ends glued in a hole. Another way of providing the user with something to hold would be to drill through the mouth for an endless rope loop to serve as reins (FIG. 9-5D). Reins and handle might both be fitted.

Thoroughly round the body parts, both in cross section and at the ends. The top of the back shown is straight, but it could be hollowed, because that is the shape of a horse and it helps to keep the rider on.

The rockers have a maximum width of 4 inches and curve up to 1½ inches at the ends. The curve (FIG. 9-4E) could be drawn with a compass made from a strip of wood with an awl through it, or you can get a satisfactory curve by springing a batten through the points and drawing round it (FIG. 9-4F).

Mark where the top edges of the rockers should come on all legs and cut off the legs to the same amount of overlap. To take the footboard, the top edges of the rockers have to be beveled. Find this angle (FIG. 9-4D) with a piece of wood across the rockers temporarily in position. Although only the centers have to be beveled, it looks better to plane the whole length.

The footboard should extend to the outer limits of the rockers (FIG. 9-3C). Do not make it longer so there will be no risk of the child stepping on the end and tipping the horse. Round the outer corners and all edges.

If the horse is to be used on a carpeted surface, round the bottoms of the rockers to minimize damage to the carpet. It is unlikely that a child could rock the horse so far that he tipped it endwise, but to prevent this, screw rubber door stops to each end of the rockers.

Punch any visible nail heads below the surface and cover with stopping before painting. The simplest finish is an overall painting in a horse color. Black is used to indicate hair and eyes. Black and white or other two color coats and more details can be painted on the face. The ears are pieces of leather or soft plastic. You can glue on and nail some plastic straps to represent a harness (FIG. 9-5E). Another piece of plastic could be attached over the body to look like a saddle.

PLAYHOUSE

This is a playhouse large enough for one or two children to use with their small furniture and to equip with their toys and belongings (FIG. 9-6). Sizes shown are to be cut from stock sizes of plywood or hardboard, but they might have to be modified to suit the space where the house is to be used. If made of suitable materials, the house could be used outside as well as indoors. The necessary materials are found in TABLE 9-3.

The two end walls are divided vertically and are hinged to the front and rear walls. There is a loose floor and the house could be used with or without a lift-off roof. For packing, the floor and roof can be removed, then the walls folded flat to not much more than 4 inches thick (FIG. 9-6A).

The design shows one door and one window in the front wall only (FIG. 9-6B), you can provide other openings. If the playhouse will normally be used in a corner of a room, it might be better to have windows in one end and the door hinged so that it opens back against a room wall. If the house is to be used away from the room wall, you could also put a window in the rear wall. The loose floor holds the end walls in shape and prevents them from folding unintentionally. If you want to make the house without a floor, use hooks or catches to keep the end

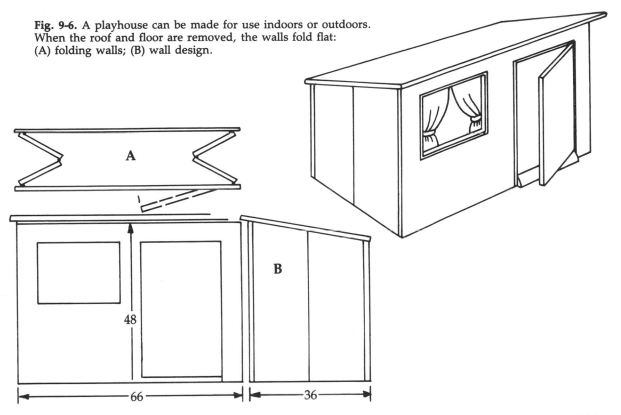

Fig. 9-6. A playhouse can be made for use indoors or outdoors. When the roof and floor are removed, the walls fold flat: (A) folding walls; (B) wall design.

walls straight. The roof also helps to hold the walls in place, but this would be insufficient alone.

The construction will involve gluing and nailing, using 1-×-2-inch battens throughout. The battens can be half-lapped at the corners and at intermediate joints (FIG. 9-7A). This would be advisable with hardboard panels, but if you use ¼-inch plywood, that would probably provide enough stiffness to support simple butt joints (FIG. 9-7B).

Start with the front panel (FIG. 9-8A). This is framed around with other battens outlining the door and window, as well as providing stiffness. At the bottom of the doorway the batten should go across. You could develop the batten into a doorstep with another piece outside (FIG. 9-7C).

Although the edges of the doorway can be left with the plywood or hardboard edges exposed, it would be better to frame around the openings with strips having projecting rounded edges (FIG. 10-7D). I would not advise you to glaze the window. It is better to leave it open with a curtain hung inside.

The back is made like the front, but should be 6 inches lower (FIG. 9-8B). How much stiffening to provide depends on the panel material, but you can assume that the children will be knocking furniture against it. Therefore, put intermediate framing accordingly.

Although each end is in two parts, you should lay out at least one end completely to ensure that the slope matches (FIG. 9-8C). You will have to bevel the top edges of the front and back of the house to match the slope of the sides, so allow for the angle of the roof that goes through to the outer edges (FIG. 9-7E).

Table 9-3. Materials List for a Playhouse.

1 front panel	48 × 66 × ¼ plywood
3	2 × 66 × 1
4	2 × 48 × 1
3	2 × 32 × 1
1 rear panel	42 × 66 × ¼ plywood
3	2 × 66 × 1
4	2 × 42 × 1
4 end panels	18 × 48 × ¼ plywood
8	2 × 48 × 1
8	2 × 17 × 1
1 bottom panel	34 × 63 × ¼ plywood
3	2 × 63 × 1
4	2 × 34 × 1
1 roof panel	3 × 68 × ¼ plywood
2	2 × 68 × 1
7	2 × 40 × 1
2 door panels	24 × 42 × ¼ plywood
2	2 × 42 × ¾
2	2 × 24 × ¾
2 door frames	1¾ × 42 × ½
1	1¾ × 24 × ½
4 window frames	1¾ × 24 × ½
1 door step	2 × 24 × 1

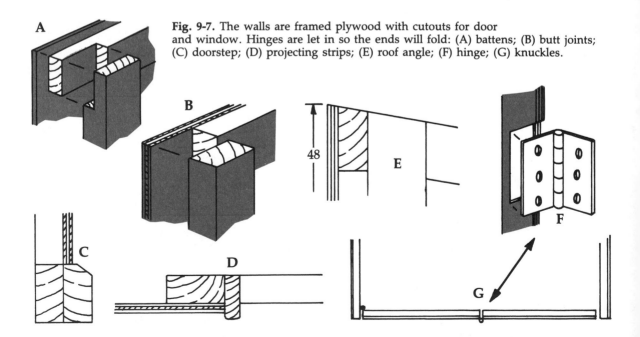

Fig. 9-7. The walls are framed plywood with cutouts for door and window. Hinges are let in so the ends will fold: (A) battens; (B) butt joints; (C) doorstep; (D) projecting strips; (E) roof angle; (F) hinge; (G) knuckles.

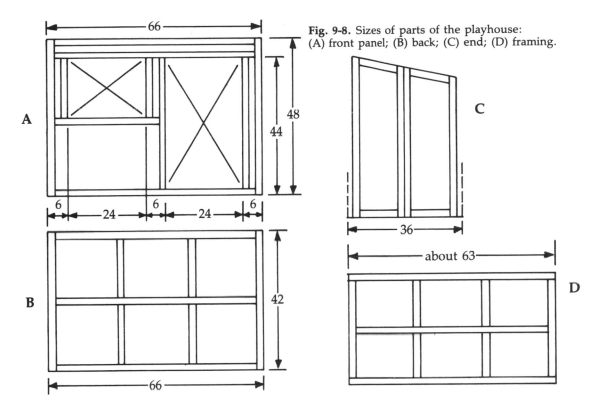

Fig. 9-8. Sizes of parts of the playhouse: (A) front panel; (B) back; (C) end; (D) framing.

The ends will fold inward. For the sizes given there is plenty of clearance, but if you make a much shorter house, it must not be so short that the folding ends would meet before falling flat.

Use strong butt hinges. For the neatest ends let the hinges into the meeting edges (FIG. 9-7F) with the knuckles inside at the corners and outside at the center (FIG. 9-7G).

The front door can be made by framing one panel, but to reduce risk of warping, it is better to have two panels with framing between. Reduce the thickness of the framing so that the door is no thicker than the wall (FIG. 9-9A). It might be best not to put any fasteners on the door, but there should be knobs or handles inside and out. If you want to include a catch, use simple strips of wood as turn buttons inside and out (FIG. 9-9B). These should be located where a child could reach through the window and turn if the door is locked on the wrong side. Pieces of plywood across the top and bottom corners of the doorway will act as stops (FIG. 9-9C).

Obtain the actual sizes of the bottom from the assembled house. Even if the wall panels are hardboard, you will probably want to use plywood for the floor so there is less risk of it becoming damaged. Use sufficient framing to provide stiffness (FIG. 9-9D). If you want some means of lifting out the floor, put a pair of finger holes near one or both ends (FIG. 9-9D). Usually it is sufficient to simply tilt the house and slide the floor out.

From the roof similarly to other parts, but be sure it overhangs all around (FIG. 9-9E). Obtain its sizes from the assembled walls. The amount of overhang back and front can be any amount you desire, although a wider overhang at the

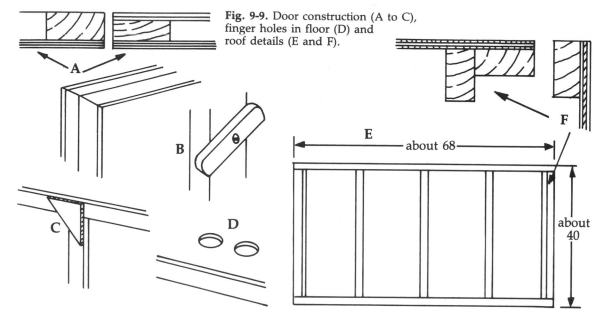

Fig. 9-9. Door construction (A to C), finger holes in floor (D) and roof details (E and F).

front improves appearance. At the ends arrange the overhang so strips can be put inside the framing to project downward inside the end walls (FIG. 9-9F) to hold them in shape. If these strips extend between the front and rear walls, there should be no need for other strips along the length to prevent the roof from slipping.

The bare house will probably be all that is needed to provide enjoyment as children arrange things inside to suit themselves. However, you might want to provide some hooks or pegs for hanging things. They should be located so they do not interfere with folding. There could be strips of wood to rest across battens to act as shelves that can be lifted out for folding, or you might want to hinge them on battens so that they can be folded up into recesses.

TOY TRUNK

In illustrations to children's stories, the pirate's treasure, the loot a highwayman takes from a coach, and all the wealth of a robber baron are in trunks with rounded tops. The shape has a romantic appeal to a younger reader or listener. If you provide the child with one of these trunks in which to pack toys, you might encourage the child to be more tidy. Such a box makes a good storage place in any case.

This trunk has a deep lift-out tray with hand holes at each end, which can be removed easily by a child when the lid is raised (FIG. 7-8). The list of necessary materials can be found in TABLE 9-4.

Construction consists of plywood framed inside. The framing is mainly there to provide extra thickness at overlapping joints. The main strength is in the plywood. This means that most of the framing strips can be attached with glue and nails without bothering to cut joints where they meet. If they are cut close together that will be sufficient. An exception is the central strip under the lid, which should be half-lapped at its ends. To ensure that the lid fits well on the box, first make both parts as one, then, after most of the assembly work has been done, cut them apart.

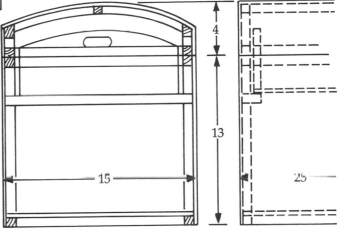

Fig. 9-10. A trunk for storing toys has a large lifting tray and a curved top for appearance and to increase capacity.

Table 9-4. Materials List for a Toy Trunk.

2 ends	15 × 17 × ¼ plywood
2 sides	16 × 25 × ¼ plywood
1 bottom	15 × 25 × ¼ plywood
1 top	20 × 25 × ¼ plywood
2 bottom frames	⅝ × 15 × ⅝
2 bottom frames	⅝ × 25 × ⅝
2 joint strips	⅝ × 15 × 1½
2 joint strips	⅝ × 25 × 1½
2 tray rails	⅝ × 15 × 1½
3 top rails from	3 × 15 × ⅝
1 tray bottom	14 × 24 × ¼ plywood
2 tray ends	5 × 14 × ¼ plywood
2 tray sides	4 × 24 × ¼ plywood
Tray framing from 4	⅝ × 24 × ⅝

All of the plywood parts are ¼ inch thick and most of the framing is ⅝ inch square. The trunk shown is 15 inches wide, 25 inches long, and 19 inches high. If you increase these dimensions be sure to increase the framing sections slightly. Much larger plywood panels would require some intermediate supporting strips. The curved top might then need two or three lengthwise pieces.

Start by drawing an end full size, either on paper or on the plywood that will make one end (FIG. 9-11A). The bottom is shown inside its supporting battens (FIG. 9-11B). There is a double-width batten over the part that will be cut to separate the lid from the box. Mark the outside of the plywood with a double line all around where the cut will come.

The center for drawing the curve of the top of the lid is at the bottom (FIG. 9-11C). This is probably a greater radius than you can set with any available compass. It can be drawn with a makeshift compass made with a strip of wood and an awl at the center and notches for a pencil at the distances to be pulled around a curve (FIG. 9-11D). Mark the curves of the tray ends at the same time.

Thicken the top edge of the plywood by drawing the curve on a wider piece of wood and then cutting around inside to reduce its bulk (FIG. 9-11E). Notch the supporting strips for the tray around the uprights (FIG. 9-11F). Match the other crosswise pieces by lengthwise ones. It will help in assembly if you cut back the end pieces to allow for the lengthwise ones, rather than trying to fit the lengthwise strips between the crosswise ones. Notch the center of the top curved piece to take the central lengthwise pieces (FIG. 9-11G).

Next, prepare the wood for the lengthwise parts. The top two pieces have to match the slope of the curved top (FIG. 9-12A). Bring them close to size, but leave a little for planing true after assembly. Have the bottom plywood ready to fit in.

Glue and nail the bottom in place in the ends. Add the side plywood panels, with their lengthwise strips fitted at the same levels as the matching end parts. Assemble on a level surface and see that there is no twisting. Leave for the glue to set.

Try the top plywood in position. It helps in bending to have the outside grain lengthwise and the panel an inch or so too wide, so the edges can be forced down by an assistant while you nail along the sides.

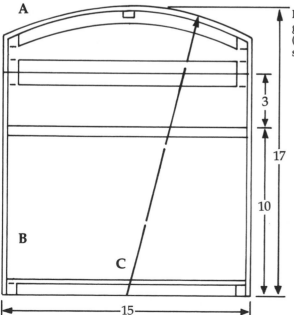

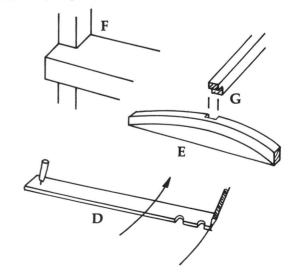

Fig. 9-11. The end of the trunk is drawn full-size to get the shapes of the main parts: (A) end; (B) bottom; (C) center; (D) strip of wood; (E) curved wood; (F) supporting strips; (G) notched center.

One edge can be completely nailed, then the plywood sprung to its curve. If there is much stiffness, the edge can be clamped while the glue sets, with a post pressing from the roof or wall (FIG. 9-12B).

Trim the plywood level all around the edges. The outside should be smooth everywhere before you separate the lid from the box. Saw around to part the lid from the box (FIG. 9-12C). Mark the lid and box so they are not turned in relation to each other. Plane the sawn edges and do any necessary cleaning of surplus glue from the insides. Join the two parts with surface hinges (FIG. 9-12D), which can be plain or decorative. You could also include a strut or cord to prevent the lid from going back too far.

The tray should rest on supports across the ends and stand above the box top when the lid is opened. It can be made of the same plywood as the trunk, with framing in the angles (FIG. 9-13A). You could also use solid wood or ½-inch plywood for the sides and ends. Then there would be no need for framing (FIG. 9-13B).

The end curve matches that of the lid and the hole should be long enough for an adult hand (FIG. 9-13C). Round the inside of the hole and the curved top edge.

Make sure the tray is an easy fit in the box. You could include one or more divisions in the tray. The dividers will strengthen it, but unless there is something specific to be fitted, it is usually better to leave the tray open.

Rope handles at the ends will match the pirate's or seaman's chest idea. Another type of trunk handle consists of two blocks of wood screwed from inside, with a piece of dowel rod set into holes in them (FIG. 9-13D). If a lathe is available, you could make turned handles. A simple handle is a block of wood screwed from inside, with a hollow underneath (FIG. 9-13E).

There are several ways of finishing the trunk. If you want it to look like an old sea or carriage trunk, arrange strips of plywood on the outside to simulate

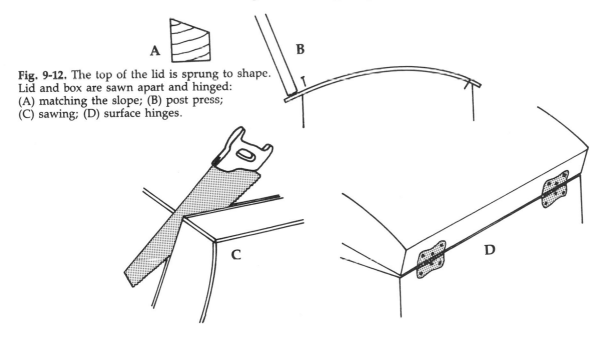

Fig. 9-12. The top of the lid is sprung to shape. Lid and box are sawn apart and hinged: (A) matching the slope; (B) post press; (C) sawing; (D) surface hinges.

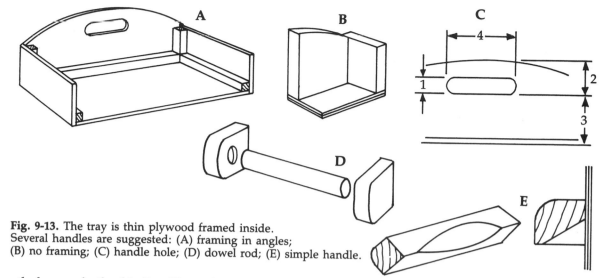

Fig. 9-13. The tray is thin plywood framed inside.
Several handles are suggested: (A) framing in angles;
(B) no framing; (C) handle hole; (D) dowel rod; (E) simple handle.

the brass or leather binding. The main part can be painted a dark color and these strips picked out in a metallic color or the whole box can be painted to look like leather.

If you don't want a traditional appearance you could use a varnished finish. A young child would probably prefer paint, either all over in one or two bright colors or with letters and pictures, possibly different on every surface. The inside could be another color and the tray yet another color. Whatever the finish, the inside should be sealed with paint or varnish to prevent the wood from absorbing dirt.

You could also include glides under the corners if the trunk is to be put on a carpet, or you could add casters so a child could move the trunk around. The corners would then have to be thickened with wood blocks under the bottom.

PLAYPEN

This pen allows the parent to put a baby down with his toys and know that the child cannot stray. The size has to be a compromise between something that provides a large crawling area but can be stored compactly. There does not have to be a base to a playpen, but it will protect the floor covering and stop the child from pushing the whole thing about as he gets stronger. The one suggested drops in, so it could be added later if required. TABLE 9-5 lists the necessary materials for this playpen.

Table 9-5. Materials List for a Playpen.

4 rails	$1\frac{3}{8} \times 36 \times \frac{7}{8}$
8 rails	$1\frac{3}{8} \times 20 \times \frac{7}{8}$
40 rods	$\frac{1}{2}$ diameter $\times$ 24

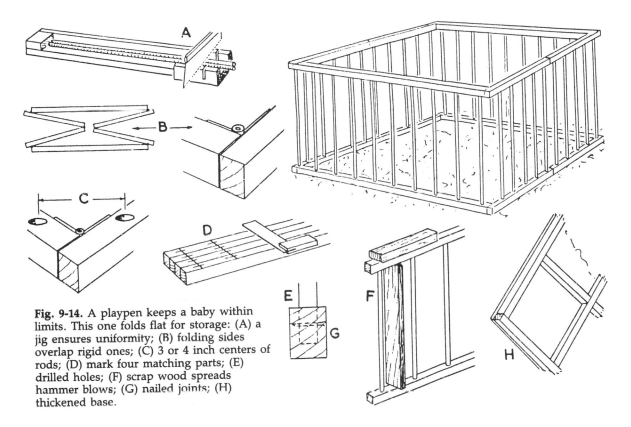

Fig. 9-14. A playpen keeps a baby within limits. This one folds flat for storage: (A) a jig ensures uniformity; (B) folding sides overlap rigid ones; (C) 3 or 4 inch centers of rods; (D) mark four matching parts; (E) drilled holes; (F) scrap wood spreads hammer blows; (G) nailed joints; (H) thickened base.

Other dimensions are affected by the available dowel rods. Those suggested are ½ inch diameter and 24 inches long. If longer dowel rods have to be cut, make up a jig to ensure uniformity (FIG. 9-14A). The top and bottom rails can be softwoods, but will be more durable if made of a light hardwood. A section about 1⅜ inches deep and ⅞ inch wide should be strong enough to allow the rod holes. The suggested size is 36 inches square, but allow for the folding sides overlapping the rigid ones (FIG. 9-14B).

Arrange close enough for there to be no risk of a child getting through the rods or getting his head stuck. Somewhere between 3 inch and 4 inch centers of rods should do, but be careful at the corners that the diagonal measurement between dowels does not exceed this (FIG. 9-14C). Some adjustment of measurements will have to be made along each side to get an even spacing. Mark out the hole positions across all four matching parts at the same time (FIG. 9-14D).

Holes should be drilled about three-quarters of the way through at each position (FIG. 9-14E). Use a depth stop on the drill or on the drill press. The folding sides meet closely at their centers so they can be marked and drilled in the same way as the rigid sides, except spacing must allow for rods coming equally on each side of the center.

Take sharp edges off rails. See that ends are cut squarely. Sand the parts before assembly. Although drilling all the holes with a depth stop should ensure accurate assembly, it is best to cut two spare pieces of wood to length as distance gauges.

To assemble a side, glue the dowels into the holes in one rail, put glue on the other ends, and tap on the other rail, using the distance gauges between top and bottom rails, as well as a scrap piece of wood to spread the hammer blows (FIG. 9-14F). It should be strong enough to only glue the joints, but to prevent movement before the glue has set, drive a thin nail across each joint (FIG. 9-14G). Check squareness by measuring diagonals and make sure that opposite assemblies match before the glue has set.

The folding joints are made with 12 backflap hinges. If the playpen is to be used without a base piece, use fasteners to hold the folding sides straight. There could also be a hook and eye on the top surface at each center joint. A base piece fitted inside will prevent folding unintentionally, even if there are no fasteners.

The base is a piece of plywood that fits easily into the bottom frame of the pen. It should be thickened around the edges and across the center (FIG. 9-14H). If you use plywood without thickening, there is a risk that a pushing child could lift the edge of the pen enough to slide over a thin base. If a base in one piece is too large for storage, it could be made in two parts divided across the center.

TOY BOX

This is a smaller toy storage box, with shelf space at the side (FIG. 9-15). The main box has a lifting top, which swings on a narrow strip at the back so when the box is against a wall the lid can go a little way past vertical and is unlikely to fall forward unintentionally.

The front and ends are paneled so decorations like wallpaper with a nursery rhyme theme, cut-out pictures or cartoon characters can be included. With the decoration confined to these areas, the main parts can be stained or varnished or brightly painted. For a complete materials list for this project, see TABLE 9-6.

The main parts can be ½-inch plywood or ⅝-inch particleboard with wood veneer or plastic surfaces. The front panel is thinner plywood and there is a plywood back. The best method of construction uses a few dado grooves, but if the material you choose is difficult to cut for joining in this manner or if equipment for grooving is unavailable, you can make satisfactory joints with wood

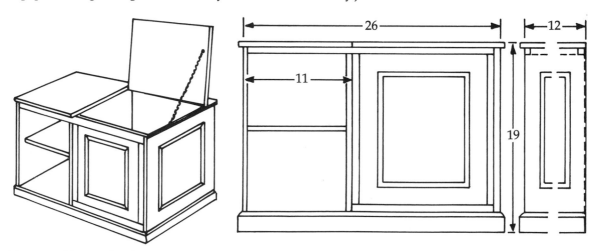

Fig. 9-15. This toy box has access from the top and shelves at the side. It can be decorated with colored panels.

Table 9-6. Materials List for a Toy Box.

2 ends	12 × 19 × ½ plywood
1 divider	12 × 17 × ½ plywood
3 lips	½ × 19 × 1
1 bottom	12 × 26 × ½ plywood
1 top	12 × 13 × ½ plywood
1 top	3 × 15 × ½ plywood
1 lid	10 × 15 × ½ plywood
9 top lips	½ × 15 × 1
1 shelf	10 × 12 × ½ plywood
1 shelf lip	½ × 10 × 1
1 back	17 × 26 × ¼ plywood
4 frames	¾ × 26 × ¾
4 frames	¾ × 12 × ¾
2 frames	¾ × 17 × ¾
1 lid stop	¾ × 12 × ¾
1 front panel	15 × 17 × ¼ plywood
4 panel moldings	½ × 12 half-round
2 panel moldings	½ × 10 half-round
2 panel moldings	½ × 8 half-round
1 plinth	2 × 28 × ½
2 plinths	2 × 13 × ½

fillets in the angles. The plinth is of the external type instead of one that is set back under the bottom.

If you use plywood, lip the exposed front edges and a border around the front and ends of the top parts (FIG. 9-16A). If you use surfaced particleboard cover these edges with matching ironed-on veneer.

Start by making the two ends and the divider (FIG. 9-16B). The ends should go to the floor, but the divider should finish at the box bottom, preferably in a shallow groove (FIG. 7-16C). Mark the shelf position on the divider and on one end. Under the top and bottom there will be ¾-inch square strips. Mark where they will come on the ends. These strips will pass through notches in the divider. Shallow notches on the inner edges of the strips provide accurate location points (FIG. 9-16D).

The back goes over the divider and bottom and into rabbets in the ends, or against strips screwed to the ends. In any case the divider and bottom must be narrower than the ends by the thickness of the back.

The front panel of the boxed part fits into plowed grooves in a frame, the top of which is also the lengthwise front strip under the top. This will only require a groove for the width of the box, but if it is continued over the shelf part, it will be easier to cut and is unlikely to be noticed.

Next make up the top frame. Corners could merely butt, but rabbet and dado joints would be better. Note that it is the long parts which go right through (FIG. 9-16E).

Make the frame under the bottom in a similar manner; however, you don't need to plow a groove or make a divider notch.

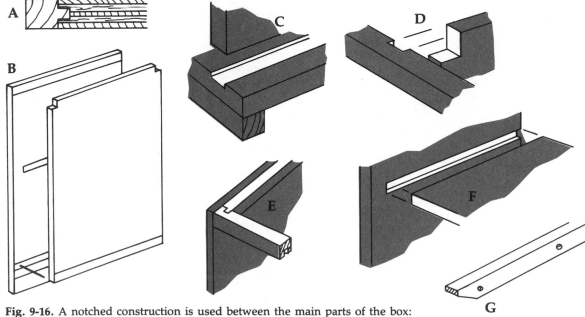

Fig. 9-16. A notched construction is used between the main parts of the box: (A) lipped front; (B) ends and divider; (C) divider; (D) notches on inner edges; (E) long parts; (F) shelf; (G) battens as supports.

The shelf is best supported by a stopped dado joint at each end (FIG. 9-16F), although it could also be supported by battens (FIG. 9-16G). It need not be brought to the front edges of the uprights, but could be set back to the end of the dado.

Now, assemble the top and bottom frames. The bottom frame can also be attached to the plywood bottom. If the bottom of the divider is not to go into a dado (FIG. 9-16C), use a strip of wood to secure it inside the box part (FIG. 9-17A). Position the divider between the frames and bring the frames to the ends. Put glue in the joints and drive screws through the frames into the ends.

Fit the shelf at the same time. Check squareness with diagonal measurements and leave the assembly for the glue to set. If there are any doubts about it retaining its shape, tack a piece of wood temporarily diagonally across the back.

The frame for the front of the box is made of square grooved strips (FIG. 9-17B). There is no need for cutting joints at the corners. Simple butts will do. Check that the frame parts will fit in the opening, then put the plywood panel between the side frame pieces and the bottom. Lift this assembly into the top part so that it can be pressed into position with glue between the meeting surfaces. A few fine nails can be driven inside (FIG. 9-17C).

Make the plinth from strips of wood beveled at the top edges (FIG. 9-17D) or use a prepared molding (FIG. 9-17E). If you buy the molding already shaped, it might be necessary to modify the height of the bottom when setting out the original design.

The plinth is decorative and does not carry much load. Miter its corners and attach it with its upper edge level with the surface of the bottom.

Next make the paneling with borders of half-round molding about ½ inch across. It can be put on the front of the box only, or it can go on one or both

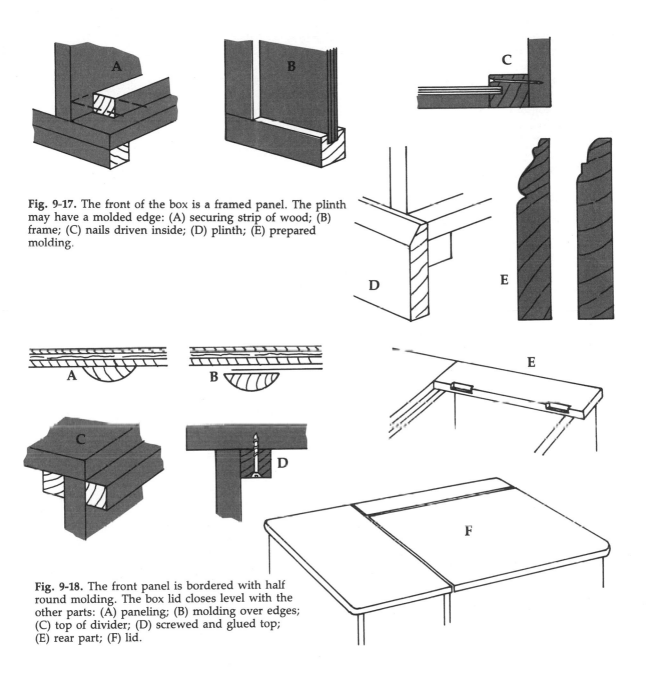

Fig. 9-17. The front of the box is a framed panel. The plinth may have a molded edge: (A) securing strip of wood; (B) frame; (C) nails driven inside; (D) plinth; (E) prepared molding.

Fig. 9-18. The front panel is bordered with half round molding. The box lid closes level with the other parts: (A) paneling; (B) molding over edges; (C) top of divider; (D) screwed and glued top; (E) rear part; (F) lid.

ends as well. You can glue and pin the paneling directly to the wood (FIG. 9-18A). Any pictures could be fitted inside.

It is easier to get a neat result and better protection against pinched fingers if the paper if first pasted on and left sufficiently oversize for the molding to cover its edges (FIG. 9-18B). If you do this before painting the whole box paint the molding before fitting it, so there is no risk of paint going on the paper.

Attach the back panel with glue and close nailing to the divider as well as to the ends and framing. A heavy toy knocked against the inside of the box could put strain on the back joints.

The top is made in three parts: the piece over the shelves is fastened down and a narrow strip is fastened down behind a lifting lid over the box. Put a strip across the top of the divider to act as a bearer for the lid and one on the other side for screwing on the top (FIG. 9-18C). Drill the parts where the screws will be driven upward into the top. Then screw and glue the top (FIG. 9-18D). Let the edge toward the box come exactly along the edge of the divider. Make the rear part come behind the lid and prepare its edge for hinges before screwing it into place (FIG. 9-18E).

Next, make the lid and hinge it in place, then trim around the top piece edges to give a neat uniform line, with rounded edges and corners (FIG. 9-18F). Do not allow the lid to fall back when in use, or the hinges and their screws might be strained. If there is one, a wall behind the box can act as a stop, otherwise there can be a cord between screw eyes to restrict movement. If there is a danger of the lid closing on a child's hands, it would be better to fit a folding strut.

The shelf part can be given a door, with the shelf front kept far enough back to admit it between the end and the divider. To match the rest of the box, a paneled door would be better than a solid one, although you can give the plywood door a paneled effect with half-round molding.

PLAY CORNER

If available space for a child's activities is limited, it is a good idea to make as much use as possible of the corner of a room. This unit has a surface at a suitable height for activities while standing (FIGS. 9-19 and 20). Underneath is storage space that can be open shelves, but is better enclosed with a door. There is also a tilting bin opening towards the end.

The part of the unit in the corner extends upward with two shelves that could hold books or toys. The space below them might be used as a sort of bulletin board where the child can put his own decorations and change them around. At the back there is a framed chalkboard. This allows plenty of room for drawing and prevents damage to the wall. The whole unit could be freestanding, but a few screws into the wall would aid rigidity and prevent the child from moving the unit.

Most of the parts can be made out of plywood (TABLE 9-7). For a painted finish that would hide the plys, there would be no need for lipping the edges that show. The material list does not allow for lipping, but for a clear finish, use lipped edges. Similarly, the back plywood is fitted over the edges without rabbets, but for a quality finish, you have to use some more advanced joints.

Particleboard can be used for some parts. Whatever material you use for the top, you could cover it with laminated plastic to give an attractive appearance and an easily cleaned surface.

Unlike most furniture construction, this piece is best started with the back sheet of plywood. Except for the plinth, it reaches the edges all around. Mark on it where everything else will come and it will serve as a full-size drawing for the other parts (FIG. 9-21A). If the bottom and the edge that will come in the room corner are made at right angles to each other, a little surplus can be left on the other edges for planing to size after assembly.

Mark the board that will make the front upright from the back plywood (FIG. 9-21B), and from this, mark out the divider (FIG. 9-21C). The top is a plain rectangle,

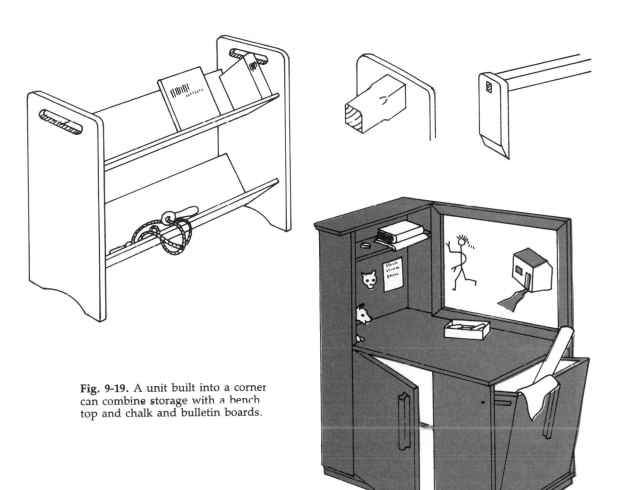

Fig. 9-19. A unit built into a corner can combine storage with a bench top and chalk and bulletin boards.

except the joint to the upright ought to be a dado for strength (FIG. 9-21D). At the back it will be nailed through the plywood and supported by a strip of wood as far as the divider (FIG. 9-21E). The bottom is made in a similar way, but you can notch it around the upright without cutting that away.

At the top of the upright the covering shelf could overhang a short distance and the upright be notched into it (FIG. 9-21F). However, a simple nailed joint would do for a less important piece of furniture. The other shelf could fit into a dado or be supported on a batten. At the back join both shelves to the plywood with battens (FIG. 9-21G) that come against the chalkboard frame.

For the chalkboard paint the back plywood with nongloss black or gray paint and frame around. Make the framing out of strips that have rounded edges and fit directly to the surface (FIG. 9-22A). Miter the corners. It is best to first make a trial assembly, then remove the framing for painting and leave its permanent fitting until you put the whole unit together.

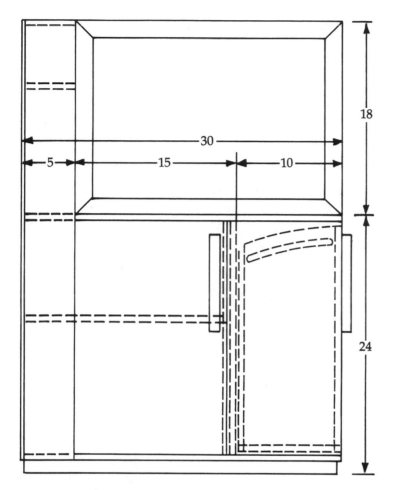

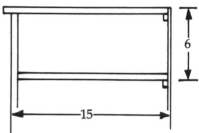

Fig. 9-20. Suggested sizes for a play corner.

The shelf will be supported on battens and its front kept far enough back to give clearance for the door. Do not notch it into the upright as this would bring its edge too far forward. Although you can attach the shelf to its battens, it might be preferable to keep it loose so it can be removed for cleaning.

The front over the bin compartment overlaps the divider (FIG. 9-22B), going partly on to a strip of wood that reinforces the joint and acts as a door stop. A similar strip could be put at the back of the divider if there is a risk of nails going through the back directly into the divider and splitting it.

The thick plywood front will be stiff enough at the bin opening without further treatment, but at the back the ¼-inch plywood should be stiffened with solid wood wide enough to give a good overlap on the pivot and stop positions (FIG. 9-22C).

With all of the parts prepared, attach the battens and strengthening pieces that are needed at the back. Put another piece of thin plywood behind the end extension. Where the plywood overlaps the upright, nail directly, but where it meets the back plywood, put strips along the edge of the back between where the various horizontal parts come (FIG. 9-22D).

Table 9-7. Materials List for a Play Corner.

1 back	30 × 42 × ¼ plywood
1 extension back	15 × 42 × ¼ plywood
1 upright	5 × 42 × ⅝
1 top shelf	5 × 17 × ⅝
1 book shelf	5 × 15 × ⅝
1 top	15 × 30 × ½ plywood
1 bottom	15 × 30 × ½ plywood
1 front	10 × 22 × ½ plywood
1 divider	15 × 22 × ½ plywood
1 door	15 × 22 × ½ plywood
1 door stop	¾ × 22 × ¾
1 shelf	15 × 22 × ½ plywood
2 chalkboard frames	2 × 25 × ½
2 chalkboard frames	2 × 18 × ½
2 plinths	1¼ × 30 × 1¼
2 plinths	1¼ × 15 × 1¼
2 handles	1 × 7 × 1¼
1 bin front	14 × 22 × ½ plywood
2 bin sides	10 × 22 × ½ plywood
1 bin back	14 × 20 × ½ plywood
1 bin bottom	10 × 14 × ½ plywood
1 back bin stiffener	3 × 22 × ½

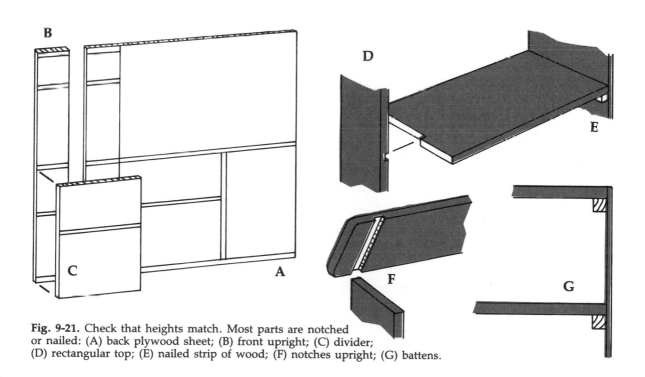

Fig. 9-21. Check that heights match. Most parts are notched or nailed: (A) back plywood sheet; (B) front upright; (C) divider; (D) rectangular top; (E) nailed strip of wood; (F) notches upright; (G) battens.

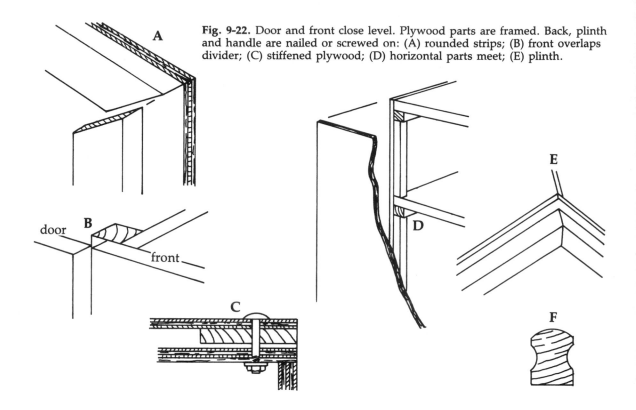

Fig. 9-22. Door and front close level. Plywood parts are framed. Back, plinth and handle are nailed or screwed on: (A) rounded strips; (B) front overlaps divider; (C) stiffened plywood; (D) horizontal parts meet; (E) plinth.

Next, assemble the top, bottom, and shelves between the back and the upright. Put in the divider and the front. With the back plywood squared, there should be little risk of the assembly being out of square, but check diagonals across the front in case there is any tendency to twist.

The door is a piece of plywood to match the front. Hinge it to the upright. Fit a catch inside, either to the shelf or to the door stop. The plinth is solid wood, mitered and attached under the bottom (FIG. 9-22E) in a way similar to earlier parts.

The operation of the bin and its construction are similar to the one already described. Measure the actual assembly and mark out a bin side. Cut this out and locate the position of the pivot point. Use this as the center for drawing the curves of the top and the slot. Try this side in position to check its clearance when it is swung. If this is satisfactory, make the other side and other parts to assemble the bin.

Upright handles are shown in (FIG. 9-20). These should be the same on the door and the bin and can be made to section (FIG. 9-22F) in a long length. Screw from inside.

HOBBY BENCH

An older child often needs somewhere to carry on a practical hobby that involves hammering and cutting as well as causing dirt and mess that might not be acceptable on a regular table. The child needs some sort of a bench, yet it need not be as large or substantial as that used for woodwork. After all, there might not be space for a permanent bench of sufficient size in addition to all other furniture in a room.

This fitment is intended to provide a strong enough working top at a convenient height, yet the whole thing only projects 6 inches from the wall when folded (FIG. 9-23). There is storage space for tools and equipment needed for the hobby. For the materials list, see TABLE 9-8.

Because the bench will be attached to a wall, choose a wall that is strong enough not to be damaged if heavy work is done. Also, the bench should be

Fig. 9-23. A hobby bench can be attached to a wall and arranged so the bench top and legs fold into a shallow unit.

Table 9-8. Materials List for a Hobby Bench.

2 sides	6 × 47 × 1
1 top	7 × 34 × 1
3 shelves	5 × 31 × 1
1 top rail	2 × 31 × 1
2 support blocks	3 × 12 × 1
1 leg stop	2 × 15 × 1
1 bench top	18 × 30 × 1
2 long legs	3 × 26 × 1
2 short legs	3 × 21 × 1
4 leg rails	3 × 14 × 1
1 crossbar	3 × 34 × 1

located where secure attachments can be made. It might be best to alter sizes so screwing to studding is more easily arranged.

The key measurements are those needed to fold a pair of legs with some clearance between them (FIG. 9-24A). Those legs should then open to support the bench top, which should not extend more than a few inches further than where the legs come in the open position. The width of the flap determines the total height of the whole thing, as it swings up into the top part (FIG. 9-24B). The legs open to the same breadth as the bench top and are held in position by a crossbar that hooks on to the legs. The crossbar can then be stowed behind the top when the bench is folded (FIG. 9-24C).

As shown, the whole assembly is made of 1-inch boards. This is not the sort of construction that should be made with plywood, if it is to stand up to

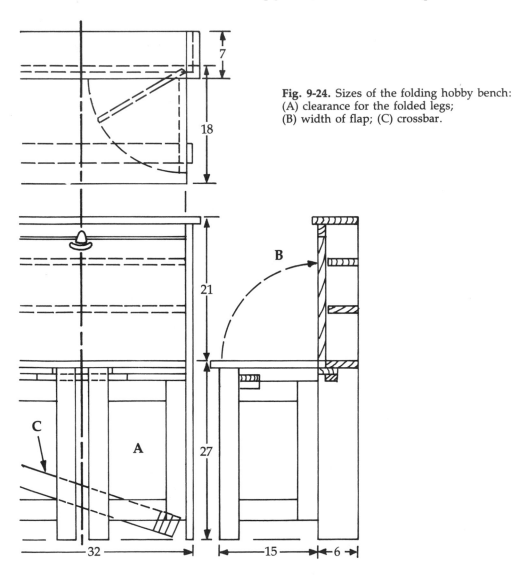

Fig. 9-24. Sizes of the folding hobby bench: (A) clearance for the folded legs; (B) width of flap; (C) crossbar.

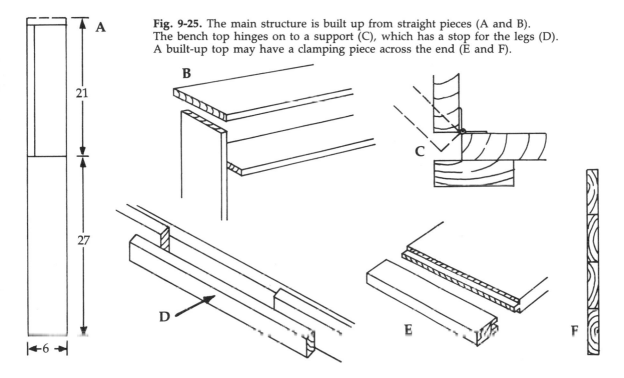

Fig. 9-25. The main structure is built up from straight pieces (A and B). The bench top hinges on to a support (C), which has a stop for the legs (D). A built-up top may have a clamping piece across the end (E and F).

hammering and levering. A light structure might also suffer from vibration, which would be a nuisance when a hobby invokes reasonable precision.

Begin by making the two sides (FIG. 9-25A). Two shelves are shown, but the top part can be fitted for tool storage or the shelves pierced with holes to take tools. The shelves fit between the sides and the top overlaps (FIG. 9-25B). All of these joints can be doweled or dadoed.

Determine how far to set the main shelf back by the amount the bench top needs in order to be flush with the outside when folded. Set the shelves above the main shelf back a little more to provide clearance, although the top one could act as a stop. There could also be a plywood or hardboard back to the storage compartment, so racks for tools are more easily arranged.

The main shelf should be the same thickness as the bench top so when it hinges down, its lower edge will rest on blocks extending below (FIG. 9-25C). One strip right across would interfere with the legs folding, so there should be two parts with another piece linking them to act as a stop for the folded legs (FIG. 9-25D). The blocks take the weight of the bench top and so relieve the strain on the hinges.

There should also be a bar across under the top, but the width of this depends on the width of the bench top, which should fold close to it for neatness. What the bench top is made of depends on its intended use. Solid wood braced across the ends makes the sturdiest top (FIG. 9-25E). If boards have to be glued to make up the width, the risk of warping can be reduced by having the curves of the grain in opposite ways (FIG. 9-25F). The tongues should be cut on the main part and the grooved end pieces made slightly too thick, so they can be planed to match after assembly.

You could also use thick plywood for the bench top or two ½-inch pieces glued together. Blockboard would also be suitable. Whatever material you choose, there should be solid wood edging.

The hinges on the bench top could be stout ordinary ones, possibly three along the edge, or it might be better to use T hinges, with the long legs on the flap. In any case the knuckles of the hinges should come on the top of the joint when the flap is down, so the blocks underneath take a share of the load.

The legs are made up in gate form and hinged on the inside edges of the sides (FIG. 9-26A). The main load will be taken on the long uprights, but the hinges should be stout ones. The gates are the same. The height of the long upright should be correct to hold the bench top level. This means a fairly close fit into the stowed position.

How the gate parts are joined depends on your level of skill. You could use mortise and tenon joints (FIG. 9-26B). The tenons need not go very far into the uprights and there could be dowels across them. If you dowel the joints, drill fairly closely, so there is a good glue area on the maximum number of dowels (FIG. 9-26C). The parts could be half-lapped, with screws or dowels across the joints (FIG. 9-26D).

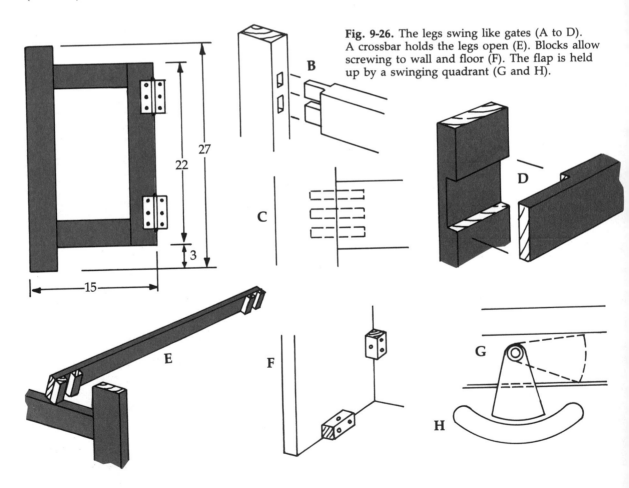

Fig. 9-26. The legs swing like gates (A to D). A crossbar holds the legs open (E). Blocks allow screwing to wall and floor (F). The flap is held up by a swinging quadrant (G and H).

Check squareness of the gates and see that they match each other. The long uprights can be left a little too long until after assembly, then trimmed to length in position.

The gates open out so when the bench top swings, their outer edges are level. Dowels or other fasteners to locate the parts in relation to each other would mean projections from the raised flap. Instead there is a separate crossbar. When the legs are folded the crossbar is stowed behind them in the lower compartment, but in use it fits over the top parts of the gates (FIG. 9-26E).

The crossbar is a straight piece of wood with square blocks across it, arranged so they can be pressed down on the gates to prevent them from swinging in or out when the bench top flap is lowered on to them. When in use the main loads are downward to the floor, but the attachment to the wall must prevent the bench from tilting.

You could also use screws going into the wall through blocks attached to the inner surfaces of the sides (FIG. 9-26F). Two will be enough in low positions, along with two more to the floor. Additional screwing points should be higher on the sides and under the top. As an alternative to wood blocks, you could use metal angle brackets.

When the two legs are folded they should stay in position without any catch or fastener as their feet will be touching the floor. The bench top flap should be secured when it is folded as an unexpected fall could be dangerous and might damage the attachment points. The arrangement shown locks by gravity, so it is very nearly impossible to put the flap up without it becoming locked there. A positive action will be needed to release it.

The lock is a quadrant of plywood or hardboard. It pivots loosely on a screw between two washers. Because of its shape, its weight makes it hang down, unless it is deliberately lifted (FIG. 9-26G). To provide a grip for pulling out the flap, there is a matching arc of similar wood attached to the flap below it (FIG. 9-26H). These two parts have carved decorations or they can be made into a badge with the initials of the owner.

The finish calls for a two-part treatment if the complete unit is to be in a normal room and not a workshop. The outside could be finished to match other furniture or be painted a suitable color. When the legs are out and the flap is down, it is probably best if the working surface is left as bare wood, but the storage shelves or tool racks should be painted not too darkly. A light gray makes a good background, so the things stored are clearly seen.

Index

Other Bestsellers from TAB

☐ **33 USEFUL PROJECTS FOR THE WOODWORKER—Editors of** *School Shop* **Magazine**

A wealth of information for beginning and advanced hobbyists . . . tools, techniques, and dozens of exciting projects. Here's a handbook that deserves a permanent spot on every woodworker's tool bench. Packed with show-how illustrations and material lists, this invaluable guide provides you with a wide variety of useful, and fun-to-make woodworking projects: a spice rack, a wall clock, a plant stand, a cutting board, a wooden chest, a magazine rack, a serving cart, a child's playhouse, and more! 160 pp., 122 illus.

Paper **$10.95** Hard **$12.95**
Book No. 2783

☐ **MAKING ANTIQUE FURNITURE—Edited by Vic Taylor**

A collection of some of the finest furniture ever made is found within the pages of this project book designed for the intermediate- to advanced-level craftsman. Reproducing European period furniture pieces such as a Windsor chair, a Jacobean box stool, a Regency table, a Sheraton writing desk, a Lyre-end occasional table, and many traditional furnishings is sure to provide you with pleasure and satisfaction. Forty projects include materials lists and step-by-step instructions. 160 pp., fully illustrated, 8½ " × 11".

Paper **$19.95** Hard **$25.95**
Book No. 3056

☐ **A MASTER CARVER'S LEGACY—essentials of wood carving techniques—Brieuc Bouché**

Expert guidance on the basics of wood carving from a master craftsman with over 50 years experience. All the techniques for making a whole range of woodcarved items are included. You'll learn how-to's for basic chip carving, the basic rose, cutting of twinings, a classic acanthus leaf, and a simple carving in the round. In no time at all you will be making many of the projects featured. 176 pp., 135 illus., 8½ " × 11".

Paper **$17.95** Hard **$24.95**
Book No. 2629

☐ **THE FRUGAL WOODWORKER—Rick Liftig**

Who says you need an elaborate workshop to fully enjoy your woodworking hobby? And who says you have to spend a small fortune on expensive materials to produce pro-quality furniture? *Certainly not Rick Liftig!* And neither will you after you get a look at the expert advice, money-saving tips, and practical low-cost projects included in this exciting new woodworking guide. You'll find invaluable advice on where and how to acquire wood at bargain prices, even for free! 240 pp., 188 illus.

Paper **$10.95** Hard **$12.95**
Book No. 2702

☐ **COUNTRY FURNITURE—114 Traditional Projects— Percy W. Blandford**

Show off a house full of beautiful country furniture— you created! There is an undeniable attraction about hand-made furniture. Whether the craftsman is an amateur or professional, individually made furniture carries on the tradition of the first settlers and their ancestors. Blandford captures the rustic flavor in these traditional projects—and shows how you can too! Projects range from simple boxes to more elaborate cabinets and cupboards. 260 pp., 246 illus.

Paper **$19.95** Hard **$24.95**
Book No. 2944

☐ **DESIGNING AND BUILDING COLONIAL AND EARLY AMERICAN FURNITURE, WITH 47 PROJECTS—2nd Edition—Percy W. Blandford**

Original designs that allow plenty of room for creativity! This volume captures the spirit and challenge of authentic Early American and Colonial craftsmanship. Blandford, an internationally recognized expert in the field, provides first-rate illustrations and simple instructions on the art of reproducing fine furniture. Every project in this volume is an exquisite reproduction of centuries-old originals: drop-leaf tables, peasant chairs, swivel-top tables, firehouse arm chair, ladderback chairs, tilt-top box tables, hexagonal candle stands, trestle dining tables, wagon seat benches, jackstands, dry sinks, love seats, and Welsh dressers. 192 pp., 188 illus.

Paper **$15.95** Hard **$21.95**
Book No. 3014

Other Bestsellers from TAB